# *Four Eternal Women*

Toni Wolff Revisited – A Study in Opposites

# Four Eternal Women

## Toni Wolff Revisited – A Study in Opposites

Mary Dian Molton

and

Lucy Anne Sikes

*Four Eternal Women:*
*Toni Wolff Revisited – A Study in Opposites*

Copyright © 2011 by
Mary Dian Molton & Lucy Anne Sikes
First Edition
ISBN 978-1-926715-31-5 Paperback

Published simultaneously in Canada and the United States of America by Fisher King Press. For information on obtaining permission for use of material from this work, submit a written request to: permissions@fisherkingpress.com

Fisher King Press
PO Box 222321
Carmel, CA 93922
www.fisherkingpress.com
info@fisherkingpress.com
+1-831-238-7799

This publication, including its accuracy, does not reflect the views of Fisher King Press. Every effort has been made to trace all copyright holders; however, if any have been overlooked, the authors assume full responsibility and will be pleased to make the necessary arrangements at the first opportunity. Concerning citations: Every effort has been made to insure the accuracy of quoted material and sources. In the case of inaccuracies, including the misspelling of names and titles, the authors accept full responsibility, apologize, and kindly ask that you contact the publisher so that these errors can be corrected for future printings of this publication.

Many thanks to all who have directly or indirectly provided permission to quote their works, including:

Excerpt from p. 25 (266 words) from BALANCING HEAVEN AND EARTH: A MEMOIR BY ROBERT A. JOHNSON and WITH JERRY M. RUHL Copyright © 1998 by Robert A. Johnson and Jerry Michael Ruhl. Reprinted by permission of HarperCollins Publishers. (See Four Eternal Women Page 137.)

**Copyrights notices continued on page 304**

*To the Memory of Toni Anna Wolff*
*and to*
*Warren Lane Molton, Charles Arthur Stevens,*
*Donna Jean Ham, and The Cousins*

# Acknowledgements

Kathy Agee, Toni Baker, Mary Alice Bird, Helga Beuing, Echo Bodine, Glen Carlson, Jean Carlson, Donna Childs, Dory Dingell, Eileen Duggan, Jean Erwin, Clarissa Pinkola Estes, Melanie Fleishman, Elaine Fleming, Virginia Fortner, Marianne Foster, Lorna Frojd, Lorna Grochowski, Libby Grout, Pamela Galvin, Soraya Hamid, Gary Hartman, Randy Hearne, Bernice Hill, Susan Houseman, Elnora Huyck, Franz Jung, Cheryl Juneau, Kansas City Friends of Jung, Cynthia Killion, Linda S. Leonard, Rosealine Leonard, Wendy MacLaughlin, Brock Masterson, Mel Mathews, Lucretia McClure, Laura McGrew, Elaine Mills, David Molton, Jennifer Molton, Steve Molton, Robert Moore, Karen Moyer, Dwight Munn, Gene F. Nameche, Jo Ann Neff, Maggie Neff, Lynn Nelson, Susan Nestor, Mary O, Neenya Ostram, Carole Jane Ryan, Laurens van der Post, Nancy Qualls-Corbett, Patricia Radell, Jo Beth Reese, Hester Sikes, Marion Sikes, Ellen Sheire, Aaron Siemers, Lou Sondern, Donna Sperry, Janna Star, Eileen Terrill, Gary Toub, Anne Lou Turner, Jennifer Tuttle, Margaret Wallace, Freda Walrod, Tom Willard, Cynthia Wilson.

A special thank you to our Kansas City Clients and Study Groups, and the Tucson Clients and Study Group. We would like to mention you by name, but are of course constrained by the rules of confidentiality. Knowing that you know who you are, we offer our deepest gratitude.

We are indebted to help from publishers Daimon Verlag in Switzerland, who own the reprint rights to the early translation of Toni Wolff's work, "Structural Forms of the Feminine Psyche." Daimon Verlag will be publishing a new translation of Wolff's collected essays in the near future.

# About the Authors

Lucy Anne Sikes, MS, ARNP, is a Senior Diplomate Jungian Analyst and is an Advanced Registered Nurse Practitioner. She is in private practice of Analysis and Psychotherapy in Prairie Village, Kansas, close to Overland Park, Kansas and Kansas City, Missouri. She currently serves as a lecturer in Jungian Theory and Practice and is past Coordinator for the Kansas City - St Louis Training Seminar of the InterRegional Society of Jungian Analysts.

After her retirement in 1983 from a full career as an educator and later an executive for the Public Broadcasting System, Mary Dian Molton began her Jungian studies and took an advanced degree in clinical social work. She has studied at the C.G. Jung Institute in Zurich, has trained extensively in psychodrama, and has worked as a Jungian psychotherapist since 1987. She also holds a BFA in Fine Arts, and an MS Ed. with a specialization in Secondary Theater Education. For several years she wrote, produced and chaired a weekly television series which showcased creative teaching.

# Table of Contents

## Section Two: The Impersonally Related Archetypes
## AMAZON and MEDIAL WOMAN

# Prologue

Early in the preparation of this work, the writers were challenged both by what we found to be the relevance and importance of the project, and also some unexpected stumbling blocks. While our friendship was strong, we began to see that each of us had a very different way of working and establishing priorities that were indeed alien, even painful, to the partner.

First of all, we decided to apply Wolff's theory to our own lives, discover what our own first ego choices had been over the years, and what truthfully motivates us now. We worked on our individual histories in order to decide which of the four types Wolff so carefully described, (the MOTHER, the AMAZON, the HETAIRA and the MEDIAL WOMAN), represented our individual paths. This turned out to be somewhat of a surprise. The more we studied Wolff's theory, the more we realized what a powerful tool it was for becoming conscious of ourselves for personal growth. While we were engaged in this reflection from all angles, the picture gradually became clearer. The one of us who thought she was the consummate MOTHER found herself, at this stage of her life, deeply engaged in her AMAZON pursuits. The one who had believed herself best described by the HETAIRA profile began to suspect that she was actually working more from what Wolff described as a MEDIAL WOMAN perspective.

We began to rearrange our self-understanding by the combined descriptions of both the familiar and the shadow possibilities of Wolff's categories. Each of us realized that what we knew of ourselves was better described, at this stage of our lives anyway, as AMAZON and MEDIAL WOMAN, who are, in Wolff's schemata, diametric opposites. (See Wolff's Model, p. 26) Thus, it was by reading about the opposites that we were best able to find ourselves. And that was when things began to clarify.

It had all begun for us, in high spirits in 1997, with a decision to mount a film series for our local Jungian community illustrating Toni Wolff's four types, (first published in Bern, 1951). This successful effort generated numerous workshops and conferences in several states, and one abroad. The enthusiasm that developed along the way among our participants provided the impetus for gathering many more personal stories, applicable films, and book suggestions for illustrative material. We both began using Wolff's model in our private practices, and sharing the results with each other.

But the greatest realization and surprise was that we found our own opposite ways of working, thinking, producing and interpreting Wolff's material became more smoothly operational, and we were able to realize that Wolff's best known published work itself was actually a study of the very opposites that had become at first our nemesis, and ultimately our most profound personal help. The realization moved us far beyond what had first appeared to be simply an interesting schemata for thinking about feminine psychology.

In time, we presented the four types as dynamic pairs of opposites, instead of clockise, as Wolff represented them pictorially in her original diagram. A further study of Wolff's article helped us to realize that her presentation had actually been conceived to emphasize the oppositional nature of the four types. That perspective had been overlooked, even lost in the general commentaries of the work, which has been presented and published elsewhere. An even more dynamic energy developed among those who came to our seminars and workshops as we began to give stronger emphais on the concept that a consideration of the balancing of opposites actually leads to the method in which women could grasp what their own personal ego preferences are, what they have been, and what they are capable of becoming as they mature.

We found that adding this more distinct application of the tension of opposites provided an additional stimulating dynamic to Wolff's material. Those who have followed Jung's individuation path will recognize aspects of the Transcendent Function. As our readers and workshop participants became personally aware of their own type preferences, and how some aspects of shadow may be present in the 'opposite' partner's characteristics, an additional dynamic was added to the material.

It is of course true that the original intent of the nature of 'balancing opposites' in Jungian analysis is primarily offered as an intra-psychic concept. But it also carries an important application in the inter-psychic relational aspects of personalities as they co-exist in our everyday lives. Something of our own natures was challenged and refined by Jung's strong validation of the importance of this fluid principle. We actually reached for and experienced some startling moments of true enantiodromia. We learned a great deal about ourselves, each other, and women in general.

It seems reasonable to hope that this could happen for our readers as well.

# An Introduction

## Four Cardinal Concepts

2

# I

## On The Importance of Balancing Opposites

"The opposites are the ineradicable and indispensable
preconditions of all psychic life."
—C.G. Jung[1]

To begin this study of Toni Wolff's published work, "Structural Forms
Of The Feminine Psyche"[2] your writers decided to start with Jung's
statement that lies imbedded in the Jungian cannon as an important
cornerstone of all Jungian work. The significance to us personally has
been almost beyond measure. (See Prologue)

---

1 C.G. Jung, *The Collected Works of C.G. Jung*, (Princeton, NJ: Princeton University Press, 1970), "The Personification Of The Opposites," CW 14, ¶ 206. Note that CW refers throughout to *The Collected Works of C.G. Jung*.
2 Toni Wolff, "Structural Forms of the Feminine Psyche"(Bern: *Der Psychologie*, Heft, 7/8 Band III, Herausgecber: Dr. phi. G.H.Graber, 1951). First read in 1934 for the Psychological Club, Zürich; a more detailed version was printed at the C.G. Jung Institute in Zürich.

# II

## Toni Wolff: A Chronology

This section is intended to provide a touchstone, drawing forth significant points in the life history of the author of "Structural Forms Of The Feminine Psyche." The time line forms a context for our homage to a great life and a splendid, disciplined mind. A formal biography of Toni Wolff does not exist as we go to print, and information about her is sparse. Gerhard Wehr wrote:

> Jung made it extremely difficult for his biographers to shed any light on this intimate relationship. He destroyed his letters to Toni, which were returned to him after her death in 1953, together with those she had written to him.[3]

Similarly, according to our research, Toni's sister, Susanne said that Toni gave her diary to her other sister, Erna, who probably destroyed it. This chronology is based on documented facts, and first-hand impressions of those who knew Toni in a variety of contexts, including: her sister Susanne Trüb, C.G. Jung Letters, and her colleagues, friends, analysands and students. We also found secondary sources, including entries about her life in biographies of Jung, and assorted statements in other writings. Included are notes from Gerhard Adler, Deirdre Bair, Irene Champernowne, Barbara Hannah, Ronald Hayman, Helena Henderson, Joseph Henderson, Sonu Shamdasani, Laurens van der Post, Gerhard Wehr, and Joseph Wheelwright. Assistance included that of librarians at the Countway Library at Harvard Medical School in Boston, Barbara Scheietzler at the C.G. Jung library in Küsnacht for eulogies made at Toni's funeral, from translations provided by Tomas Willard, and other translations by Gary Hartman. Considerably more information is given in the HETAIRA profile, along with contrasting data from the lives of other important HETAIRA women, such as Simone de Beauvoir and Lou Andreas-Salomé.

---

3 Gerhard Wehr, *Jung: A Biography* (Boston: Shambhala, 1987), 143.

1888 On September 18 Toni is born, a native of Bern, Switzerland, first child of Anna Elisabeth Wolff (formerly Stutz), and Konrad Arnold Wolff.

1890 Sister Erna Wolff, (later Naeff) is born.

1892 Toni's only other sibling, Susanne Wolff (later Trüb) is born. Toni and her sisters enjoy the privileges as children of the first families of Zürich. She enters finishing school in French Switzerland, and later attends extended classes in England for six months, learning the language as well as history and culture. Toni attends the University of Zürich as a non-matriculated student of philosophy and poetry. Toni has a relationship with Hans Trüb, who later married her sister, Susanne.

1909 Toni's father dies of a heart attack, at about 63-64 years old. She is 21 years old. She suffers a deep depression.

1910 Toni's mother brings her (age 22) to Dr. C.G. Jung (age 35) for analysis.

1911 Jung writes to Freud on August 29, (Of those who will come with us to Weimar) "a new discovery of mine, Fr. Antonia (sic) Wolff, a remarkable intellect with an excellent feeling for religion and philosophy..."[4] Toni attends the Third Psychoanalytical Congress at Weimar Sept 21-22. She is one of the 46 people (of 55 attending) who posed for the official photograph. Following termination of her analysis, her depression re-occurs. She became an active member of the group of students surrounding Jung, and was in consistent contact with him.

1912 Toni is age 24 when Jung's conflict with Freud is rendered visible to all, with his publication of *Wandlungen und Symbole der Libido*, (later published in English as *Psychology of the Unconscious* in 1916). Toni is a member of a committee that meets with Jung on a regular basis, whose purpose was investigation and discussing Psyhchological types. This committee included Emilio Medner, Adolf Keller and some theologians who focused on terminology for three types. Toni was also instrumental in introducing the functions of sensation and (along with Moltzer's earlier contribution) on intuition.

---

4 C.G. Jung and Sigmund Freud, *The Freud-Jung Letters* (Princeton: Princeton University Press, 1974), 440.

1913 On December 12, Toni (age 25) accompanies Carl Jung in his 'descent into the unconscious, also called his *nekyia*, serving as his analyst in the process, which she had undergone earlier herself with his guidance.

1915 By this time, Jung and Toni are known to have an intimate physical relationship, the duration of which is not known. She remained beside him, as peer and collaborator, until her death, some thirty-eight years later.

1916 Toni Wolff is elected first president of an informal organization called The Psychological Club, consisting of Jung's current and former analysands and students. She served in this capacity for seventeen years. This group became very strong and lasted nearly 40 years. It was a solid intellectual as well as social community for the growing number of Jung's students and professional associates.

1921 Toni is 32 years old, Jung is 46. Jung publishes his book, Psychological Types, which begins with documentation of the historic work of his predecessors in the field of psychological typologies. This history formed a basis from which his own new dynamic model grew and flowered, along with the cooperative efforts made by a joint committee of peers, of which Toni is a lively contributing member.

1922 Toni is a frequent lecturer at The Psychology Club in Zürich.

1923 Jung's mother dies. Construction begins on the first tower of Jung's retreat at Bollingen, where Toni visits and works many hours.

1929 Toni spends a month visiting England at the home of Barbara Hannah's family. Jung acknowledges Toni as his capable assistant, to whom he refers patients for analysis. Often, patients see both Jung and Toni for sessions.

1933 Jung calls a particular encounter, "One of the most curious events of my life"[5] Jung and Toni experience a mutual vision that both fully believed actually happened during a trip to Ravenna. The mosaic in the church in Ravenna, which Toni and Jung 'saw' was of Christ holding out his hand to Peter, who was sinking beneath the waves. The original mosaic was a gift from Empress Galla Placidia (d. 410, A.D.) in gratitude for her rescue from the storms in

5 C.G. Jung, *Memories, Dreams, Reflections* (New York: Random House, Vintage, 1965), 285.

her ocean crossing. Only later, when Jung asked a colleague visiting in Ravenna to bring back a picture postcard of this mosaic, was it discovered that the mosaics, which he described, were actually destroyed by fire many years prior to their visit.

Toni takes notes on Jung's first informal lecture at the Eranos Conference, 'A Study in the Process of Individuation.'

1934 Toni, who is 45 years old, presented her first reading of her original monograph, "The Individuation Process In Women" at The Psychology Club, Zürich.

1935 Toni compiles a comprehensive testimonial volume entitled "The Cultural Significance of Complex Psychology," for Jung's 60th birthday celebration. Toni acts as Jung's hostess during his Tavistock Lectures in London, arranging his time for social visits from friends and students.

1946 On May 10, Toni delivers her paper, "Christianity Within," in London to the Guild of Pastoral Psychology.

1948 Toni presents her work, "Structural Forms of the Feminine Psyche" in a reading at The C.G. Jung Institute, Zürich, the year of its founding.

1951 Wolff's work, "Structural Forms of the Feminine Psyche," first appears in public print in DER PSYCHOLOGIE, Bern.

1953 Toni Wolff dies of a heart attack on March 21, the Vernal Equinox. Her funeral is held at The Church of St. Peter, Zürich. Many of her analysands and colleagues speak during the service. Jung is ill and does not attend. Note: Jung wrote concerning this event in a letter to James Kirsh on May 28,1953, when he was 82:

> On the day of her death, even before I had received the news, I suffered a relapse and had a bad attack of tachycardia. This has now subsided. But it has left an arrhythmia, which hampers my physical capacities very much.[6]

1956 "Structural Forms of the Feminine Psyche" is privately printed for the student association in Zürich.

1958 March 18, Jung writes to Dr. Daniel Brody (Proprietor of Rheim-Verlag, Zürich), whose publications later included all of Toni Wolff's written material:

---

6 C.G. Jung, *Letters, 1951-1961* (Princeton: Princeton University Press, 1975), 117.

I feel the need to recommend the collected papers of Toni Wolff to your attention. As president of the Psychological Club in Zürich for many years, she had a unique opportunity to get to know the ambience of analytical psychology from all sides  as well as hosting its representatives from practically all the nations of Europe and all the Anglo-Saxon countries.[7]

1958 June 18, in a letter written to Carol Jeffrey by Jung, age 83:

It is unfortunately true that when you are wife and mother you can hardly be Hetaira too, just as it is the secret suffering of the Hetaira that she is not a Mother. There are women who are not meant to bear physical children, but they give rebirth to a man in a spiritual sense, which is a highly important function.[8]

1959  Included in Jung's *Collected Works* (Vol. 10, pp. 887) is his Introduction to Toni Wolff's "Studies in Jungian Psychology":

In writing this introduction I am discharging a debt of thanks; the author of the essays, printed in this volume, was my friend and collaborator of more than forty years, until her untimely death in 1953 at the age of sixty-five. She took an active part in all phases of the development of analytical psychology, and to her we owe the expression 'Complex Psychology' as a designation of this field of research.

At Toni Wolff's death, Jung showed Joseph Henderson the Toni Wolff stone carving in his garden, which he had made and inscribed:

Toni Wolff
Lotus
Nun
Mysterious

---

7 C.G. Jung, *Letters, 1951-1961*, 424-425.
8 C.G. Jung, *Letters, 1951-1961*, 455.

# III

# An Introduction to Wolff's Four Feminine Archetypes

Instead of the use of the customary early mythological figures to illustrate the archetypal credibility of Wolff's categories, these first illustrations of the four types have been selected from four different periods of history. This may help to illustrate the 'eternal' nature of the archetype for the reader. A more thorough historic overview is presented and illustrated in the opening chapters of each of the following four sections, wherein each type is more fully discussed and illustrated, including Wolff's words (translated) concerning them.

Wolff presented the four types in a clockwise order in her model, MOTHER, AMAZON, HETAIRA and MEDIAL WOMAN, with the opposites forming a quadrant. We present the types in our text in the order of her text, as pairs of opposites, in this introductory section, which retains the quadrant image, but emphasizes the nature of the oppositional quality of relationship. Both ways of understanding her model are important. As you will notice, she maintained that of the four major archetypes, two (MOTHER and HETAIRA), represent *personal relationship*, while (AMAZON and MEDIAL WOMAN) represent the *impersonally related* types. Further into the material, the reader will grasp the importance of the maturing factor of each type. As each of us becomes familiar with both the personal and the impersonal characteristics of our own preferred type, we are reminded that all archetypes live, to some degree, in all of us. Her point is that our growth depends on our ability to integrate and assimilate into consciousness an understanding of our own archetypal preference first, and the others over a period of time as we mature.

In further chapters we have added and elaborated, for each of the types, seven different perspectives: 1. An Overview; 2. Familiar Characteristics; 3. Less Familiar (Shadow) Possibilities; 4. Career Preferences; 5. Relationship to Men; 6. Relationship to Children; and 7. Relationship with the Other Types. The further sections contain extensive information: personal narratives, case studies, examples from available films, and literature, both historic and current.

The reader will find it helpful to refrain from determining her own primary type too quickly, before she has explored the types from all of these perspectives. It is also quite natural for a young woman to think she might be *all four of the types*. After all, those early years are full of experiencing, at least in fantasy, aspects of all four types. Reader may even be quite surprised when her primary preference finally becomes conscious, along with all its various attributes.

# The Personally Related Feminine Archetypes

## MOTHER and HETAIRA

## 1. The MOTHER

Everyone knows something about her...

### A Look at Hannah, and Others

Some three thousand years ago in an agrarian culture nestled in the sparse hills of what is now Palestine, a rich story of the Old Testament book First Samuel[9] tells of a woman named Hannah. She lies beside her husband, weeping in the night for the deepest longing of her heart, a child of her own. Elkhana, her husband, holds her to him, rocks her, and tries to console her. He croons, trying to kiss away her tears, and imploring, is he not more to her than sons?

---

9 *The Holy Bible*, King James, First Samuel 1: 6-8.

## Films, Books, and Stories

Wolff defined the MOTHER archetype as <u>a woman whose primary ego priority is the well-being of her children (or charges)</u>.[10] Three outstanding illustrative MOTHER films are discussed more fully in Section One: In *Bagdad* (sic) *Café*,[11] a childless woman bestows the best of the nurturing MOTHER type in a forsaken desert place. In *Hannah and Her Sisters*[12] a contemporary Hannah, as a zealous MOTHER, loses touch with her husband and inflates her sense of importance by 'becoming' MOTHER to everyone, nurturing all (children, sisters, family, and friends) except, most often, herself and her husband. The BBC film version of Virginia Woolf's novel *To the Lighthouse*[13] presents an extensive amplification of the darker side of the MOTHER archetype, as she reveals her indomitable will-to-power over those she loves the most, and feels she must extend her attention far beyond the scope of her immediate friends and family.

## Narrative: Susan's Story

My mother is in her late 80's. We have never been close, but she doesn't know that. For Christmas day, my husband's sister Christine invited my family to dinner. That included me and my husband, our two adult children, and my mother, who is widowed and lives alone. During dinner, my Mother kept up a steady stream of comments and exclamations about how wonderful Christine was, what a fine dinner it was, how beautifully the house was decorated, on and on.

At first I just let it pass, and thought, well, Mother is just trying to be a gracious guest. But as this went on, I began to struggle. My stomach began to churn. My heart was pounding in my chest. I finally excused myself and headed for the bathroom, dissolving into the tears, which I could not, for the life of me, hold back. Mother had not once, during the entire holiday season, touched me, thanked me, or said one nice thing to me. I had run countless errands for her, shopped for her, wrapped her gifts for family and friends, taken her to visit her friends and chauffeured her to doctor's appointments. All this I managed while holding down

10 Wolff, "Structural Forms," 8.
11 *Bagdad Café*. 1987. (Also known as Out of Rosenheim). See Film Index.
12 *Hannah and Her Sisters*. 1986. See Film Index.
13 *To the Lighthouse*.1983. See Film Index.

my own full-time job, and scheduling my work around my 'assignments' from her. She had also taken most of her meals at our house, with never a word about what went on our table. Nothing. Somehow, it all collected and hit me, at Christine's table.

This pain has been with me all my life. Why is it that I can't get over wanting her approval, when she addresses me mostly with complaints and demands? I remember only once, in 50 years, feeling even tentatively close to her. One evening, when I was maybe eleven or so, she invited me to go for a walk with her, and for some reason, to my astonishment, she wasn't cross with me. You'd think I'd learn not to long for her tenderness. But I still do.

If you asked her if she loved me, she would be shocked. 'Of course I love my daughter,' she would say. But I can't remember ever *feeling* loved. Just that once, as I said, for a few minutes, I felt not quite a fool or an idiot in her eyes. I guess I've been trying to get back to that moment ever since, even for just another moment.

We have included this painful but familiar story to help introduce the incredible power of the MOTHER archetype, which can reach far beyond even the death of the personal mother. Reviewing self-nurture is an important part of the personal development of the MOTHER type, and is presented in Section One.

# 2. HETAIRA

What's love got to do with it?

## Aspasia, The Delight of Pericles, Ruler of Athens

A much longer stretch backward in history takes us to the Golden Age of Greece, circa 450 B.C., when a famous and controversial woman, educated as a HETAIRA, finally became the wife of Pericles, the ruler of the city-state of Athens.[14] Some writers have suggested that it may have

---

14 Madeline M. Henry, *Prisoner of History - Aspasia of Miletus and Her Biographical Tradition* (New York: Oxford University Press, 1995), 9-10.

been Aspasia and not the man himself who wrote the famous orations for which he is still remembered and studied.

The HETAIRAE of ancient Athens and Sparta were women who enjoyed certain privileges that were not available to the society of the 'respectable' women of that time. The wealthy wives of the city were bound to lives of seclusion, were not allowed the privilege of literacy, nor were they educated beyond the arts of household management and child care. The Greek word Hetaira simply means 'female companion.' But it also came to be used to designate certain women, the Hetairae, who were recruited from the provinces to be educated for lives that were devoted to providing interesting and intelligent companionship for the men who were the leading statesmen and scholars of the time. The Hetairae came originally from beleaguered circumstances, and were recruited for their natural gifts of superior intelligence and beauty. Some were slaves, some free women, and some foreigners. They were brought to the cities and scrupulously trained in foreign languages, law, politics, the humanities, the arts of music and dance, the social graces and the elements of style and entertaining. In short, it was the Hetairae who provided the charming company and lent a grace and sophistication to city life. It is also true that liaisons with their male patrons customarily included their sexual favors. A few of the most accomplished, such as Aspasia and Phrene, became famous for their achievements and found their place in the historical records of such writers as Herodotus and Plutarch.

Aspasia of Miletus lived in the time just before Greece was a consolidated national entity, and was still governed by city-states, each with a measure of autonomy. Miletus was a part of a region that had recently been acquired by Athens. In the year 450 B.C., Pericles, as ruler, had declared it unlawful for an Athenian to marry foreigners, even from another city-state. But later he found this beautiful, brilliant and vivacious woman to be irresistible. By virtue of her own considerable talent she became a fascinating courtesan as well as his mistress. She was celebrated for her beauty, wit and accomplishments, and her home became a lively gathering place for the intellectual and literary elite of the city. She also became known as a scholar and teacher of rhetoric, who was often in dialog with the famous Socrates. As ruler of Athens, Pericles was not without political enemies, who agitated over their illicit relationship and publicly accused Aspasia of impiety. Playwrights of the

day also lampooned her in lively comedy. Pericles defended her successfully, however. He divorced his wife, who had borne him two sons,
both of whom were his legal heirs. He later married Aspasia, who had
also borne him a son. According to Athenian law at the time, their son
was considered illegitimate because of Aspasia's status as a 'foreigner.'
During the famous plague in Athens, both of the legal sons of Pericles
died. Later, Pericles was able to rescind the law that he had instigated,
and which had denied Aspasia's son's entitlement to Athenian citizenship and his due inheritance. Their son was named after his father and
in time became a general in the Peloponnesian War, thereby earning his
name in ancient history.[15]

Toni Wolff considered herself to be a HETAIRA, meaning, by her
definition, a woman who is primarily committed to the quality of her
relational life with her partner.[16] In reading about Toni Wolff's private
life, one wonders how her experiences in the HETAIRA mode evolved.
First, this occurred in a sense, with her own father as his intelligent
favored daughter, and later as an intimate partner and colleague of
Jung. Pondering the questions regarding all four of these relationships
motivated her work, as she struggled to understand her life, and later
develop her own AMAZON and MEDIAL qualities as an analyst, teacher
and writer. (Other famous HETAIRA women featured in Section One are
Lou Andreas-Salomé and Simone de Beauvoir.)

## Film Study: *The African Queen*[17]

The course of the genuine HETAIRA type is superbly portrayed in the
classic film *The African Queen*. The story of Rose (Katharine Hepburn)
begins with her as a spinster as well as, arguably, a HETAIRA at least in
attitude to her inept brother. She worked tirelessly to assist him as a
missionary among tribal people. Later, she skillfully unwraps the best
in her unlikely shipmate, Charlie, (Humphrey Bogart), and leads his
imagination and barely-realized talent into great and seemingly impossible achievement. In so doing, she discovers new and unexplored parts
of herself.

---

15  Henry, *Prisoner of History*, 15.
16  Wolff, "Structural Forms," 6.
17  *The African Queen*. 1951. See Film Index.

The HETAIRA type represents women whose ego priorities lie first and foremost in the subtle, dynamic qualities of their relational lives with their men. Once again, this occurs inside or outside the boundaries of marriage vows... most commonly, outside.

# The Impersonally Related Feminine Archetypes

## The AMAZON and The MEDIAL WOMAN

## 3. The AMAZON

Superior woman, or inferior man?

### Film Study: *Elizabeth I* (1998)[18]

Some eighteen hundred years after Hannah gave birth to Samuel, Queen Elizabeth I of England informed her court that she renounced all suitors and would not wed.

In an unforgettable scene in Shekhar Kapur's film *Elizabeth I* (1998) the Queen (Cate Blanchett) faces her court and advisors, and announces that it should be understood that she would marry England! Wolff's AMAZON descriptions provide a portrait of women whose personal focus, or primary ego priority, more or less unconscious, lies in the impersonal realm of collective consciousness.[19] While there have been countless others ever since recorded history gave us the word AMAZON, Elizabeth I, ambitious daughter of Henry VIII, illustrates an outstanding historic figure of female intentionality. She unquestionably followed a path focused specifically on her public. She was concerned,

18 *Elizabeth I*, 1980. (Also, *Elizabeth the Virgin Queen*) See Film Index.
19 Wolff, "Structural Forms," 7-8.

primarily, with the perilous condition and survival of the monarchy, which could only endure in the light of a favorable public consensus. She focused all of her energy on developing and maintaining the good will and well-being of her subjects.

There are numerous women that conspicuously share her focus throughout history; in fact, we seem to be currently living in the era of the contemporary AMAZON, who patterns her life in order to succeed by serving the will, needs and interests of the conscious collective sector. The mood and public taste of her time focus her attention. She makes special notice of each small detail that leads her to her ultimate goal. She is astutely aware of specifics and most often seems to know, accurately, what is possible.

## Wolff's 'True' and 'Inferior' AMAZON

Wolff also makes an important distinction in her study of what she calls the true AMAZON, one whose goals are based on a natural ambition for public achievement, as opposed to a sub-type, which Wolff designated as 'the inferior AMAZON,' one whose motivation is based on unconscious personal anger which may render her compromised in her ability to sustain personal adult relational life. She is the one who creates a battleground wherever she goes and carries the unfortunate shadow of demanding discord.[20] She represents a well-known, sometimes tragic figure among us, even today. (See Section Two.)

## Film Study: A 'True' Amazon, *Tampopo*[21]

We selected a portrait of the 'true' AMAZON nature in this prize-winning Japanese comedy in which a young mother decides to create the best ramen restaurant in Tokyo, and does so. The Tampopo story line is dispersed among other themes in the film, but the 'true' AMAZON characterization is ultimately delivered.

The film *Disclosure*,[22] reviewed in Section Two, skillfully presents seven contrasting AMAZON women, in various stages of growth, motivation and maturity.

---

20 Wolff, "Structural Forms," 8-9.
21 *Tampopo*. 1985-1986. See Film Index.
22 *Disclosure*.1994. See Film Index.

A workshop participant offered this preview of an AMAZON family member of three generations ago, in rural northern Minnesota:

## Narrative: Jo Beth's Story

I have a story, a tale concerning my mother, so I have named it, 'How My Mother Escaped Being Either A Nun Or Farm Woman.' The background must be set; Mother was the second born to a family of nine children of pure French Canadian ancestry. They lived in rural northern Minnesota, close to the Canadian border. Both her mother's and her father's families were even larger, numbering thirteen or fourteen children. Virtually all the men were farmers, and all the women were either farm wives and mothers, or nuns. The nuns between the two families in her generation numbered six or eight.

The household atmosphere was a warm, firm and close knit French Catholic home where the rule of the patriarch was absolute. French was the only language spoken by the grandparents. French holidays included the annual blessing of the womenfolk and children on New Years Day. They would all line up before my grandfather, heads bowed, on bended knees, to receive his blessing, one by one.

In the two large families of my mother's parents, all the girls were educated in a 'girls only' high school run by the Sisters of St. Joseph, some distance away from the family. Six or eight of my mother's aunts had joined the order, having gone to France to the motherhouse for final vows. All returned to North America to serve as nurses or teachers.

Here is where my mother's story begins:

Her older sister, Delia, had followed in line and attended St. Joseph's when she was eleven or twelve, and younger than most girls in her class because she had skipped a grade early on. Mother tells of Delia coming home for the holidays, and crying loudly about the harshness and strictness at school. There was never enough food to eat, and it wasn't very good. When her Mother had given her little jars of jam and jellies to take back with her on her last trip home, she had hidden them in the small drawer of the dining room where she kept her personal silverware, only to have the nuns discover her deception, slap her knuckles, and take the treats away.

Just a few years later, it came time for my mother to enter the Academy and join her sister, Delia. *She refused to go.* And her Father, the absolute ruler, would have nothing of her refusal. There was much conflict and many tears between her and her father. Her mother steered clear.

My mother wanted to go to East Grand Forks, the 'big city', and attend a coed Catholic parish school. Father would, again, have nothing of it, and it looked like she was going to have to do the proper thing and attend the all-girl school, as had all the respected young women of the family.

Now there was, in the extended family of aunts and uncles, one solitary exception among all the women who were either farm wives or nuns. Yes, Aunt Armeline was a 'career girl' who lived in Grand Forks and had an important job as private secretary to a successful attorney named Mr. Owen. She was unmarried at the time, had her own apartment, nice clothes, and such fine things as linen and china.

Somehow, it was Aunt Armeline who intervened. She found a Catholic family that needed a boarder who would 'help out,' fold and iron and so forth, and accepted my mother. So at the age of about thirteen, Mother made a dramatic change in her life when she moved to Grand Forks and began living with an unfamiliar family and attending the co-ed parish high school. Later, Aunt Armeline married Mr. Owen... (laughter from the audience). Because of her, my own life could not have helped but to have been different from that of all my cousins, and even my own siblings, because the story of Aunt Armeline has continued to shape the relationship between Mother and me. And that has made all the difference.

# 4. MEDIAL WOMAN

She could be canonized, or burned at the stake...

Wolff's final category provides us with a portrait of women whose primary focus is characterized by their basic preoccupation with phenomena related to the collective unconscious.[23] They are governed by a set of natural laws that remain mysterious, even to themselves. They are sometimes gifted with a prophetic imagination.

---

23 Wolff, "Structural Forms," 9.

## Cassandra's Gift Of Prophecy

The history and mythology of ancient Greece introduces us to this final and most difficult to grasp of the four types. Cassandra was said to have been the fourteenth child of King Pram and Queen Hecuba of Troy (circa 1100 B.C.). The earliest tales of Cassandra relate that, as a lovely young woman, Apollo gave her the gift of prophecy. Then he asked her to become the voice of the Oracle at Delphi, and also his lover. She declined. Apollo was angry. But he well knew that the gifts of the gods couldn't be taken away, once they are bestowed upon a mortal. He retaliated with his own prophetic curse, declaring that even though she had been given this extraordinary ability, people would not believe her words. Her father knew she had very special prophetic abilities, and he used her gifts freely during the famed Trojan War. If he agreed with her prophecies, she was celebrated. If he disagreed, she was secluded.

At the end of the ten year war, Cassandra was carried off, a captive, from her home in Troy to Mycenae. The conquering Greek warrior-hero Agamemnon had taken the mysterious princess as his concubine, his reward, a spoil of war.

Clytemnestra, Agamemnon's wife, stood waiting for them inside the palace with murder in her heart, for ten years. She had plotted his immediate death upon his expected arrival, in retaliation. She had suffered her rage and grief since the time Agamemnon had insisted that their first child, Iphigenia, be given as a sacrifice, to secure fair weather for launching the Greek armada to sail to Troy. As the homecoming entourage approached the palace gates, Cassandra has a vision of a great sea of blood flowing over the threshold of the palace toward her. She knew immediately of her own impending death, and that of her captor, Agamemnon. Clytemnestra murders them both.

Homer recorded her legend some 400 years later, and then after another 450 years, the playwright Aeschylus dramatized a portion of her story as part of his *Oresteia* trilogy.[24]

MEDIAL WOMAN still encounters a general lack of public credibility. Yet her type retains an indomitable tenacity.

---

24 Aeschylus, *The Oresteia*, "Agamemnon" translated by Ted Hughes. (New York, NY: Farar, Straus and Giroux, 1999), 51-66.

History records many famous women graced with these gifts, such as St. Teresa of Avila, Abbess Hildegard von Bingen, and the clairvoyant 'Seeress of Prevorst' Frederica Hauffe. Contemporary writer, Caroline Myss along with other talented MEDIAL writers of our time, has helped us to recognize the value of MEDIAL WOMAN today. On the other hand, associated with this archetype are many tragic historic records. During the Inquisition in Europe, the Vatican distributed the fatal tome, *Malleus Maleficarum*,[25] which unleashed three hundred years of severe persecution of women whose characteristics were considered MEDIAL. The idea of some women as potentially wicked and evil prevailed. The brilliant St. Teresa of Avila herself was one who barely escaped persecution. Those deemed suspect at that time were all women scholars, priestesses, herb gatherers, gypsies, nature lovers, mystics, and any female who loved the natural world. Midwives were tortured and often killed for using their knowledge of herbal lore to relieve the pains of childbirth. Such women were tried as witches, and sentenced to death by drowning or burning at the stake for crimes of heresy. Some writers have set the number of such deaths at five million women, over a three hundred year period. This persecution was not limited solely to Europe nor attributed entirely to Catholicism. The Protestant Reformation also carried a strong payload of references to women 'heretics' in the new world. The persecution surfaced in Puritanism with its tragic chapter of witch-hunting hysteria at Salem, Massachusetts in 1692, wherein nineteen people, (mostly women) were hanged, and several died in prison. (See Section 2, MEDIAL WOMAN, Chapter One.)

Toni Wolff describes the MEDIAL WOMAN as one whose imagination spans both the known and the unknown. She stands as a bridge between two worlds. Wolff describes their common characteristic as being that which is preoccupied with, and attuned to, phenomena which lie in the collective (impersonal) unconscious. Therein lies the MEDIAL WOMAN'S primary ego focus.

In our age of scientific rationalism, such phenomena are regarded for the most part unfavorably. To the rationalists, the perception of the MEDIAL WOMAN seems absurd; to some others, her visions are uncanny, scary, or perhaps pathological. Yet talented astrologers make a good living, we still read our horoscopes, consult our seers to help solve crimes, find lost treasures, and locate water hidden deep under the sur-

---

25  H. Kramer and J. Sprenger, *Malleus Maleficarum* (Cologne, 1484).

face of the earth. We read the Tarot, cast runes, and patronize contemporary psychics on matters related to the imponderables of time, chance, circumstance, and synchronicity. Examples are omnipresent. Gifted MEDIAL healers of extraordinary skill sometimes bring about scientifically inexplicable cures. The world of creative artistry has many a MEDIAL WOMAN gracing concert halls, theaters, and art galleries who enrich and enhance the range of human perception with powerful images and sublime interpretive imaginations. We depend enormously on the often MEDIAL skills of gifted hospice workers and clergy whose special calling in life enables them to smooth the path of those preparing for death. Perhaps there is even something of an unconsciously MEDIAL character in our tireless preoccupation and demand with poll taking in the political sector, as we seek through complex, extensive number systems to predict the outcomes that favor the candidates of our choice. Somehow the pollsters' results take on an almost oracular quality in the public mind, depending on which 'oracle' is favored.

MEDIAL WOMAN, in our time, may range from the familiar fortuneteller to the work of distinguished analysts and writers of impeccable training and credentials. She also may be engaged in powerful spiritual leadership. MEDIAL WOMAN is found everywhere. She is in the college dorm, the local church, the hospital staff, the trailer park, television sitcoms and advertising media. She might be the first one out with the Tarot cards, and wear a crystal around her neck. But in another mode, unforgettable accounts of her abilities gathered after her death may also be sufficient, even, to assemble the Papal Curatorium in the Vatican to review, and sometimes carefully validate, the spiritual phenomena of sainthood.

Jung maintained that most of our discomfort with occult and paranormal phenomena lies in the fact that we simply do not yet understand the laws which are operative in this way of 'knowing.' "There are things not yet true today," he once said, "perhaps we dare not find them true, but tomorrow they may be."[26]

We still want to know what seems to be unknowable. We keep looking for, and are drawn to, those who somehow remind us of the limitations of our relentless, determined, and sometimes tiresome rationality.

---

26 C.G. Jung, 1966-1977, "Two Essays on Analytical Psychology", CW 7, ¶ 201.

## Book and Film Studies

Several films are presented in Section Two that illustrate MEDIAL
WOMAN in a wide variety of ways; Meryl Streep carries the role of
Clara, the MEDIAL WOMAN in Isabel Allende's *The House of the Spirits*[27]
with graceful dignity. This story also includes a glimpse of Clara's character as a child, who had the curious gift of telekinesis. Films such as
*The Gift*;[28] *Moonlight and Valentino*;[29] and *Eve's Bayou*;[30] present similar
characterizations. (See Section Two and the Film Index).

An account of a MEDIAL WOMAN experience is included here, as a
woman called 'Ann' presented it in a workshop session:

## Narrative: Ann's Story

I want to tell you a personal story that involves my mother and her
father's property located on the  Mexican border. It's a land where
water is very precious, so it's a story about water.

Mother said, 'I found a well one time. I was out at the Placer
claim my father had on the Mexican border. That was down at
Pap's place, called Los Lobos, far from any indoor plumbing. Pap
came up and said to me, 'You could witch some water for us.' We
needed a well closer to the house. The well was a couple miles
away, and we had to haul water in big Jeep cans by burro.

There were some Mexicans working on Pap's house. They helped
haul the water and pour it into those Jeep cans. The cans were dark
green, Government Issue. The burros had wooden saddles on them
with hooks on both sides, and men roped the cans to the saddles.
That was all right. But it was a lot of hard work.

My Mother said, 'Pap got a thin green branch from a tree, maybe mesquite, since that was mostly the only tree around. I didn't
think I could do anything with the stick,' Mother said, 'It had a
fork in it, like a Y. Pap showed me how to hold each of the branches
on the sides of the opening Y, and I walked around, and the base
part of the stick began to move down when I found the water. I'd
never done anything like that before, but Pap told me to go ahead.
He thought I could do it and I did. I asked him if he could do it,
and he shook his head.'

---

27  *The House of the Spirits*. 1993. See Film Index.
28  *The Gift*. 2000. See Film Index.
29  *Moonlight and Valentino*. 1995. See Film Index.
30  *Eve's Bayou*. 1997. See Film Index.

That's what my mother told me.

I found myself in the same position as my mother was, when I was about eight years old, and my own father told me I could do that, could do what my mother had done. We were in our home, then, in Globe, Arizona.

He cut a forked branch off an almond tree, and peeled it ... put one side of the Y in each of my hands, with the base of the Y out in front of me, and I walked along, and thought, 'This is hooey.'

And it started to do it. The branch just dipped down.

Dad dug the well there, twenty-five feet down, with a pick and a shovel. It's still there, on my land. It irrigates the fruit trees...

When asked if she could still do this, Ann paused, and said quietly, 'I don't think I could do it again. You see, it's that I don't really need...to find water.'

# IV

## Knowing Your Type

Most women, when they begin to understand Wolff's construct of the four feminine forms, immediately consider which one might be their first choice to identify where they think their primary preference lies.

Wolff called 'forms' what we generally think of as 'types,' or archetypes. She added a footnote to her manuscript that clarifies her choice at that time.[31]

The four categories that Wolff describes are hardly new. In fact, they are given conspicuous illustration in all literature, and are older, even, than written language. For this reason they carry the unmistakable ring of truth. These forms represent structuring patterns of psychological behavior linked to instinct, which are evident only through their manifestations in women's behavior, and carry aspects of unconscious material.

The idea of there being a certain plasticity to Wolff's forms is helpful, once the predominant one is made conscious. The greatest problem lies when there is inflexibility to the patterns of the primary type. *To remain caught in one principal archetypal position, or self-image, is like a slow death.* Once a woman has experienced the 'just so' sense of herself, a repose and awareness is certainly very present. This is sweet, but also seductive, like a luscious fruit in its juicy perfection. But as soon as that happens, or whenever any piece of affirming reality is clutched too tightly as the *final answer*, there begins the slow decay, the disillusionment, the tendency to court the shadows of martyrdom, injustice-collecting, self-pity, illness, and an often silent bitterness. Future growth is hampered, and the personality takes on certain aspects of rigidity. It is an unconscious invitation for the shadow possibilities to take over the positive

31 Wolff, "Structural Forms," "Endnote 3, p.13: Instead of structural forms, one might just as well use the term 'structural types', since the meaning is that of imprinting or typification. But in the view of the fact that analytical psychology has by now classic application, it may prevent conceptual confusion if the term structural forms is used throughout."

qualities of the type, and sabotage them. Failing to consider, or reach for, other available options for goal setting and growth promises a predictable decline into illnesses, loneliness, isolation and even the silent specter of post-menopausal meaninglessness.

Using Wolff's schemata, your writers developed ways to assist women to identify the form most characteristic of their own personalities, and how to work with the relevant implications. When women begin to see themselves expanding their understanding of how they conduct their own lives, they are bound to consider the options Wolff presents more closely. We believe that *understanding* these primal forms can assist women in some powerful and provocative ways:

* It provides each woman with a mirror for seeing aspects of her inner life that may well be unknown to her.

* It invites women to journey further into the realms of both self-awareness and social interaction.

* It focuses a new lens of cultural awareness, as reflected in mass media, politics, religion, family and social life.

* It exposes the paradigm, or 'world view' behind these forms as applicable to women of ancient history as well as contemporary women. In that sense, the work is both timeless and dynamically relevant. On a more personal level:

* Reader will be significantly challenged to identify her own type, and seek ways to integrate the other types into consciousness as they suggest themselves to her over time.

* Reader will find the path ahead for her own personal growth to become clearer, and yes, even more inviting. The great feminine archetypes, the MOTHER, the HETAIRA, the AMAZON and the MEDIAL WOMAN are still with us, across the centuries. Their forms constitute the main archetypal grid of the adult female psyche, like a map. We find them in everyday life, as well as in history books and folklore. They are in next week's thriller, the glitz of MTV hype, the boardroom, the kitchen, the chat room, the classroom and our bedrooms. They are discussed in the diaries of our grandmothers, and parade persistently in and out of our dream worlds. The historic examples validate the tenacity of each type.

But how does this help you, reader, to figure out your own pre-dominant type?

<u>First of all</u>: Wolff points out that the original early choices women make, and the 'types' they choose to personify and prioritize, are solidified in the personality outside the realm of consciousness. That is, these behaviors and attitudes develop autonomously, for the most part, and are apt to be, at least partially, beyond conscious awareness.

<u>Next</u>: Study Wolff's diagram carefully. Each type has its own characteristic set of attitudes, preferences and behaviors common to the type. Wolff developed her model to help us understand the inter-relationships of the four types. This model will help the reader begin to recognize her own primary type.[32]

**Wolff's Model:**[33]

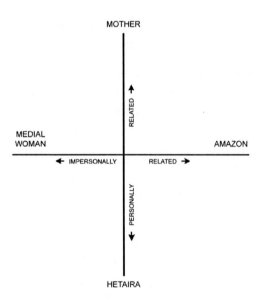

The first distinction that Wolff makes on the diagram concerns personal and impersonal relatedness:

---

32 Wolff, "Structural Forms," 11-12.
33 Wolff, "Structural Forms," 4.

## MOTHER and HETAIRA

You will notice that MOTHER and HETAIRA, are personally related to their first priorities. The MOTHER is primarily concerned with the well being of her children or charges, above all else. This, also, is a deeply personal issue related to her first and most essential priority. The HETAIRA is primarily concerned with the quality of the relationship to her man, or men. These priorities are often set deeply in the unconscious realm, and may be barely conscious to the woman until she has had some time and experience to ponder their existence.

## AMAZON and MEDIAL WOMAN

In contrast, the AMAZON and the MEDIAL WOMAN place their primary energies in manifestations of collective life, or the general public, per se. They are deeply involved with issues other than the realm of personal relationship. This collective realm also has its conscious and its unconscious life. The AMAZON is ultimately concerned, first of all, with consciousness, i.e., what is of importance in the public domain. Another way of saying it is that the AMAZON is primarily interested in what she can bring to the world that the world needs or wants. MEDIAL WOMAN'S first preference and priority is with the phenomena related to the collective unconscious. She is deeply interested in less-than-personal 'other worlds' of a spiritual nature. She stands between, mediates, two different worlds.

Beyond the opposite types, the next issue that Wolff mentions regarding the model is that each type has two adjacent types as well as the opposite type, as observed on the model. Each type knows something about her adjacent types that is familiar to her. The opposite form on the diagram is her 'fourth' type, and the one she knows the least about. (Examples: AMAZON knows something about either MOTHER or HETAIRA, or both. HETAIRA is familiar with AMAZON or MEDIAL WOMAN, or both, etc.)

Chapter Two of each of the following sections elaborates these relational qualities further. Once again, if you can choose the type that you know the least, or that interests you the least, then the OPPOSITE ONE of the diagram is probably your own preferred type.

For our workshop use, we developed a list of easily available and popular commercial films, which present lively and contrasting illustrations and amplifications of qualities that Wolff identifies for each of the types. Workshop groups, home study groups and individuals have used these films extensively, with considerable success. We suggest that our readers take the time to obtain copies of the films and view them as they are referenced throughout the book. And as the work progresses, so does the list of relevant illustrative material. All the film references are listed alphabetically with full information in the Film Index Appendix, and all books referenced are included in the Bibliography.

It is our hope that Wolff's work will significantly broaden the reader's options for personal growth.

It certainly has for us. Good hunting! And gathering!

# Section One

## The Personally Related Archetypes

### The MOTHER

### and

### The HETAIRA

# MOTHER

## A Random Scroll

**Mrs. Antrobus,** in Wilder's *The Skin Of Our Teeth* . . . **August,** in Sue Monk Kidd's *The Secret Life Of Bees* . . . **Charity Lang** in Stegner's *Crossing To Safety* . . . **Demeter** . . . **Princess Diana of Wales** . . . **Ellen O'Hara** in Mitchell's *Gone with The Wind* . . . **Mia Farrow** . . . **Frances,** in Lessing's *The Sweetest Dream* . . . **Gaia, 'Mother Earth'** . . . **Hannah,** in film *Hannah and Her Sisters* . . . **Hannah, Mother of Samuel,** *Old Testament* . . . **Hecuba of Troy** . . . **Jasmine** in film *Bagdad (sic) Café* . . . **Angelina Jolie** . . . **Emma Jung** . . . **Ethel, Jacqueline, and Rose Kennedy** . . . **Kuan Yin** . . . **'Marmie'** in Alcott's *Little Women* . . . **Maria,** in the film *The Sound Of Music* . . . **Mary, Queen Mother of England** . . . **Mary, Mother of Jesus** . . . **Monica, Mother of St. Augustine** . . . **'Mother'** in Treadwell's *Machinal* . . . **Mother Goose** . . . **Mother Meera** . . . **Mother Teresa of Calcutta** . . . **The Old Woman Who Lived in a Shoe** . . . **Rhea, Mother of the Olympians** . . . **Queen Noor of Jordan** . . . **Mamba and Haggard** in Heyward's *Mamba's Daughters* . . . **Virgin of Guadalupe** . . .

"Sometimes I feel like a motherless child"
—*Spiritual*

"Show me the child with no complaint"
—*Jacques Brel*

# Chapter 1

## An Overview of MOTHER

This study of the MOTHER type begins with a workshop report:

## Narrative: Diana's Story

My friend Elaine invited me to attend what she described would be a revelation to me. What she meant was that she knew my secular upbringing and my WASP background would be seriously challenged by whatever it was she had in mind. She was right.

We had talked about Jean Shinoda Bolen's book *Goddesses in Everywoman,* and she maintained that there was plenty of goddess worship going on in our culture, here and now. When I parried with, 'You mean New Age religious groups, like the 'Priestess' women?' She responded, 'No, not at all.' As a sort of bet, she asked me to set aside December 12th, and do what she asked. Curious, I agreed.

At five-thirty on a very cold morning I found myself standing next to her in front of a small mission church called Guadalupe Shrine in Kansas City. The sidewalk and steps outside the little stone chapel were already crowded with people of all ages, mostly Latino, many with tiny children, all waiting, stamping their feet and puffing frosty clouds in the winter air. During our wait, for what I knew not, Elaine told me that the mission was a shrine, not a full-time church. Weekly services were not held here, only special occasions like this one. Close beside the chapel was a small one-car garage with a flat roof. On top of this garage about fifteen feet off the sidewalk was a life-sized statue of the Virgin of Guadalupe. An adult-sized male image was kneeling before her, placing painted roses at her feet. Elaine explained that this was the holy day of the Virgin of Guadalupe, and we were about to see how this was celebrated.

A station wagon rolled up to the curb and men began unloading guitars and sound equipment. The crowd continued to grow. Then five or six young girls lined up on the sidewalk in front of the statue of the Virgin, and began to sing to her in lovely harmony. They were all about the same age and height, maybe thirteen to fourteen years old, and about five feet tall. The Spanish songs were completely pure and sweet, and sung with rapt attention focused on the statue. The men, probably fathers, accompanied the girls with the guitars. The music was amplified and could be heard for at least for a few city blocks.

When the girls ended their songs, about 300 people began to crowd into the chapel, filling every pew and spilling to the side aisles. As we were pressed ahead by the flow of worshipers, I was greeted with the heady fragrance of hundreds, maybe a thousand, of fresh roses, banked in tiers on three altars. As we waited for the service to begin, I noticed young parents holding sleeping little ones that grew heavy, and now and then the parents would trade off the 'holding' duties. Slightly older toddlers were bundled sleeping into pews; still older children stood quietly in place in the aisles, waiting. The energy in the room was charged with an unmistakable sense of sweetness that I could hardly explain, except by the tenderness which I saw expressed between family members, young and old, so early on the cold morning. Nobody was cross, scolding, nobody crying, there was just a quiet mood of contained expectation in the small crowded chapel.

A song began, and then came the celebrants bearing the cross and the incense up the center aisle, led by a dozen matronly women, whom Elaine whispered were probably members of the woman's guild that kept the shrine going. A very tall priest with blond hair and blue eyes led the opening prayers. Then he said something that completely surprised me.

"We are here to tell people that we know we are loved," he said.

It was his unequivocal statement of fact. Powerful. Bold. I still remember that I felt a distinct shiver. Somehow I could feel what those people felt, that a powerful bond of love was palpable, in the room. It said something about working hard, for not much money, being discouraged, and finding somehow a way to begin again, day after day, because you know you are loved. The longing for the nurturing all-loving MOTHER, is here, rising from the primal depths of the human spirit.

Later I was reminded that the Virgin of Guadalupe is honored by countless millions of worshipers worldwide. In fact, she probably commands the largest following of a divine feminine presence anywhere on earth.

Ever since that day, I have thought a great deal about how a woman's sense of being left out of the realms of power might be related to being left out, also, of the hierarchies of the godhead. It doesn't have much to do with theology. I think it has to do with an insatiable human need for the divine feminine spirit of renewal and nurture.

This story was chosen because it brings us a picture of the overwhelming power of the MOTHER type throughout the world. It speaks to the universal longing of the human race to find nurture from a maternal source.

Humans do not love perfectly. They try, stumble, fail, and are in constant need of renewal. That is the way we are. And we keep on longing for a renewal source. This is the story of our ability, or lack of it, to regenerate our capacity for giving and receiving human love. This constitutes an essential part of the drama of life, whereby the dynamics of this single primary connection between mother and child remain as potent in the mature adult as it was in the child, and finds itself acted out again and again in the same inevitable manner, on different stages, with different players. But the scenario remains tenaciously the same.

MOTHER is the most quickly recognizable manifestation of the feminine psyche to us all. Since the human race first flowered into consciousness, all members of the species capable of thought have given some attention to the nature of their mothers, and how that relationship has influenced their lives, either positively or negatively, and most often both.

Those of us who raise children ourselves also endlessly ponder the powerful and capricious nature of our personal identification with the mothering role and the impact it brings to our lives. Some of that same personal conjecture may have led us to the dim and secret regions at the boundaries of consciousness which beckon from within, and bid us search courageously for a deeper level of understanding into the enigmatic realm of the MOTHER type. While we try not to confuse the 'type' with our own experience of our personal mothers (because, of course, any archetype is much larger than any one person's experience). It serves our purpose in describing the MOTHER to acknowledge the vastness which the MOTHER type represents. She is as Mother Nature herself. Therein is stored the entire repertoire of human relational life, from the subtlest nuance of tenderness to the wildest tempests of rage, and each takes its inevitable turn upon the stage of our personal and collective history.

The MOTHER of whom Toni Wolff wrote, however, and this section of the book addresses, is just one of the four 'types' of the adult feminine psyche, and is easily distinguished from the AMAZON, the HETAIRA, and the MEDIAL WOMAN.

MOTHER, for the purpose of this study, applies to the individual woman whose ego identity is primarily described by the characteristics of the role.[34] She may have an impressive career, and a strong marriage; she may have many children, or none. Her children may move easily into adult life and competence, or find themselves suspended in childhood dependencies way beyond the natural order of maturity. Regardless, the MOTHER type still experiences herself in the nurturing role as the primary articulation of her selfhood. Wherever there is MOTHER, there is also the necessary object of attention, CHILD, or some approximation of CHILD, as in protégé, charge, patient, pupil, or even institution. And her ego is primarily invested in the well being of those within her care. Her energy is instinctive, containing, encompassing, and care-taking.

Like all of Wolff's forms, MOTHER is directed both by conscious and unconscious motivations. She is both positively and negatively experienced by her charges, who are deeply affected by MOTHER'S conscious life, as well as her unconscious history, motives and dreams. To be primarily involved in the MOTHER role means that the concerns of the children (charges, protégés, etc.) supersede all other relational life priorities, even that of the woman for herself.

It is important for us to consider here that many a personal mother is not as affected by this primal MOTHER type as powerfully as others may be, although this truth may lie out of her conscious range at the time of childbirth. The woman does not necessarily 'choose' her primary archetypal preference by her conscious will, and the other three types are also quite capable of producing healthy and productive children. The major difference is that the priorities of the other three types are apt to be arranged somewhat differently.

34 Wolff, "Structural Forms," 4-5.

# Chapter 2

## Familiar and Positive Qualities of MOTHER

Toni Wolff's ideas:

- "...cherishing, nourishing, helping, charitableness, and teaching. Her instinct relates to all that is in the process of growth, is undeveloped, in need of protection, care or assistance."

- "She does not condescend, but provides room for development and security, and finds her ego fulfillment in strengthening the object of her attention until, in the normal case, it can be dismissed from her care."[35]

Jung wrote of the positive aspects of the MOTHER archetype as follows:

> Qualities associated with (MOTHER) are maternal solicitude and sympathy, the magic authority of the female, the wisdom and spiritual exaltation that transcend reason, any helpful instinct or impulse, all that is benign, all that cherishes or sustains, that fosters growth and fertility.[36]

As we distinguish the characteristics of the type as illustrated by the quotes from Wolff and Jung, and differentiate them from our own repertoire associated with the personal mother experience, we understand once again MOTHER, in the archetypal sense, is indeed far greater than any one personal mother. The MOTHER represents a universal, timeless component of the human psyche. All of us wish, somehow, that we had been perfectly mothered as children. That ideal lies hidden in the psyche of all of us. But if we are unaware of the enormous universal collective power of this type, we will invest our own personal maternal experience with a superhuman energy, which explains the longing in the first narrative. The task of separating the longing for perfection from the experience of our personal histories with our merely human mothers is perhaps the major work of adult maturity. For that reason,

---

35 Wolff, "Structural Forms," 4-5.
36 C.G. Jung. 1959-1969, "Psychological Aspects of the Mother Archetype," CW 9i, ¶ 158.

the effect on our development as personal mothers can be contaminated by an inflation, whereby a mother-to-be may fantasize herself in a role of near-perfection.

It is important to know that this longing for perfection is also projected by the tiny infant on the personal mother, and she is therefore both the object of our longing, and the target for our ills, as seen by the 'personal' psychologies of the day. It is not only the child who unconsciously projects matters of enormous consequence to the psyche upon the personal mother. It is the literature of psychology itself that has bestowed upon her the superhuman attributes that actually belong to the archetypal vocabulary, the eternal language of our race.

Patricia Berry writes:

> If there is any concept in psychology that we have overused, it is that of the mother. And blamed her. At one time or another we have used her to explain our pathologies: Schizophrenia as her double binding. Paranoia as our inability to trust because of our need to tie our thoughts into rigid systems in compensation for her lack of order, Hysteria, a tendency to over sensitize without feeling because of her 'wandering Womb.'[37]

James Hillman also carries this idea of unfairly blaming the personal mother for all our ills as follows:

> If she is always *present*, then she fosters weakness and dependency pampering. If she nurtures *warmth* and *closeness,* then she is called *smothering* and *devouring.* If she desires much for her child and fantasizes its future from the reserves of her spirit, then she is *dominating its life with her goals.* If she is farseeing and detached, then *her wisdom is that of* a *witch.* If she delights in life, and the pleasure of the senses, then she is either *seducing her children,* or *depriving them of their lives by living so voluptuously her own.*[38]

By virtue of this type, unquestionably the most powerful of the four, we begin to see what enormous oppositional forces are at work in the psyche of the woman who takes on, unconsciously, MOTHER as the type that is most descriptive of her nature. If she is working on becoming as conscious as possible, she diligently strives to sort out her own

37 Patricia Berry, *Fathers and Mothers* (Dallas: Spring, 1990), 89.
38 James Hillman, *Fathers and Mothers* (Dallas: Spring, 1990), 105.

personal maternal history from the power inherent in the supra-human MOTHER archetype. One thing she will need to understand is that she will not be, ever, *a 'perfect'* mother. Perfection belongs to the realm of divine adulation, and by virtue of its definition, is beyond human accomplishment.

## Film Study: *Bagdad Café*[39] Part 1

This classic film carries a portrait of mothering at its human best. Jasmin (Marianne Sagebrecht), a childless matron tourist from Germany, visits America's southwest and encounters an entire family radically in need of nurture at several levels. She transforms a rundown, lonely motel/gas station/café into warm and creative life by virtue of her own MOTHER capabilities, so powerful that they transcend the familiar boundaries of race, culture, economic status, and life experience. The portrait of Jasmin in this film helps us understand the highly positive role that is possible for this type, and assists us in identifying the outstanding contributions to society that such women are able to provide.

Jasmin's mothering is entirely natural. She leaves her gruff but affable husband temporarily stranded in his inoperative car in the Mojave Desert. She sets off on foot in the blistering heat to find a place for what her spirit knows she must do, which is to nurture others with all her heart and strength.

Her spirit enters into each of those she touches, not so much with a narcissism that demands their applause, but with the genuine spirit of creative invention. Her gifts are offered to them freely. She helps each one find his or her own inner delight in life, which she seems to have in herself, in abundance. Thus, she works her magic, first with the children, then by an extended inclusion of the nearby adults. Then the scruffy cowboy artist (Jack Palance), energized by her imaginative encouragement, proposes marriage. It is already clear that she is not as interested in being a wife as she is in making things bloom in those she touches. Rather than snaring her adopted family into dependency, she liberates them. The cafe itself offers her another revolving population to nourish and encourage as well as that of her immediate adopted family. She manages her own life with enormous freedom and spirit, and thereby creates the same in others.

---

39 *Bagdad Café*. 1987. See Film Index.

The ideal of 'perfect' mothering underlies the psyche's need for divine intervention, and gives rise to the archetype of the 'fairy godmother' in our beloved childhood literature. When 'good mother' dies, the ideal remains forever in the heart and soul of the bereft child.

Here is an account of a dream Mary Dian Molton had at the time of the death of one of her own clients:

## Narrative: Mary Dian's Story and Dream

Her granddaughter Shanna and her grandson-in-law, Kram, called her The 'Mutti.' They had secured the help of Jewish Family and Children's Services to bring the little lady, not even five feet tall, all the way from Kabul to be with them, in Kansas City, in 1986. They were a part of a sizeable population of Afghanis who came to America during the time of the Russian occupation of Afghanistan. They had two small children, and the young mother felt that she needed Mutti to come to the United States where she would be safe, and also to provide some trustworthy child care so that both parents could hold down jobs and learn to support their family in this strange new country. It took a long time for the old one to arrive. The adult children had worried and worried as she wove her way through countless obstacles in leaving her home and friends: the mounds of paperwork in unfamiliar languages; traveling alone; and encountering legions of strangers speaking different tongues in refugee camps, in order to come where she was needed.

There was an awful moment when the family had gathered in the airport at the scheduled time to finally welcome her. All the passengers deplaned, and there was no Mutti. Where was she? What could have happened to her? Shanna was beside herself. She could not believe her beloved Mutti was not there. Agency workers across the country were summoned to help, telephone calls made, and finally Mutti was located. Somehow a mistake had been made concerning her departure schedule. She was finally located sitting calmly on her bed in a strange hotel in Los Angeles waiting patiently for someone to take her to yet another airport. She arrived in Kansas City, beaming, a day later than scheduled, with seemingly no ill effects.

Mutti soon took over the kitchen and the care of the little ones. Shanna, her English skills improving rapidly, found work, as did Kram. As their social worker, I was often in their home helping them through the red tape of medical examinations, dental work, licensures, vaccinations and everything else a social worker does. The fall season came for fasting and religious services, and then the winter. It was spring when I got word that the Mutti had become suddenly ill, and she died shortly after. I went to make a sympathy call, and saw the griever's wreath on the door of their modest 'Section Eight' home. I expressed my sympathy to family and friends, all crowded into the living room. Many were silently weeping, all of them distressed almost beyond words. I, too, was caught up in their grief and incantations.

That night, I dreamed that I was back there among them, grieving with them. All the men, young and old, were in a circle, a great white sheet surrounding them as they groaned and cried for the Mutti. In a similar fashion, all the women were held together in an enormous green band, or perhaps a blanket, encircling them, as they swayed and moaned for her. I walked around them, the inconsolable family and extended family of this small woman. Then in the dream, I walked around the outside of the house and there were some stairs leading downward. I began to descend into the earth. The way was dimly lighted, but from no source I could determine. I came to a very large underground cavern, and directly across from me was an enormous prone sleeping giantess, or goddess figure, unclothed, at least twenty-five feet in length, lying on her side with her head toward me, pillowed against her arm. Her skin was the color of terra cotta. I was maybe another fifteen feet across from her. I stood there watching her breathe, knowing somehow I was in another realm.

I have never tried to analyze the dream; I only know that this figure was not the spirit of the Mutti alone, but perhaps the symbol of mothering itself, coming from deep in the earth. Maybe Mother Nature herself. I don't know. But I will never forget the dream, and that image.

# Chapter 3

## Less Familiar (Shadow) Tendencies Of MOTHER

Toni Wolff wrote about the possible darker characteristics of MOTHER:
Toni Wolff's ideas:

- "The negative aspect of mother is anxious nursing and tutelage of the object when the later no longer needs it; lack of confidence of the latter's strength and independence, and interference with its development."

- "The ego is only experienced in its motherly function, and is empty without it. The specific danger involved is that unaccepted aspects of her own personality may infiltrate into the protégés and may tend to realize themselves through them."

    (Paraphrases): A negative tendency of MOTHER is anxious nursing and over-instructing, far beyond the needs of her charges. She may fail to affirm their own need for a sense of strength and independence, and thus delay the maturing process.[40]

The darker side of the MOTHER type has been characterized in countless ways in mythology, folk tales, fiction, religion, theater, literature, psychology, and throughout the arts. For example, one good look at Wilhelm de Kooning's fierce and formidable paintings of women can strike terror in the psyche, and evoke in us ancient and nearly forgotten moments of childhood when caught in the rage of the dark MOTHER. The wicked stepmothers of the fairy tales from all cultures remind us that MOTHER can be as cold and mean as she is helpful. While the idea of stepmother as 'bad' and real mother as 'good' is certainly with us from such tales, and we recognize the stereotype as distasteful; still, it reminds us that the powerful anger of MOTHER might be understood as a 'step' away from the child's longed-for ideal. All personal mothers are powerful, and are experienced *by the child* as 'good' mother or 'bad' mother, depending on her interaction with the child's wishes at any

---

40 Wolff, "Structural Forms," 5.

given moment. The child will inevitably experience both sets of reactions to the mother with varying degrees of emotional intensity. And necessarily so, because within the early interaction of mother and child, the vast repertoire of human emotions is developed and imprinted.

However, another great conflict arises when the ego of the personal mother is unable to relinquish her charges in a timely manner. If she continues to direct, cajole and instruct long after it is either necessary or useful, the child will react in one of two ways: Either the child develops a resentful alienation (most often buried deeply within), or an unconscious accommodation, in an effort to try to meet the mother's ego needs, by remaining dependent. If the anxious tutelage continues, the maturing process is compromised, and there will be a serious outcome for both parent and child.

At this crucial time when the personal mother must release her own ego from its total preoccupation with her children, the woman is in danger of becoming *consumed by the MOTHER archetype.* She may also lose track of her own selfhood as even existing beyond the needs of her charges. Her own personal ambitions are lost to her, as she, indeed, may find her ego empty of meaning outside the role of MOTHER.

The film *To the Lighthouse,*[41] based on the novel written in 1927 by Virginia Woolf, gives a powerful portrait of this phenomenon:

## Book and Film Study: *To the Lighthouse* Part 1

The story develops the figure of a mother, Caroline Ramsey (Rosemary Harris) whose classic mothering extends not only to her six children, her professor husband, a chosen student of his, and their other omnipresent house guests, but also to the vacation summer seaside house, garden, neighborhood and the surrounding local inhabitants. She is the undisputed commander of an entire social unit.

Unknown to her consciousness is the fact that she is consumed, or imprisoned, by the MOTHER archetype, and she becomes somehow omnipotent. She embodies the flow of time and the changing seasons, which finds the family in its own well-known place. Every year, the same ceremonies are held, in much the same way. She also benevolently

41 Virginia Woolf, *To The Lighthouse* (New York: Harcourt Brace, 1986), 62.

mothers the neighboring local townspeople, as she tends a sick woman in the neighborhood at night. She moves from one aspect of her domain to another, sweeping the landscape, anticipating in advance what to her are 'the needs' of all in her purview, children, guests, schedules, food, entertainment, all of it. A brief moment in the film shows her sitting exhausted by the rolling sea, contemplating its vastness, and one senses her aloneness. Her subtle orchestration of everything that goes on, from the cricket game beside the sea to her daughter's engagement, is dictated entirely by her wishes and planning. She has become, and maintains, the figure through which all nurturing sympathy flows. There is no 'Caroline,' outside the MOTHER role which has consumed her.

The youngest son, seven-year-old 'James the sixth,' is indulged and spoiled by her. At one point, she goes to his room in the early dawn while he is sleeping soundly, and picks him up. She carries his gangly body across the dewy grass, cooing and singing to him for the entire world as if he were a fussy baby who had summoned her. This act is undertaken entirely for her own needs. Under Mother's protective care, 'baby' James is barely influenced by his father's rules, and never seems to make it 'to the lighthouse' until after his mother's death. Only then, when he is a sullen teenager, can he achieve his father's companionship and praise for his abilities.

Hanging in young James' room is an animal skull that he likes, a relic of nature, which would interest any growing boy and inspire his emerging curiosity about the natural cycles of life. It is covered by Mother's shawl, an apt metaphor.

Caroline Ramsey's husband, Michael (Michael Gough), is also 'mothered' by her. He serves as an important mirror of her own importance as well. He shows up like clockwork for each of her planned rituals and games over which she presides. He has little or no time for his own pursuits, and is querulous, since he is unable to find the necessary hours of quiet either for his own writing or for consultation with the 'promising' student who has been invited to share the family vacation and receive advice on his thesis from his professor. Ramsey can't even find the necessary energy, time, or concentration to compose an important guest lecture due in the fall at the University of Cardiff. His best professional work, he fears, is behind him. Caroline addresses his career not with encouragement for the work he still longs to produce, but for the past accomplishments that have established his reputation. A frustrated man, he is very easily enraged over small incidents. But even his furious outbursts serve Caroline's needs, for then she becomes the stoic, benevolent and subtly martyred absolver of his sins, entirely misunderstanding his real needs. She comforts him as she would a child, and still insists on his full participation at every level of family life. He seems to have been subtly rendered impotent by too much mothering. Interestingly enough, the narrating voice of the story is articulated by another house guest, the talented artist Lilly Briscoe (Suzanne British), a single woman, who tells the tale of the Ramsey household as she experiences it over several summers. At one point blossoming daughter Nancy, who dreams of a more private life independent of Mother's constant perusal, confides to Lilly with the wistful report that Ramsey's aren't allowed to have secrets. Gradually, Lilly herself begins to realize that Caroline too is subtly patronizing her, and she finally bursts forth:

Lilly: "Is my situation so different than yours? Children? A man always to share your bed, and I have none? Do minds ever open? Should love claim so much?"

Mrs. R: "Poor Lilly...."

Lilly: "You must not say that. Why must you always insist that the likes of us stand outside the gates of bliss just because we are not married? It is true; I do not have a man to serve. Am I not permitted to be happy on my own? Can you care for the whole world, Caroline?"

Mrs. R: "You just don't understand...."[42]

Caroline can only react to Lilly's accusation with a patronizing dismissal. Another houseguest, Augustus, Ramsey's old college bachelor friend, seems dissipated while Caroline is alive. He presents himself at the family picnics and gatherings as gruff, unfocused. He drinks in his room at night. Only after her death does he return to his successful writing of soul-fulfilling poetry.

Each member of the family and some of their annually returning guests find their lives somehow stopped just short of their own self-actualization. Such is the result of the unchecked voracious archetypal

42 *To The Lighthouse.* See Film Index.

MOTHER. The subtle emotional development of each member of the family folds silently into Caroline's needs for constant affirmation of her own 'usefulness.'

Yet Caroline could never believe that she was behaving in any manner other than that of a self-sacrificing, kind and generous mother. That she believes all women should go and do likewise is perfectly clear to the observer, but not to Caroline herself, who would never acknowledge such an uncompromising position. She is entirely beyond any reproach, in her own mind, and is utterly convinced of her invincibility. Also, even the reader or audience member cannot help but feel drawn into Mrs. Ramsey's world, and fall prey to her self-aggrandizing charm of selflessness, which means, in her mind, unselfishness as a cardinal virtue.

According to Analytical Psychology, however, "selflessness" could also mean to be absent from the self in its entire unconscious potential. Caroline confesses to a terrible fear of being alone ... that is, of having any private serious interest of her own outside of her MOTHER role. She is very uncomfortable when it occurs to her that she just might be as smart as her husband, or that being alone, a feeling of intolerable pain for her, might be necessary in order to learn what her responsibilities to that undiscovered self might require. For example, that she might relate to the other adjacent types for which she has undoubted talent and ability, AMAZON or MEDIAL WOMAN, has never occurred to her.

She is constantly in motion; as if to stop would mean that she was somehow useless. In this state, where she moves from one aspect of the MOTHER archetype to another, she is never at rest in her own center, but always in the milieu of others, managing, planning, reflecting, deciding what is 'best' for everyone, and unconsciously creating dependency upon her, which fortifies her ego position. By so doing, she exhausts her own strength, and much of that in those around her. Caroline still believes herself to be both everything, and nothing. There is no grounded center of personhood, only a glittering mirror for the flow of admiration from others.

At first, Lilly seems enthralled, for the most part, by Caroline's charm and grace. When she returns to the summer house some years after Caroline's death, her imagination objectifies and focuses all that she has experienced of Caroline, whom she also deeply loved and admired. She makes several variations of a painting of the house and garden trying to understand Caroline's spell of enchantment over her, and the entire place. Finally, Lilly is able then to achieve her own spiritual freedom, and be ready to tell the story with compassion, objectivity, and grace.

Perhaps the most touching of all the elements that make up the experience of MOTHER in *To The Lighthouse* is the stunning lack of consciousness that Caroline brings into her role as MOTHER. The tangle with the archetype has become so overwhelming that she believes in her own indisputable rightness, and sometimes, even in her omniscience. In this great work, what Caroline sees as nurture and benevolence to all, tragically become a legacy of crippling dependence and unfulfilled longing for those she truly loves the most.

* * *

When the mother loses her entire selfhood into the all-encompassing MOTHER archetype, then the indictments of which Hillman and Berry wrote as 'unfair judgment' may indeed influence the future of children far beyond that which she can begin to imagine.

The influence of the mother takes on an unconscious autonomy that is carried out endlessly in the relational life of the adult child, long after the contact with the personal mother has died or been resolved on an adult plane. In still easier terms, in the personality of the adult, the MOTHER type combines with the personal mother history and continues operating in the psyche in ways that seriously influence adult life.

The long–term effect of an omnipotent and dark MOTHER on one tragic daughter is the subject of the following Broadway play early in the 20th century. It presents a superb study of the power inherent in the negative mother-daughter relationship.

### Brief Theater Portrait: *Machinal*[43]

This powerful play was written by Sophie Treadwell, and presented on Broadway in 1928 starring Clark Gable and Zita Johann. The story depicts the struggle of a young woman whose bondage to her ferocious,

---

43 *Machinal*, a play by Sophie Treadwell, played first in London 1928, and later on Broadway, as an example of expressionist theater, based on the true story of a tragic convicted murderess Ruth Snyder. Revived in 1994 by Laurence Olivier.

all-consuming mother leads her, with a dreadful inevitability, to commit a tragic crime. Because of the mother's insistence on the invincibility of her point of view, her lovely daughter Helen never experiences one moment of freedom, either in her imagination, her body, or her own destiny. Having never experienced a sense of personhood independent of her bondage to mother, she projects her sense of inferiority and deference first unto her demanding husband, and remains psychologically captured and abused by him. Later, a transient terrorist lover seduces her with his tales of wild pseudo-freedom and she becomes a helpless accomplice in his crimes of violence and death committed upon his own captors. There was never really a 'Helen.' Only a tragic enslaved 'daughter.'

There are many stories about the maternal shadow, and its painful after-life in children. Most of them are tales of too much mothering, or not enough. Again, the best thing we can do is realize that the role itself is far bigger than human, and never truly gets done 'perfectly.' (See MOTHER as Scaffolding, Chapter 6).

# Chapter 4

## MOTHER and Some Career Thoughts

Wolff wrote:

- "In the case of maternal professions, the place of the home is taken by institutions and organizations of public utility."

  (Paraphrases): Schools, hospitals, and service professions attract the MOTHER type and provide the culture with enormous strength and pioneering achievement. The nurturing skills of the MOTHER are highly adaptable to public service, and can enrich the culture with great strength and effective leadership.[44]

The nurturing skills which the MOTHER type has honed to a high degree are essential to any society. If she chooses to follow a career, she has some excellent choices available to her in many fields, including teaching, medicine, psychology, children, personnel work, social work, plus all that involves household management in design, food, etc.

Three reports from one workshop reflected the intrinsic differences between personal mothering and attitudes about professional nurturing. An adjustment might be required.

Carol, a woman in her mid-forties, was a teacher during the early years of her parenting. She decided to work on a master's degree in clinical social work.

### Narrative: Carol's Story

Right away as I began the program, I was given a practice assignment in a residential treatment center for boys, ages five through twelve. I worked four eight-hour days a week, and was assigned the

---

44 Wolff, "Structural Forms," 5.

role as therapist for three boys and their families. I knew practically nothing about doing this kind of work, but there was a strong support system for me in the night classes at the university, and a resident professional therapist on staff at the center, so I jumped in.

Among my charges at the center were six-year-old Jason, and his mother who lived in a nearby town. Jason was a lovely little boy with soft brown eyes and yellow curly hair. He suffered from epilepsy, attention deficit disorder, depression, hyperactivity, and mild retardation. One session with mother and him together made it clear that the mother wasn't in much of a position to help him. Actually, she wanted Jason to tell her that he was fine. In effect, to nurture her. So that's what he did. He was far from fine. Midway into our work together, Jason began 'going off' in school. I had read in his chart that this had happened to him before, but up until that point, it hadn't happened on my watch. He began suffering terrible rages, so that he had to be isolated and wear a football helmet to keep him from injuring his head, which he banged helplessly against the wall of his isolation chamber. He was unable to sleep or eat. Under heavy medication, he would finally settle down and be able to reenter the life of the school and the household program with the rest of the boys. Then the spells would repeat.

I found that when Jason was enduring these dreadful episodes in the isolation room, I would carry my anxiety and discomfort about him home with me after work hours, no matter how hard I tried to let thoughts of him go. I knew, in my head, that there were capable staff people attending to him in my absence, but my ability to care for my own family and get my schoolwork done really suffered. I would dream about him at night, get up, and call the night staff at the Center to check on him to see if he was all right. My husband was concerned, and mentioned that maybe I was too tenderhearted for this work. My instructor at school told me I needed to get a hold of myself, and if I didn't learn how to do that, I would burn out in a hurry.

What I realize now is that I was carrying the MOTHER archetype with me into a situation which I did not cause, and might not be able to fix. And that the feelings I was experiencing were absolutely appropriate for a mother who had a seriously ill child, but useless as a professional person trying to do a competent and caring job.

Jason opened in me all the maternal ideals that the MOTHER type cherishes, like being 'the one who nurtures selflessly, far beyond the call of duty.' But I needed to develop new (AMAZON) skills to make the professional relationships as important to me as my personal ones, but less personal.

I also know now that it is possible to remain deeply sensitive to the pain of those around me, and still be able to help without being consumed, or neglectful of my own health and the needs of my own family.

After an extended maternity leave followed by a stretch of classroom teaching at the junior high level, and while her own children were still young, Barbara made a career change to a corporate setting as a resident educator:

## Narrative: Barbara's Story

I entered the office setting and sort of unconsciously became, over a period of time, something of 'den mother' to the office personnel. I listened to all the stories about their families and children, and exchanged anecdotes on a daily basis with just about everybody, including my immediate boss, who liked to stand at the door of my office and talk about his kids and tell jokes.

Gradually I came to understand that the new program I had been hired to design didn't have the budgetary support necessary to do the job. There was no real commitment to the task at the higher levels of the administration. It seemed that perhaps the job assignment had been a sort of token effort to appease some people.

I finally realized that if I really wanted to see my program fly, I would have to find my way from mid-management to the executive level of the organization. Actually, I was excited by that challenge. And I began to suspect that the role of 'mother to all' might not be appropriate, if I really wanted to be taken seriously, and not to be so dependent on being Mrs. Wonderful to everybody around me.

I became, little by little, less involved with everyone's personal stories. I started to feel the pull of a genuine ambition outside of my personal life. But still, I remained friendly and affable. I began studying the financial structure of the company, and strategizing just where the new program could find the necessary funds, and some genuine executive support. It was a little lonely for me. My boss stopped by less often. People just assumed I was really busy, I guess. But it paid off. I finally went to the boss with a full fiscal plan, and asked if I could present it to the corporate heads. Not only was it funded; I was given a staff, and ultimately a VP title in the whole development section of the company. Best of all, I got to develop part of myself that I hardly even knew existed.

One of Barbara's adjacent types, the AMAZON, was assimilated success-fully.

As an opposite scenario of the effects of mothering on career life, there is the story of a young woman who, caught unconsciously, chooses a career that her mother had wanted, and misses an experience for which she may have been ideally talented and suited.

## Narrative: Roxanne's Story

> I never wanted to be a hairdresser. That was the career my mom wanted very badly, and never got to follow. She had lost a leg in an accident as a child and was on disability, so her career options were really limited. She used to brush my hair, and hers too, for hours and hours.
>
> And she made me go to beauty school. I worked as a hairdresser for fifteen years, and never liked it. After Mom died a few years ago, I thought I should do something else, but continued at the salon, day after day. I was sick often and missed a lot of work. Then there were several pesky surgeries. So finally I just quit. My husband was great about it, and said he could take care of us. But you know, as soon as I'm feeling better, maybe I can find something I'd really enjoy, and I might even go back to school. I know I need to 'get a life,' as the kids say.

This story may help the MOTHER type, and her children as well, address her own personal needs for the development of her talents and interests. Her efforts to integrate the characteristics of the other forms into her consciousness and embrace some of them as her own will also be of significant help to her. If she is able to do this, she offers her children and those around her a powerful example, and as was not the case for Roxanne, freedom from having to carry her mother's dream.

# Chapter 5

## Of Men and MOTHER

Some of Wolff's thoughts about men:

> (Paraphrases): The relationship (of MOTHER) to the male is determined by his aspects of husband and father, so his workplace place in the world is protected and promoted. Whatever he experiences as the deepest utterances of his private soul, aside from his career aspirations, may be suppressed by her, and he thus becomes a necessary fixture. He will probably exaggerate his virility in male company among his male friends. MOTHER may unconsciously ascribe the role of FATHER to him in the outside world, so that his relationship to her is circumscribed by his role as parent.[45]

How often we hear the MOTHER type say, of her three children, 'I have four children, you know,' as she jerks her thumb toward her husband, out of earshot across the room. The busy world with her children becomes, day in and day out, one that is tutorial. She unconsciously may become tutorial with her husband as well, instructing him on how to 'be,' and what is 'best' for the children and all concerned, as she sees it. In so doing, she may be unaware of his private longings, hopes, ambitions and fantasies that may not necessarily fit exactly into the provider role or offer the pattern of solicitous care that she feels is appropriate as FATHER.

He may indeed be a very good father, but that is not all he is. He is a unique individual as well. Both were human beings with hopes and dreams, long before they became parents. And she too may have completely lost track of her own selfhood outside the MOTHER role. If so, she not only instructs the children, but the husband as well, in how she perceives his role as FATHER, and in almost everything else. If this is the case, it puts great stress on the relational life. They are no longer peers. She is the one who *knows everything*. While this profile is unpleasant,

---

45 Wolff, "Structural Forms," 5.

it is also very familiar. The seeds of serious marital discontent are obviously inherent in this scenario.

## Book and Film Study: *To the Lighthouse*,[46] Part 2

In this film version of Virginia Woolf's famous novel, Michael Ramsey is assigned the fatherly responsibility for the behavior of what he calls 'the animals' (in this case, the children). In watching the film of the traditional family outing of a cricket game by the sea, the audience might cheer for him as he blows up when seven-year-old James behaves like a silly baby who decides he does not have to play cricket by the rules. James thinks he has special favored status as the youngest. Father irritably hauls him off to 'feed him to the fishes.' Yet Father is so disagreeable in doing so, his fury is hardly concealed. Caroline seems silently martyred by Father's behavior, which takes the pressure off James. The audience is subtly maneuvered to believe now that Father is somehow also an 'animal', and that Caroline is the only fair and sane parent. In truth, this is exactly what everyone within her purview seems to be subtly, and semi-consciously, seduced to feel.

## Film Study: *Hannah and Her Sisters*[47]

Woody Allen's screenplay and film, *Hannah and Her Sisters*, illustrates Toni Wolff's description of the MOTHER type admirably. The protagonist Hannah (Mia Farrow) is so determined in her desire to produce and raise children that she loses sight of her husband's inner life entirely. They agree to a surrogate insemination and she becomes pregnant with twins. She is enamored, preoccupied and captivated by her new MOTHER role. She and her husband become merely 'friends,' they divorce, and she proceeds to reenact a similar ego preoccupation with her next husband, even when she acquires his several children. Soon this second husband seems to need another female companion. Hannah's own need to care for others extends to her 'mothering' her own mother and her adult sisters, all of whom might well need to learn how to take care of their own lives. Even more tragically, she is unable to take much of any serious interest or pleasure in the excellent career options

---

46 *To the Lighthouse*. 1983. See Film Index.
47 *Hannah and Her Sisters*. 1986. See Film Index.

available to her outside her rapidly expanding home life. She is amaz-
ingly virtuous and long-suffering. That her virtue smacks of possible
self-righteousness and infallibility does not reach her consciousness,
or that of those around her. The MOTHER archetype now owns her,
and is functioning as an autonomous authority which unconsciously
relegates all her other ego priorities to a lower status.

## Clinical Study: *An Angry Wife*

Connie was a woman who was very angry with her husband and considering divorce. She unconsciously began manipulating her young
children to want Mommy more than they want Daddy to tend to their
needs, such as the nightly bath time, or taking them with him when he
goes on errands.

She reported that the children liked her more than they liked their
father because she 'played with them more and made them laugh.' She
added that she was 'more fun' than he was.

The therapist asked her if he was cruel to the children, or if he would
hurt them. She replied firmly that he was not cruel, and would never
hurt them. She was beginning to feel uncomfortable with the questioning. She added that he was really just not very comfortable with
children.

The therapist asked if she thought that he loved the children. She
looked stunned. She finally replied that she thought he loved them.
Then she added, 'he ... deeply...loves them.' It became clear that Connie was setting up her children to confirm *her* dislike of Daddy, which
was a sad mistake for all concerned. She had been unaware that this was
what she was actually doing.

Lest this portion of the work be misunderstood, the father also bears
some responsibility for understanding the 'types' available to him in
his psyche, and for his own self-nurture. (See *King, Warrior, Magician,
Lover*[48] by Moore and Gillette, who recently produced seminal work on
the masculine archetypal structures.)

---

48 Robert Moore & Douglas Gillette, *King, Warrior, Magician, Lover* (New York,
NY: HarperCollins, 1990).

It is important to know that many MOTHER types cannot believe that they have anything more to learn about their partners than is already known to them. His secret longings, fantasies, oblique ambitions and needs for encouragement or new creative opportunities, may be entirely out of MOTHER's conscious range. In Connie's case, FATHER is the role into which her husband is cast. Unconsciously she wants to see him fail, to validate her desire to end the marriage. All other parts of him are not required by her ego, and therefore hardly exist, or may be, indeed, pieces of him that she vaguely senses, but which make her distinctly uncomfortable, and she consequently represses. She may be out of touch with parts of herself, as well. Learning something about the HETAIRA may help her gain a new understanding of her problem.

# Chapter 6

## Of Children and MOTHER

Wolff's thoughts:

> (Paraphrases): Once she realized her primary preferences as MOTHER, she may arrange the rest of her life life accordingly, either through marriage or a motherly profession and activities. Marriage is perceived through the point of view of insuring optimal home and school conditions, social position, security and career opportunities.[49]

When considering Toni Wolff's thoughts about the MOTHER type, it seems prudent to pause for a moment of reflection on the manner in which the culture has shifted in the half century since she wrote "Structural Forms of the Feminine Psyche." At that time the world was just recovering from a debilitating war, the population had been depleted, and the building of new young families was a powerful personal, as well as collective, high priority. The Baby Boom was in full swing. But it was also true that women who wished to live sexually active lives with their male partners had very little security regarding the prevention of unwanted pregnancies. In our time, with the availability of reliable birth control, decisions regarding if and when to bear children are or course considerably more flexible. Women have more options regarding career choices and managing their own time lines in building families. Also, the defining factors of what constitutes a nuclear family have been revised by a rapidly changing culture. All this change has come about very abruptly, and requires a periodic review regarding the positive and negative aspects of the archetypal roles.

It is useful to remember that Wolff herself was a HETAIRA, and neither a wife nor a mother. The MOTHER type, by her own definition, is the one with which she was the least familiar or comfortable.

Nevertheless, keeping these ideas in mind when we read Wolff's words, 'Once the primary motherly structure is recognized, the MOTH-

---

49 Wolff, "Structural Forms," 4-5.

ER type will....' The words have the ring of truth, even though they imply a consciousness which was not then, nor is it now, necessarily characteristic only of the MOTHER type of women who bear children.

The only difference between the natural MOTHER type and the other types, at the juncture in their lives of deciding to have children, might be in the arrangement of their priorities. For example, a MOTHER type will target her lifestyle toward meeting the child's needs as she sees them, first and foremost. The AMAZON and MEDIAL WOMAN types, however, might be inclined to also consider other factors as well, such as their own educational or career interests. Such issues as 'making a home where children will be safe and economically secure' may still be a high priority for at least three of the four types of women who become mothers, regardless of their natural type. The Hetaera's priorities regarding childbearing may be more diffused, and will be discussed in the next half of this section.

Toni Wolff's concept of MOTHER as nurturer is two-fold. The first one is the other-related 'outer life' MOTHER, nurturer to child (protégé, student, patient, etc.) The object of her nurturing is both personal and external. Issues relevant to how she may work with her charges are reviewed herein. The MOTHER archetype naturally assumes the presence of the object of her nurture.

This outer MOTHER and CHILD is presented first, and will be followed by a section on Self-Nurture.

## Of MOTHER and Child

The next segments illustrate various possible aspects of mothering, which once encountered are easily recognized and acknowledged.

## Scaffolding

The image of 'scaffolding' as descriptive of the maternal task was the metaphor used of the Russian psychologist, L.S. Vygotsky.[50] MOTHER needs to build emotional and physical scaffolding, which holds the child safely while she/he grows into being able to stand securely in place alone. Metaphorically, scaffolding is a container of sorts. It sup-

---

50 L.S. Vygotsky, *Mind in Society: The Development of Higher Psychological Processes,* (Cambridge: Harvard University Press, 1978), 80.

ports both the builder and the growing entity. In the literal sense, not all the work is necessarily finished on the inside of the building before the scaffolding can come down. This 'inside of the building,' which is tantamount to the psyche of the young adult, is the work of self-nurture.

One well known script is as follows: Women who grew up with heavy-duty servant roles to fulfill in their girlhoods sometimes prolong the irresponsibility of their own daughters, and continue the servant shadow by waiting on them beyond the time of the child's actual need. This relieves mother's unconscious pain for a tiny moment only; the servant shadow festers, and succeeds only in prolonging the daughter's immaturity. But it does nothing permanent to heal the original pain of the mother, and constellates other issues with the daughter, who may truly feel that she is entitled to be waited upon, and may even project an unconscious sense of 'entitlement' on others with uncomfortable, possibly co-dependent results.

Janet, the headmistress of a K-12 independent school tells this an-ecdote:

## Narrative: Janet's Story

Pat was a woman who did some housework for me, and she told me once about an experience she had with her seven-year-old daugh-ter. At the time, I was talking to parents who had children with a minimum ten years between two of their children, just to see what they thought they had learned about parenting from one child to the next. We had talked about this idea from time to time. I was thinking about setting up some interviews with parents and maybe doing a book on the subject. I didn't get it done, but Pat's story made the rounds among my staff of teachers.

Pat has a nineteen-year-old son in college, Ben, and her daugh-ter is Laurie Ann. Once after the holidays, when her son had been home from school, I asked her how that was, to have Ben home. She shook her head. 'Truthfully,' she said, 'it was awful. It was *environmental rape!* Everything in the refrigerator belonged to him and his friends; his stuff was strewn all over the house; he would leave his car parked so that neither Bill nor I could get our cars out of the garage and get to work, while he slept until noon. So we had to nearly fight with him to get to work on time. So help me, I vowed Laurie Ann would not grow up like that.'

I asked her to keep me posted on how she planned to accomplish that.

A few weeks later when she arrived at work, on time as usual, she said, 'Hey, I really got it together with Laurie Ann this morning.' I asked her what she did. 'Well,' she grinned, 'You know, I'm supposed to get to work here by eight o'clock, and Laurie Ann's bus picks her up at the corner at seven-thirty. So at about seven twenty five, she comes into the kitchen where I'm finishing loading the dish washer, and she is whining, 'I can't find my shoes, and I'm gonna miss the bus...' I stop what I'm doing, pick her up, twirl her around the kitchen like I always do when I play with her, and plunked her down on the counter. I knew she was working me to stop what I was doing and find her shoes for her. And I knew if I did, I'd be late for work. Then I look straight into her eyes, and say, 'You know, Laurie Ann, I think you are just about the smartest seven year old I ever met. You know what else I think?' Her eyes open wide, and she answers, still whiney, 'No, what?' I reply, 'I truly believe, as smart as you are, that you *can* find your shoes. And you *might* miss the bus!'

I was impressed. 'What happened?' I asked.

Pat went on. 'Well, she giggled, and jumped down from the counter, and ran off and found her shoes. She made it to the bus.'

I needed further confirmation. 'What would you have done if she hadn't found her shoes?' I asked.

Pat smiled. 'I had it all figured out in about three seconds. I would leave at my right time so I would not be late for work. My husband works nights and was due home before nine, so I would have called him and related the story. And I would have called my next door neighbor, told her the situation, and ask her if Laurie Ann could call her if she needed something, until my husband got home. And then I would have just kissed her goodbye, told her she had time to find her shoes now, and maybe tomorrow she would remember where to put them at night. And then I would have left her, guiltlessly, and gone to work.'

I thought that was pretty good parenting. Good scaffolding. I told her so.

In 1998, the Washington Monument was being resurfaced and repaired. The scaffolding was up so long that people in the city became used to it; some came to think of it as part of the permanent design, even to like it. And when it came down, they missed it. But only then could people clearly see the original intent of the designer, and to appreciate the building's true character. Even after the scaffolding came down, extensive work was done to increase the beauty, safety and efficiency of the structure, and considerably increase the view of the city, from the inside. The analogy created by the metaphor of 'scaffolding' is that the ultimate character and purpose of the structure is fulfilled by the maturing child, not just by the MOTHER. So it is with human beings. MOTHER, at her best, is sturdy scaffolding.

## Perfectionism

For those who are aware of the issue among some mothers of 'hanging on too long' as descriptive of the shadow, it may be helpful to remind us that MOTHER has to undergo painful relinquishments in the course of raising a child. The ideal of 'perfection' raised in Chapter One may linger in the unconscious, and is just one of the relinquishments necessary in parenting. Inherent in the archetype of MOTHER is the archetype of CHILD, and the nature of CHILD is to want MOTHER to behave in the way that suits child's wishes. Of course it is neither possible nor healthy to give the child the total right-of-way in the equation. Along side those two is her desire to be perfect at the job of being Mother.

She may be inclined to ignore the existence, in her psyche, of the ideal longing for perfection that may be lingering in her unconscious. Human beings love passionately, but not perfectly. We are just not wired for it. MOTHER might want to understand how important and crippling an 'addiction to perfection' can be, for both parent and child. Also, it is helpful later for the child to realize that the mother does not think of herself as perfect, nor is she, nor he. We can learn to forgive ourselves, and each other, when we experience our often-painful mistakes along the way. (See Marion Woodman's work, *Addiction to Perfection*.)[51]

## Clinical Study

Anne is forty years old, and is five years into her second marriage. Her new husband had a son by a former marriage, which had ended tragically with the mother's death by suicide. Anne adopted this boy in the second year of her marriage, so she became a mother for the first

---

51 Marion Woodman, *Addiction to Perfection* (Toronto: Inner City Books, 1993).

time to eight-year-old Bill. This was an important event for all concerned, and she took her new role very seriously. After a year or two, it was reported to her that young Bill was exhibiting some episodes of strong and seemingly uncalled for anger at school. The parents found a competent counselor for him, a man named John. After Bill and John became acquainted and began seeing each other regularly, the episodes of inappropriate anger subsided. By all reports, the boy made a good adjustment to a change of schools, his early puberty later, and his life in general. He enjoyed his friends, and was known by peers and teachers as one who was sensitive to the feelings of his classmates. Bill's visits to talk with John had enabled him to recall and reflect helpfully upon his early memories of his deceased mother.

Anne has graduate credentials in a helping profession, and works as a consultant part time. She has strong intellectual, spiritual and artistic interests, and wanted to direct her future toward a path that explores these further, but was undecided about which direction she might take. So she decided to do some exploratory therapy for herself.

One morning, Anne came to her session disturbed about the fact that as she had left her house, Bill had asked where she was going, and she had fabricated a story about 'errands.'

As she began to explore the reasons why she had not mentioned to Bill that she was in therapy, she herself was mystified at first. Finally she realized that she feared that her seeing a therapist might make him anxious about her, and worry that there was something wrong with her. His experience with his natural mother's death haunted her, even though Bill now seemed to be able to talk about it with some freedom.

Further exploration of the issue of her discomfort about hiding the truth from him, which was not her normal way of relating to anyone, was based on her unconscious desire for him to think she was a perfect mom, who had immediate answers for all, or at least most of the questions of life. She could hide her therapy, and still appear at least semi-perfect. But she could not hide from herself the fact that she had deliberately misled her son.

As Anne began to understand her experience with Bill and her desire to maintain an infallible persona, she also realized why she had not been able to address the problems she had experienced with her own 'perfect' mother, in her own therapy.

Subsequently, Anne told Chris that she was doing some therapy to help her make some decisions. He listened carefully, said, "Like me and John, huh?" and went off to ride bikes with his pals.

The unconscious image of perfect mothering takes on super-human proportions very quickly. It is sometimes difficult for the MOTHER type to understand that presenting her own human fallibility to her children also helps them to accept, and come to terms with their own human-ness, both in its splendid possibilities and its imperfections.

## Compensatory Mothering

If a mother knows that she suffered a great deal in her own childhood from needing material necessities, or if she needed much more of her personal mother's time, love, attention, encouragement, or tolerance, then she may bestow more of these bounties upon her child/children than they actually require. If so, this may delay their maturation, and encourage their dependency upon her.[52] In the worst scenario, this may even deprive them of their own responsible adulthood.

If Mother is able to develop the skills of attentive self-nurture, it is possible to experience some relief from these ancient inner pains. Once it is identified, the process of working out the underlying conflict and trauma is best undertaken with the help of a trained professional. Some 'good Mother energy' can be brought to bear upon her own early memories, pain and trauma. The original pains can begin to subside, her centering balance can be restored, and she can address her child's needs more realistically in a non-compensatory manner. But this is very difficult work, and is best done, as mentioned, with professional help. Analyst Laura McGrew calls this issue 'compensatory mothering.'

Still, the phenomena must be addressed in this chapter, as well as the term 'compensatory mothering,' and given its important place in discussing the self-nurture of the MOTHER archetype.

## Film Study: *Bagdad Café*, Part 2

In another scene from the film mentioned in Chapter 2 from *Bagdad Café*, Brenda, (C.C.H. Pounder), the resident beleaguered mother, is trapped in an awful situation. While trying to manage a wreck of a café,

---

52 C.G Jung, "Psychological Aspects of the Mother Archetype." CW 9i, ¶167.

raise her children, staff the Motel and attend to the trucks and cars arriving for service, she presents another aspect of mothering that helps
us see how the unconscious pain of the mother affects the child. Here
is the scene:

Brenda is enraged, and yelling at her useless husband who refuses to
help with any of the chores associated with the motel and restaurant.
Her daughter, age twelve or thirteen at most, rides up to the gas station
on the back of a huge motorcycle, operated by a large hairy man in full
cavalier hippie regalia, and whose face the audience doesn't see. (The
camera suggests that his face isn't seen by anybody else, either.) The
daughter jumps off the back of the huge cycle, and sidles up to Brenda,
all sweetness, and gives her a manipulative story, with her hand out-
stretched, ending each sentence with a little question in her voice: 'Uh,
Mom, we just need a little. . .uh. . .bread? So we can go to this, err- concert?'

Pointing to the biker, she continues, 'This guy, his name is, uh,
Rock?'

Mother Brenda, with glazed eyes still smoldering with anger at her
husband, reaches into her pocket, and hands over a wad of her hard-
earned money, without a word. Nothing is said about when to expect
the girl home. The little daughter flies off into a situation that the view-
er senses she is hardly mature enough to handle, and Brenda returns to
her miserable squabble with her husband. The scene appears to have
three or four people in it, but psychologically, one can see three generations, at least, of painful history. Somewhere under Brenda's preoccupied half-aware mothering response is that of a young teenager,
her own painful girlhood self, strapped for money, and on a very tight
leash at home, for whom any sort of 'fun' was scarce indeed. As we
watch Brenda in this scene, her eyes reveal that her focus on her 'real'
daughter, in that moment, is nonexistent, as if she were oblivious of
the actual young girl in front of her. She is responding completely from
the original pain and trauma of her own unconscious past, and her
ever-present frustrations.

## A Primer on Adult Self-Nurture

The second manner in which Toni Wolff's remarks are directed in the
MOTHER quotations have to do with how MOTHER self-nurtures. But

it is also true that much of the entire subject of self-nurture is common to all four types. Each type experiences motherhood somewhat differently.

Self-nurture characterizes how a woman, regardless of her type, may relate to her own selfhood: her talents, health, needs for growth and challenge, pleasures, tastes, self-respect, and how she talks to herself, (the 'inner speak'). All of this is 'self-nurture.' It is the presence of a nurturing, forgiving, and friendly attitude toward one's self. You recall that Wolff points out that the MOTHER type may be very good at taking care of her charges, but inept in her capacity for self-nurture.

The care and nurture of one's own selfhood is simply not a high conscious priority for the mother at the time of her child's infancy, beyond keeping her body able to function properly. It is also true that in our time, fathers may take on significantly stronger participation in the care-giving needs. Nevertheless, the woman can become a different and nearly unknown person to herself as she matures. If she suffers a bit of an inflation of her own new importance as a mother, for some women the experience is the first genuine adult power that they have ever known.

The matter of neglecting her own selfhood has to do with the duration of that particular condition, and the tenacity with which the woman maintains her newly acquired power. At what point does her natural desire to stabilize a new life become what Jung calls the 'hypertrophy of the maternal element?

Jung describes this issue in psychological terms:

> Her own personality is of secondary importance; she often remains entirely unconscious of it, for her life is lived in and through others, in more or less complete identification with all in her care.... The less conscious she is of her own personality, the greater and more violent is her unconscious will to power.... The mind is not cultivated for its own sake, but usually remains in its original condition, altogether primitive, unrelated and ruthless, but also true, and sometimes as profound as nature herself.[53]

Sooner or later, attention to the personal development (self-nurture) of all women needs to be examined. The issue of self-nurture that Wolff raises, is appropriate for the MOTHER study in that it is an area in which

---

53 C.G. Jung, "Psychological Aspects of the Mother Archetype." CW 9i, ¶167.

the MOTHER type nurtures her own life as well as that of her charges, or fails to do so. However, the issue of self-nurture does not exclude the other three types by any means, as mentioned. The MOTHER type, who is particularly a nurturer by nature, is not necessarily skilled at taking care of her own needs at all, any more than the other three types.

Carol Gilligan, in her first book, *In a Different Voice,*[54] comments on the strange disappearance of selfhood that is noticeable among young girls just as they commence their menses. It is as if they loose much of the promising self-motivation and individuality which they seemed to embody as youngsters, and become, rather, stereotypes at about the time they sense themselves to be sought after by the male population. In her later work, *The Birth of Pleasure*[55] Gilligan explores young girls even further, and postulates a remarkable paradigm for the emerging young woman learning to trust herself, as the entire culture begins to unravel the tangled web of patriarchy. This phenomenon of inter-relational life between the sexes, which has been with us for thousands of years, will not yield without objective observation and evaluation of the manner in which both men and women are mothered, as well as fathered.

Remaining conscious of one's selfhood during the process of motherhood is hard work. Only since the world has become aware of female psychology has it even become important. The woman herself will have to struggle for consciousness about her own life, even somewhat apart from the demanding MOTHER role.

## Film Illustration: *Runaway Bride*[56]

A film portrait of this concept of regaining the sense of selfhood is presented in this comedy wherein Maggie (Julia Roberts) enacts the familiar scenario of a young woman whose tastes, goals and sense of herself seem to be dictated by the men who court her, until finally she disengages from the field of courtship, goes off to live alone, acquires some sense of her own true preferences (eggs fried or scrambled?), develops some goals, and figures out her own talents and abilities.

---

54 Carol Gilligan, *In a Different Voice* (New York: Random House, 1982).
55 Carol Gilligan, *The Birth of Pleasure* (New York: Alfred A. Knopf, 2002).
56 *Runaway Bride*. 1999. (See film index.)

In doing so, she gradually becomes ready for a wiser approach to choosing a mate, or at least a healthier one, provided she is able to hold on to her self hood when she returns to being courted again. In the last scene when Maggie describes what she has discovered about herself to the future husband (Richard Gere), she displays a lovely careful patience with, and acceptance of, herself.

* * *

The episode is brief, but the essence of her self-nurture is not only what she has learned, but also the manner in which she has quietly acquired the comfort zone of being alone with herself in a gentle, nurturing manner.

While the film does not deal directly with the MOTHER type, it does speak to the need of all women for realistic and kindly self-nurture, hopefully before undertaking responsibility for adult relational life. Still, a woman must start where she is, and do the job, respectful of her own process. It is this middle ground, this invaluable time between girlhood and parenting, that is only age-appropriate in the ideal world of time and movies. It can only happen when the woman becomes aware that it is needed, no matter how old she is. To learn something of one's own selfhood, and take responsibility for it, is the challenge of which Wolff is speaking.

In our adult life, it is important to know that in order to live our lives responsibly and remain flexible and centered, self-nurture remains a necessary ingredient for our self-renewal process, for as long as we live. How is an adult woman to be nurtured? This is about learning what she needs to do for herself.

## The Inner Voice

If you were mothered or fathered by being scolded and bullied, then that is the way you will probably treat yourself, with constant self-criticism, shaming and guilt. You will be very poor company for yourself, as you grow up, uncomfortable about being alone, and feel 'one down' in most social situations. You are, in effect, bullied by your own scolding, and quick to do the bidding of others, in order to keep at bay the angry parental voice inside of you. If you were allowed to suffer through your mistakes and failures with understanding, encouraged to take heart, forgive yourself and begin again, rather than being lectured, blamed and scolded, then you are fortunate indeed, and might learn to do the same for yourself.

The task is to pay attention to the inner speaking – what we are saying to ourselves, all the time. You can start talking to yourself with words of encouragement, nurture and acceptance. This single reverse of a longtime habit is an enormous change, and a huge step in the right direction. Jungian Analyst Laura McGrew calls this, "When I began to speak myself into being."[57] John Bradshaw calls this, "Taming the Shameful Inner Voice."[58]

Learning adult self-nurture may be an entirely new idea for some women. In addition to the rudimentary basic health care, safety, fairness and money management, it means learning to nurture one's own talents and interests, bring them to the world in a useful form; encourage one's own growth, and discover some genuine joys, which are distinctly different from having 'good girl' feelings for following someone else's agenda. All are important parts of the self-nurture process. They are necessary for the woman who is involved in, and accountable for, her own life, regardless of whatever type she is. But as a MOTHER, it is the essential work that keeps all the other tasks of parenting on target, and her shadow as conscious and in check as possible.

One of the many rewards of this endeavor for children is that when MOTHER takes care of herself, they are released from feeling that they are solely responsible for the success or failure of mother's life and happiness. It follows, as night follows day, that children can begin to understand that they are ultimately responsible, in kind, for their own lives, and their own genuine happiness.

---

57 Laura McGrew, "Shame and the Paralysis of Feminine Initiative." (Chicago: The C.G. Jung Institute of Chicago, Graduate Thesis, 1989), 76.
58 John Bradshaw, "Taming the Shameful Inner Voice," *Meeting The Shadow*, (NewYork: G.P Putnam's Sons, 1991), 290-292.

# Chapter 7

## MOTHER and The Other Types

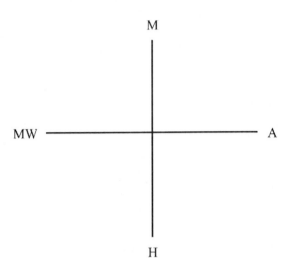

Wolff's thoughts:

- "All the four structural forms are inherent to every woman. If possible she will realize the one that is most consistent with her nature. By and by, a second form will assert itself from within."

  (Paraphrases): The AMAZON and the MEDIAL WOMAN are the two adjacent forms for MOTHER. Wolff maintains that if a gradual integration of the next form does not take place, the first one will begin to turn negative. Gradually a third form will begin to become more clear. The fourth one is the hardest to assimilate, and is sometimes quite difficult.[59]

According to Wolff's model, the woman who carries MOTHER as her primary characteristic type knows something of, and is also comfortable with, aspects of both the AMAZON and the MEDIAL WOMAN. The

---

59 Wolff, "Structural Forms," 4-5.

most difficult archetype for the MOTHER to integrate is the HETAIRA, which is the one opposite her in Wolff's diagram.

For example, Hildegard of Bingen, (See MEDIAL WOMAN, Section Two.) who was a prominent Abbess of the twelfth century and achieved world renown, was honored as MOTHER to the younger nuns of her order. She was also a visionary who personally experienced the divine voices known to the gifted MEDIAL WOMAN, and exhibited some strong AMAZON qualities of political astuteness and leadership. Most conspicuously missing concerning opposite types are the attributes of the personal HETAIRA, which bears out Wolff's model concerning opposite types. As primarily 'MOTHER,' some of her biographers consider her to have been strict. However, her personal life was decidedly influenced to a great measure by the painful absence of her own mother, and her introduction to the harsh disciplines of convent life at the tender age of eight years. She was known to have had some deeply personal relationships, including her surrogate mother, the beloved Jutta. The achievements that characterized her life attest to a remarkable diversity of abilities, and a richly invested energy. Missing, of course, is the HETAIRA sensibility.[60]

For the most part, the MOTHER finds the HETAIRA to be somewhat of a mystery. Often, she is denigrated by the MOTHER type. The MOTHER sometimes seems to need all 'others' (meaning children, friends, husband, acquaintances), to be diminutive in relation to her own 'important' self. If the marriage begins to frazzle at the edges due to the engulfing characteristics of the MOTHER, she might do well to look at HETAIRA a little more closely, and extend her imagination further into her partner's world. Not all men who become fathers are as totally consumed by the FATHER archetype, as their spouses are apt to be, by the all-powerful MOTHER.

## Two HETAIRA Dreams

Women of one type often dream about the missing 'opposite' parts of their personalities, who show up as shadow manifestations:

One dream is fairly common: A wife lies in bed with her husband, and there is an unknown woman also there with them, perhaps lying nearby.

---

60 Fiona Maddocks, *Hildegard of Bingen* (New York, NY: Doubleday, 2001).

One interpretation might be that husband is also 'with' a part of the wife that she herself does not know, a shadow wife, a part of her own self that she cannot, or no longer can, access easily.

* * *

In another more specific dream, the woman dreamer is in an apartment building awaiting an ascending elevator. The door opens, and her husband is in the elevator, holding and kissing Goldie Hawn, (or some other HETAIRA type of woman), who reciprocates warmly.

Clearly, some playfulness and relaxed attention on behalf of the wife, who is consumed with MOTHER duties, is called for. Goldie stands in for the consummate HETAIRA, in the 'ups and downs' of life, to remind the wife that pleasure, Eros and joy, also might need to be present in the mix.

Somehow, Goldie seems to find a way to hang on to her own happiness, in most of the roles she plays.

* * *

## Film Study: *The English Patient*[61]

This film offers a study of two very different women who, in the context of the film, never actually meet. One, Katharine Clifton (Kristin Scott Thomas) is the consummate HETAIRA. She and her lover are ultimately stranded in an ancient cave where she has suffered a broken leg and is unable to walk. He must leave her to make the long trek across the desert, in some hope of finding help. With a powerful and passionate devotion to her illicit love, she hangs on, alone in the darkness, to the last breath of her life.

The other woman, Hanna (Juliette Binoche), is the consummate MOTHER type, a devoted nurse. She struggles against enormous odds in wartime Italy to take care of her lone dying patient. She has set up a hospice of sorts for him in a ruined and abandoned villa, keeps him fed, reads to him, and tirelessly cares for his fatal wounds as best she can. During this time she falls in love with Lt. Kip Singh (Naveen Andrews), a skilled demolition expert, who deactivates perilous land mines lo-

---

61 *The English Patient*. 1992. See Film Index.

cally. Their love story is dramatic, sensual and tender. Yet she chooses her destiny as 'nurse' to this one dying patient to be more compelling in the long run than any possible future with this lively and adoring man. She mournfully waves goodbye to Kip from the back of a truck, and lets him go. There seems to be no plan for after the war, or hope of reunion somewhere, sometime.

The contrast between the two women is startling, and undeniable. Neither one is 'better' than the other; and each is courageous in her own way. But their choices and priorities are entirely different. In the film, these two women never meet. MOTHER and HETAIRA rarely do. If they did, they might have little in common, and very little to engage them to pursue a personal friendship. It is interesting to think about how they might see each other if they met years later in life, and exchanged stories.

* * *

This film gives a lively treatment to some adjacent and opposite types:

### Film Study: *The Grass Harp*[62]

The Talbo sisters live in a large well-kept Victorian house, in the early part of the 20th century. The AMAZON sister Verena, (Sissy Spacek), provides the bulk of their livelihood by owning and managing a thriving dry goods store. Her MEDIAL sister, Dolly (Piper Laurie), has a small business on the side. She gathers medicinal herbs. Using a formula gleaned from some traveling gypsies, she prepares and bottles a pain-killing elixir. Her little enterprise is growing steadily, aided by Catherine (Nell Carter), the family household retainer, a woman of the earth similar to Dolly. Unexpectedly, an orphaned young nephew is brought into the household to live with the three women. Both Dolly and Catherine do a good job of taking on MOTHER nurture when young Colin is added to the daily family life. AMAZON Sister Verena has a brief fling with a traveling salesman, who turns out to be a crook, and she is left sadder and wiser. She hasn't done as well at trying for (a HETAIRA style) romance as she had hoped, and has made an embarrassing, foolish and costly choice. MEDIAL WOMAN sister Dolly, who gathers her herbs and hears the grass sing, turns down an offer of marriage from an adoring

---

62 *The Grass Harp*. 1996. See Film Index.

and highly suitable widower, Judge Charley Kool (Walter Matthau). She chooses to favor that which she wants to accomplish in the world with her small business and her own MEDIAL talent. She also wants to attend to the needs of the household as a surrogate mother for Colin. The dynamic between the AMAZON and MEDIAL sisters is very interesting, and they end up realizing that they really do not understand, or really even like each other, but they truly need each other, and Colin needs them both.

In this film, the HETAIRA role is glimpsed by both sisters, but rejected. Dolly connects to herself through her MOTHER love and devotion to Collin, and Verena keeps the household financed through her strong AMAZON skills. (See Part 2 of this film, Section 2, AMAZON, Chapter 21.)

There is always a struggle, as women, try to work their way out of patriarchal culture patterns, to re-imagine ways of relating to their opposite type, other than through the huge archetypal roles they predominantly carry. How does MOTHER meet HETAIRA? Or vice-versa? How does AMAZON finally meet MEDIAL WOMAN?

If their understanding of each other, or lack of it, remains unconscious, they will either instinctively oppose each other's lifestyle and secretly long for the benefit they might see in the opposite position, or project their anger upon their opposite in a general manner, perhaps politically or socially.

The important thing for all women to consider is that understanding these archetypes makes it possible to extend their own consciousness and give some validation to other perspectives.

# HETAIRA

## A Random Scroll

Aphrodite . . . Sophia Baddele . . . Denise Scott Brown . . . Elizabeth Barret Browning . . . Bastet . . . Bathsheba . . . Baucis . . . Simone de Beauvoir . . . Boubelina, in Kazanzakis's *Zorba The Greek* . . . Lucretia Borgia . . . Calypso . . . Camilla, in Virgil's *Aeneid* . . . Camilla, Duchess of Cornwall . . . Camille Claudel . . . Circe . . . Cleopatra . . . Colette . . . D.H. Lawrence's *Lady Chatterley* . . . **Matty** in Byatt's *Angels and Insects* . . . Madame Curie . . . Delilah . . . Ariel Durant . . . Maleva Einstein . . . Eve . . . Euridice . . . Veronica Franco . . . Nell Gwyn . . . Gomer . . . Queen Guenevere . . . Pamela Harriman . . . Helen of Troy . . . Heloise . . . Katharine Hepburn . . . Inanna . . . Isis . . . Ishtar . . . Isolde... Juliet . . . Lady Luck . . . Lilith . . . Monica Lewinsky . . . Marilyn Monroe . . . Mae West . . . Mary Magdalene . . . Messalina . . . Anais Nin . . . Georgia O'Keeffe . . . Yoko Ono . . . Phyrene . . . Madame de Pompadour . . . Nancy Reagan . . . Lou Andreas-Salomé . . . Sappho . . . Scherazade . . . Shekina . . . Wallace Warfield Windsor . . . Theodora . . . Thisbe . . . Violetta, in Verdi's opera *La Traviata* . . . **Belle Watling,** in Mitchel's *Gone With The Wind* . . . Toni Wolff . . .

"What's love got to do with it?"
—Tina Turner

# Chapter 8

## An Overview Of HETAIRA

"You alone are real to me."
—Lou Andreas-Salomé[63]

The real story about the HETAIRA is ... just that. The 'story.'

For the HETAIRA, there is always a story, one that enthralls her companions, herself, and those who overhear it. They will pass it on with gusto, continuing as it winds into the delight, horror, sorrow or just plain gossip of today's news.

Like the MOTHER, HETAIRA is primarily described within the context of highly personal relational life. Some of the finest encounters of lovers are described in the HETAIRA literature. As part of those mythic love stories, the Egyptian lore records that when the great God Osiris was torn into pieces and scattered across the earth, his Queen Isis picked up the pieces one by one, put him back together again, and restored him to life; thus, by virtue of her being the actual means of his resurrection, she somehow gained her primary position in the mythic duo. We hear of them as 'Isis and Osiris.' Yet in the listings of the HETAIRA literature, the feminine partner's name most often follows that of her male counterpart. One does not commonly hear of 'Isolde and Tristan,' or 'Juliet and Romeo.' One must admit that of the most famous HETAIRAE of history, few rarely rose to, or surpassed the notoriety of their partners. Most of us know the name of Pericles, but few of Aspasia. The HETAIRA is apt to be obscured in that manner. But her stories remain among the most challenging and romantic of the archetypes.

This is an important caveat. In like manner, for the HETAIRA there is also apt to be the 'Yes, but...' quality to her story, or the 'If only...' non sequitur. This 'Yes, but...' quality is powerfully expressed by the early twentieth century poet, Rainer Maria Rilke:

---

63 Lou Andreas-Salomé, *You Alone are Real to Me* (Rochester, NY: American Reader's Service Series #6, BOA Editions, 2003).

## Hetaira – Tombs

*In their long hair they lie*
*with brown faces gone deep into themselves.*
*The eyes closed, as if before too great a distance.*
*Skeletons, mouths, flowers. Inside the mouths*
*The smooth teeth like a pocket chess set*
*Lined up in ivory rows.*
*And flowers, yellow pearls, slender bones,*
*Hands, tunics, fading fabric*
*Above the caved-in heart. But*
*There beneath those rings, talismans,*
*And eye-blue stones (cherished keepsakes)*
*The silent crypt of the sex still stands,*
*Filled to its vaulted roof with flower petals.*[64]

As Anne Carson observed in her book, *Eros the Bittersweet*, myriads of poets have tried to describe the experience of falling in love, as did the ancient Sappho:

Eros once again limb-loosener whirls me
sweetbitter, impossible to fight off, creature stealing up…
—Translated by Anne Carson.[65]

Eros is complicated. Carson comments on Sappho's use of the word 'sweetbitter', mentioning that the English version, bittersweet, actually inverts the terms of Sappho's compound word, *glukupikon*. The word 'sweetbitter' carries a significant HETAIRA connotation in that it is characteristic of the excitement and anticipation of love, while 'bittersweet' connotes the memory of lost love in retrospect. These two ideas resonate and describe the HETAIRA experience, as they move fluidly back and forth in her moments with her lover. She represents the image of a woman who is attached to her male partner, rarely through marriage.

---

64 Rainer Maria Rilke, *New Poems 1907* (New York: Farrar, Straus & Giroux, North Point Press, Bilingual edition, Translated by Edward Snow, 1984), 167.
65 Anne Carson, *Eros the Bittersweet* (Normal: llinois State University, Dalkey Archive Press, 2003), 3-4.

Characteristically, it has been through the context of her sexual behavior that she was known and identified culturally as a HETAIRA. But that image has changed somewhat, with the identifying qualities assigned to the archetype by Toni Wolff and others within the past one hundred years. Now, if she is married or unmarried, has one lover, none, or many, how then are we to understand her, in this day and time?

For the contemporary HETAIRA, the first priority of her world goes to the quality of her relational life with her lover.[66] Whether consciously or unconsciously, her primary objective and the anchor of her ego orientation lies in the arena of her personal relational life with her partner. This personal dynamic remains also true of the MOTHER, but the object of the MOTHER attention goes first, of course, to her children or charges. Yet, as with all four of the types, if the HETAIRA remains unable to grow and develop her own inner life, she carries a lonely and often tragic shadow. As she loves greatly, she may also suffer greatly, and her greatest suffering comes when she loses connection to herself by becoming totally absorbed by her relational life.

We know many names for her, strewn across the continuum of her history. Among her endless descriptive titles she has been known as trollop, street walker, prostitute, femme fatale, femme inspiratrice, seductress, courtesan, lover, anima, anima woman, the beloved, call girl, geisha, hetaira, hierodule, whore, mistress, companion, escort, goddess, special friend, slut, partner, girl friend, creative collaborator, etc.

For the HETAIRA in the ideal sense, romantic love can become that which inspires her partners to the best and most noble of their creative abilities, and the experience is reciprocal for her as well. At her least evolved, romantic love becomes its opposite, in which she provides a moment of sexual relief in return for a subsistence living, and sex falls into the impersonal public shadow. In this case, instead of Eros as her personal joy, she settles for the illusion of genuine Eros and it becomes her merchandise for sale. In either case, her world is focused primarily on the male world, and is tailored to engage, accommodate, satisfy, comfort, energize, delight or stimulate male attention. In this sense, historically she was most often looked down upon by conventional society. Even more recently, she was considered an inferior element by the early feminist interpreters of culture. But if she happens to be closely associated with her own partner in a professional and/or marital

---

66 Wolff, "Structural Forms," 6.

partnership, such as that of the brilliant scientists Marie and Pierre Curie, or the talented theater duo of Jessica Tandy and Hume Cronyn, she is able to contribute distinctly to the world something of her own independent achievement, and ultimately earns respect in her own right.

However society sees the HETAIRA or does not see her, the fact remains that she can be, by virtue her own nature, a nurturer of an element in the male world which is most often noticeably missing, that of intense, creative, relational, and joyous sexual, spiritual, and intellectual interaction.

## From *The Mythic Tradition*[67]

We recall that ancient societies of the Middle East in the area of the Fertile Crescent known as the Cradle of Civilization were agriculturally based; the earliest known deities were the manifestations of the feminine earth mother, goddess of all fertility. Each geographic locale within the Fertile Crescent personified her in their creation mythologies. The moon, the morning star, the seasons, weather, plant and animal life, and human sexual regeneration represented her. To appease and please her, humans courted her favor, thereby assuaging their omnipresent fear of disastrous floods, hurricanes, volcanic eruptions, famine, pestilence, or their own possible failure to reproduce. She was their spiritual refuge through the cyclic years, and the source of the renewal of hope in the human heart.

The great fertility goddess was known by many names, each of which eventually evolved into a successive one over time. She was known in Egypt as Hathor, and later Isis/Nieth and Bastet. She was first Inanna/Ishtar among the Babylonian/Assyrians, and Ishtar/Astarte among the Semitic tribes. She was also called Queen of Heaven, the Morning Star, the Moon, and the Heavenly Virgin. In all three regions, the goddess was accompanied not by a male of equal power and authority, but by a handsome male consort representing her glorious lover-husband-son-brother. Each of the three cultures, somewhat independently, worshiped her through their ceremonial observances of the grievous death of her beloved in the late fall of the year, and her courageous part in his regeneration and resurrection in spring.

---

67 Robert Graves, *The Mythic Tradition* (London: Hamlyn Publishing Group, Ltd. 1985).

Astarte was the Semitic name for her. Recent excavations of ancient lands now known as Israel unearthed the first small clay images of her, found in great numbers. She stands quietly erect and inviting, offering her breasts and a little smile. She was the goddess for whom the Israelites burned incense, offered wine and prepared food in defiance of Jeremiah's God, during the early years of 1,000 B.C., some two thousand years after a fragment of Babylonian hymn to Tammuz was recorded in pictographs. Eventually, navigation, colonization, warfare, territorial concerns and religious observances banished her, and the new Hebrew law of Jeremiah, 'One God' overcame her temples. In time, the physical/ sexual aspects of the feminine deity were declared evil. She became the 'Whore of Babylon' during the early centuries of 1,000 B.C.

## Aphrodite

The mythic prototype of the HETAIRA archetype is captured in the legends associated with this Grecian goddess of human sexuality. Among the several mythic tales of her birth, one of the earliest creation myths comes from the pen of Hesiod, writing about the beliefs of the ancient Assyrians [paraphrased.]:

Gaia (earth) and her husband Uranus, (heaven) created children, but he refused to allow them to emerge into the light. It was finally their son Kronos (time) who took a sickle, lopped off his father's genitals, and tossed them backwards into the sea. It was from the sea that the beautiful Aphrodite was born, rose amid the foam, and the lovely, laughing goddess was carried by the tides of time to the island of Cyprus. The early Phoenician navigators of the Mediterranean probably brought their goddess worship to the island of Cyprus, where the stories of her evolved and combined with the existing feminine deities of the island over time. There are several other later tales of her birth; among them is that of the early Greek historian Herodotus. He wrote that she was the daughter of Zeus and a Dione, (a priestess of the groves where tree spirits lived).[68]

The Greek writers were the best to describe the joyous subtleties of Aphrodite. She is gloriously beautiful; she loves laughter, wonderful robes and colors, five-petaled flowers, and incense offered in her honor. She is utterly pure, and associated with the breathless beauty of cre-

---

68 Graves, Introduction. *The Mythic Tradition,* 130-135.

ation. She became the goddess principally of lovemaking, in the holiest tradition of honor, back before the time when sexuality and spirituality were fragmented into oppositional elements of our human nature.

The Aphrodite story places the principle of sexual union among the very first divine elements of the later Greek pantheon, even before Zeus. So the essence of sexual life was present as the uniting principle of earth and sky, and carried to the Island of Cyprus via time and the tides of the sea.

In the first great temples to Aphrodite built on the island, the practice of introducing young women to their sexuality by sacred prostitutes was the custom. This was carried to mainland Greece, and continued in countless temples throughout the centuries of Greek and Roman rule up until the time Christianity was declared the official religion of the Emperor Constantine in 315 A.D. It was known to have flourished in countless other regions of the Fertile Crescent.

## Prostitution: Sacred and Profane

For more than two thousand years during the era 2000 B.C. and forward until the third century A.D., sacred prostitution was an accepted cultural phenomenon. 'Common' or 'profane' prostitution was also existent, a very different social manifestation of the sexual act.

Jungian Analyst Nancy Qualls–Corbett in her book *The Sacred Prostitute*[69] describes sacred prostitution as a 'coming-of-age' ritual for the well-bred maidens of the ancient culture. Prior to marriage, young women were brought to the temple compounds by the priestesses and educated in the facts and subtleties of adult lovemaking. They consecrated their bodies to the goddess Aphrodite, and then were taken to the temple proper, where they would sit devoutly waiting 'the stranger,' who would toss coins into the lap of the maiden he choose. The coins were given for the support of the temple. The man involved was regarded as 'the stranger,' in the religious tradition of his being a god in disguise, or of standing in for a god in this ritual. The experience was never an orgy of lust, but a sacred occasion. The sexual act was to be joyous, free-spirited, open, and in every way blessed by the goddess. The stranger was to be welcomed and nurtured as if he were, indeed,

---

69 Nancy Qualls-Corbett, *The Sacred Prostitute* (Toronto, ON: Inner City Books, 1988), 21-51.

the god, and she the goddess. Once the young woman had been consecrated in this manner, she was allowed if she wished to return to her
home and prepare for marriage. She was now ready to have a family.
Should she arrive at home pregnant, the resulting child was honored
and accepted into the family and community as a special gift, without
stigma.

Qualls-Corbett:

> However they came to the temple of love, by law, dedica-
> tion or servitude, of royal or common birth, for a night or
> a lifetime, we know that the sacred prostitutes were many
> in number. They were accorded social status and educated.
> In some cases they remained politically and legally equal
> to men.[70]

> Special legislation in the code of Hammurabi, King of
> Babylon, (1800 B.C.) concerned the rights and good name
> of the sacred prostitute; she was protected from slander,
> as were her children, by the same law that upheld mar-
> ried women's reputation. Also by law, the sacred prostitute
> could inherit property from her father and receive income
> from the land worked by her brothers.[71]

The profane, or 'common' prostitute, however, who lived in the great
cities concurrently during this time, was the opposite story. She worked
principally in brothels, taverns and public entertainment places. There
were no privileges and no respectability. She was required to dye her
hair in garish colors of yellow, red or blue; strict dress codes forbade her
from any attempt to pass for a respected woman; no jewelry, no gar-
ments made of the genteel purple cloth. She was prohibited from riding
in vehicles, mingling with society, participating in ritual ceremonies, or
enjoying the privileges of citizenship. Qualls-Corbett mentions these
women were bought with public money and placed in state-owned
brothels, their earnings going to state coffers. Their children were not
allowed citizenship and were considered as bastards.

Over time, as the upper levels of society in the city states of Greece
began to develop a more urbane culture; the young, beautiful and intelligent women who might have otherwise become common prostitutes

---

70 Qualls-Corbett, *The Sacred Prostitute*, 37.
71 Qualls-Corbett, *The Sacred Prostitute*. Citation: W. Sanger, MD, *History of Prostitution,* (New York, NY: Harper and Brother, 1859), 37.

out of necessity, were singled out. They were among slaves, poor families of indentured servants, or from rural areas where poverty was most often the rule. They were brought to Athens, Sparta or Corinth to be groomed in the arts, languages, music, dance, and public ceremonies. They were taught how to conduct charming conversation, and how to make themselves agreeable to men. They provided color, enthusiasm and style for the sophisticated social life of the leaders of these cities.

The Hetairae of ancient Greece developed in a rapidly growing sophisticated culture. In contrast, married women of respected citizens were allowed virtually no life outside that of the household, and little education beyond the domestic arts. Like the early Amazons, the Hetairae became almost a counter-culture development in total contrast to how 'respectable' women were expected to behave.[72]

## The Absence of Aphrodite

Scholars of classicism report that in the rituals associated with polytheism, it was always the overlooked god or goddess that mapped the downfall of the human being. Women well might speculate about what was lost by the disappearance of Aphrodite, and along with her the last vestiges of the sacred feminine goddess of sensuous sexuality. Certainly the aspects of joyous lovemaking made sacred by the act itself are not a commonly understood element of our spiritual lives. The mutually nurturing and welcoming aspects of the ancient cult have been all but lost. Impersonal sexual prowess has been consigned to the mundane shadow of a competitive and somewhat banal pastime. One wonders what happened to women, when the idea of 'joyous welcome and nurture' was removed from the sexual act? Could 'joyous welcome and nurture' instead, have been dedicated only to children, the sick, the aged, and the infirm? Could this have dehumanized our sexuality, to some extent? Half of our most celebrated marriages falter, and the sense of the 'sacred' part of our sexuality has long been overlooked, over-burdened with pseudo-religious legalism, or trivialized into degrading commercial titillation. When sex is overlaid with legalism, whether public or private, and void of the element of personal enrichment, dry laws contaminate its magic, prudery becomes prurience, and our sacred sexual

72 Katie Hickman, *Courtesans* (New York: HarperCollins Perennial, 2003), 13-16.

images become pornographic. Conversely, we might consider, also, that we are apt to idealize sexless spirituality itself in a manner that carries us into flawed and dangerous psychological areas of guilt, depravation, perversion and/or unconscious compensation. For example, MOTHER, when she forgets the aspect of herself and her partner as joyous lovers, may unfairly fear HETAIRA as the great oppositional threat to 'family life', and HETAIRA blames MOTHER for relegating her attention and nurture skills to children only, and neglects her male partner as well as her own needs for creative, loving and joyous sexual renewal. With such opposing attitudes, the female sex has become ruthlessly characterized by the simplistic categories of 'virgin' and 'whore.'

Early feminism, on the other hand, worked from the root metaphor of the 'equality' ideal for both men and women. Writers questioned the idea of the HETAIRA aspect of the feminine nature of a woman as one of living enmeshed in the life of her man, or men in general, to the neglect of her own selfhood. Simone de Beauvoir expressed her disdain of the HETAIRA type both in her early autobiography and her later work, *The Second Sex*:

> I use the word hetaira to designate all women who train not only their bodies but also their entire personalities as capital to be exploited. Their attitude is very different from that of creative workers who, transcending themselves in the work they produce....
>
> And the hetaira does not reveal the world, she opens no avenues to human transcendence, on the contrary, she tries to captivate the world for her own profit. Offering herself for the approbation of her admirers, she does not repudiate that passive femininity which dedicates her to her man: she endures it with a magical power that enables her to catch the men in the snare of her presence and batten them off; she engulfs them along with her immanence.[73]

Thankfully, de Beauvoir, who by Wolff's broader definition was actually a HETAIRA herself in relation to Jean-Paul Sartre, modified her position. She did allow for the accomplishments, relative freedom and creative achievement of "a few hetairae, courtesans, and geisha, those of exemplary intelligence who manage to self-actualize and share,

---

73 Simone de Beauvoir, *The Second Sex*. Translated and edited by H.M. Pashley (New York: Random House, Vintage Edition, 1989), 568.

through their powerful lovers, in the government of the world, as well as develop their creative lives, and live with some degree of freedom."[74] Confined to this early narrow rubric, had it not been possible for us to overlook the single most essentially feminine principle of all, for both men and women, *that of the ability to remain connected to one another,* in whatever manner is appropriate? As we shall see, this element of the HETAIRA archetypal nature was the most significant piece for Toni Wolff. Her work considerably broadens the defining characteristics of the HETAIRA archetype beyond that of de Beauvoir's earlier characterization.

Toni Wolff wrote just a few years before de Beauvoir. She saw the role of the HETAIRA in a different light, principally that of companion, friend and peer of the man in order to assist him to achieve his best development and accomplishment, as well her own. In that sense, she felt her own life to be dedicated not only to a man and their life and work together, but also to the study of the distinct ways in which women relate to themselves and the world through archetypal roles. Her understanding of this places the HETAIRA rightfully among them. De Beauvoir spoke confidently of the social structures concerning that of HETAIRA in a societal sense. Wolff looks at the psychological, spiritual and historical constructs of the type. Our task is that of re-evaluation of the HETAIRA'S role as Wolff understood and experienced it. This more relevant representation of HETAIRA seems to be correcting itself in this 21st century by a chorus of healthy women who genuinely love men, have *not* been terrorized by them, and are as eager to assist the men among us who have also suffered from centuries of patriarchal practice and upbringing. From their vantage point, they have seen that both sexes have suffered. Women are also beginning to see that in some ways, they too have seriously perpetuated the system of patriarchy, particularly in the manner in which they raise their children. What is missing in some of the early feminist conceptualizing is that both sexes need to become responsible for both mutual, and self-nurture in the development of selfhood. Most certainly, this mandate may include genital sexual activity, but it is no longer defined solely in that manner.

When HETAIRA learns self-nurture, she begins to strive for the middle ground. As she matures, she realizes that she may be, or may have been, inclined to pander to the collective shadow of impersonal sex.

---

74 Beauvoir, *The Second Sex.* 569.

She might have settled, for a time, with being 'admired' rather than being involved in the enormous and challenging task of nurturing her own individual personal life as well as that of her partner. This offers us a serious challenge. The manner in which HETAIRA has developed culturally over the centuries, and is still doing so, is the HETAIRA 'story.'

## The HETAIRA in History: Heloise, A Scholarly Medieval HETAIRA

Heloise Abelard was a reluctant twelfth century wife. She preferred her HETAIRA stance with her brilliant clergy-scholar-lover, only marrying at his insistence, after their affair and her pregnancy were discovered. Her reluctance to marry was rare, yet inherent in her point of view, which she articulated consistently during their correspondence in later years. She described her passion in ways that were both literary and lively, thereby fusing her own joyous acceptance of her lover with his strictly rational mind. She expressed this in the first letter written to Abelard some fourteen years after their final separation:

> But you kept silent about most of my arguments for prefer-
> ring love to wedlock and freedom to chains. God is my wit-
> ness that if Augustus, Emperor of the whole world, thought
> fit to honor me with marriage, it would be dearer and more
> honorable to me to be called not his empress, but your
> whore.[75]

Abelard was a renowned and respected philosopher and theologian. He was also a canon, scholar and keeper of the semi-clerical vows associated with his position as newly-named head of the incipient school at Notre Dame de Paris. This meant that he could not marry, but he was entitled to earn money for teaching and maintaining his own private household if he chose to do so. For many canons, keeping a mistress was also an accepted arrangement, if not entirely proper for a semi-cleric. Such things were customarily managed in a discrete manner. He was a handsome man of forty years, with a brilliant intellect and wit, which assured his popularity with the students who flocked to his lectures. His reputation was so esteemed that he is still known as the man

---

75 James Burge, *Heloise and Abelard: A New Biography* (San Fracisco: Harper San Francisco, 2003), 20. This quote is from Heloise's first letter.

who founded the Notre Dame style of rhetoric, and who coined the word 'theology.'

Abelard knew of Heloise before they met by virtue of her own prodigious accomplishments as a scholar. She lived in the household of her uncle, Canon Fulbert, also of Notre Dame, who was proud of her accomplishments. She had received an education at the convent at *l'Argenteuil*, near Paris. It is believed that she might even have been born and raised at the *l'Argenteuil*. Another writer, who mused that perhaps she was the daughter of a former abbess, agreed that Heloise's father remained also unknown. What is actually known, however, is that at a young age, she was already adept at Latin and the literature of the classics, and her scholarly accomplishments were well known in the circle of academics and clergy that constituted the fairly enclosed cultural life of the *Ile de la Cité*. Canon Fulbert had offered lodging rooms in his household to the renowned Abelard, and probably a suitable stipend, in return for undertaking direct supervision of further scholarly studies for his precocious niece.

Scholars do not agree about Heloise's actual age when she began studies with Abelard. In fact, all the dates of this period are subject to a somewhat fluid scale. Some say she was still in her teens, others that she may have been over twenty. Whichever, soon there was a flaming romance. The affair, which lasted some fifteen months, was conducted right under Fulbert's nose. Shortly after the affair and her pregnancy were discovered, Heloise, dressed as a nun, slipped out of the house in the night with Abelard, and they traveled four days to his family home in Brittany. Their son, Astrolabe, was safely delivered under the care of Abelard's family members. Once Heloise and their son were settled, and knowing that he had to face Fulbert and come to some agreement about the future, Abelard returned alone to Paris.

Fulbert was furious. He felt the family honor and his own reputation had been attacked, and he demanded that Abelard and Heloise be married. Even knowing that this was totally against Heloise's will, Abelard finally yielded to this arrangement, provided that Fulbert agreed that the marriage be kept secret. At Abelard's insistence, Heloise returned to Paris and the marriage was performed in a small church.

After the marriage, Heloise returned to the convent of her earlier years, *l'Argenteuil,* without her uncle's knowledge and at Abelard's request, since it was of course impossible for her to remain in her uncle's household. It was arranged for her to live at *l'Argenteuil* without taking final vows, by virtue of her being an earlier student and resident there, and the lovers were at least able to see each other. There are charming accounts in the literature of their finding ways to manage a little clandestine time alone in one corner or another. Canon Fulbert, when he discovered Heloise was at *l'Argenteuil*, thought that Abelard was planning to divorce his niece. Again, the canon was furious. He felt he had been tricked once again by Abelard. Enraged, Fulbert hired his own servants and another accomplice to enter Abelard's apartment while he slept, and castrate the man. Soon, of course, all of Paris knew the story.

Denied of his full career options and humiliated by the violence done to his body, Abelard once again insisted that Heloise follow his wishes rather than her own. He knew that his only recourse was to take holy vows, and ultimately enter the monastery at *St. Denis*. In order to protect Heloise from Fulbert, and perhaps fearful that she might one day marry again, Abelard insisted that his wife take her final vows as a nun. And so, once again, she set aside her own preferences and did as he requested, not in order to please God, but to please Abelard.

As the story unfolds, Abelard's career was also shattered. His treatise, *On The Unity and Trinity of God,* was condemned by the Council of Soissons and burned without even having been read. He entered the cloister at *St. Denis* as a monk in 1119, but he suffered a series of discords wherever he went, in spite of his scholarly fame.

After several moves, he finally built himself a hermitage on a remote property assigned to him, and began first to build a retreat, and then as before, to teach. The buildings became both shelter and inspiration, and were consecrated as a formal monastery. Abelard named it, lovingly, The Paraclete (the Divine Supporter, or Holy Spirit). Several years later, Abelard accepted the position of Abbot of St. Glides in remote Brittany near his family home, and left The Paraclete. By a strange coincidence, Heloise's convent at *l'Argenteuil* was 'closed' as deemed morally 'unfit,' for reasons that were probably political, and the property was given to *St. Denis*. Some of the nuns, who chose to remain under the care of Heloise as Prioress, were in need of a consecrated home. Abelard offered them the use of The Paraclete, which ultimately became a famous and highly respected convent under her direction, and she became Abbess.

It was while she lived there that Abelard's autobiographical account of his life with her, History Calamatium, came into her hands, and their correspondence began. Another set of very early letters, discovered in 1980 and edited in the 16th century by a monk named Johannes de Vepria, is now believed to have been written by the lovers, exchanged on an almost daily basis during their actual love affair.[76]

Most relevant to our study of HETAIRA is the determined effort of Heloise to maintain a relationship with Abelard in their correspondence that included their great friendship, their common philosophical and spiritual lives, and the memories of their joyous physical passion as well.

## Courtesans

As the power of the early Christian church spread across Europe, the documented stories of HETAIRA are difficult to uncover, and all but disappeared as a social phenomenon. But they surfaced again a thousand years later during the Renaissance when the word 'courtesan' began to be heard. It was at first associated with the mistresses taken by the Papal court during a period when the papal retinue was nominally celibate at best, and mistresses were brought to the court. Katie Hickman describes this in her book, *Courtesans*:

> The Master of Ceremonies at the Papal Court, who was responsible for hiring them, referred to them picturesquely as 'our respectable prostitutes' but they frequently became much more than that.
>
> Alexander VI, who was elected Pope in 1492 when he was sixty-one, was already the father of no fewer than six children by his lover Vannozza dei Cattanei. He later fell in love with Giulia Farnese, who joined him in the Vatican when she was just seventeen, and later became the model for Raphael's fresco of the Madonna in the Pope's private apartments. By the beginning of the sixteenth century the usual term for any high-class prostitute *meretrize* was beginning to be replaced by the politer *cortegiana honesta*, [...] meaning 'honest' or 'honored' courtesan.[77]

---

76 Burge, *Heloise and Abelard: A New Biography.*
77 Katie Hickman, *Courtesans*, 15.

Conditions for women throughout Europe at this time, particularly in Venice, approximated, in many ways those of ancient Greece two thousand years earlier. Wives were strictly repressed, stayed home, took care of their households, and supervised their children. Their arena of public visibility was firmly controlled. Prostitution flourished as always, and men took mistresses. But there grew a separate society across Europe of women who first imagined, and then achieved, a grander visibility.

Courtesanry grew and flourished for nearly five hundred years, and this lively sector of *the demi monde* became a substantial part of the culture. This 'smaller world' was enormously colorful and provided society with the glamour bestowed in today's world on film and television stars and famous fashion models. The courtesan was not to be discussed in polite company, by the established wives of the upper levels of society. However, aristocratic husbands lavished money, houses, jewels and exorbitant gifts upon their libertine favorites. Unlike the prostitute, prepared to sell her favors indiscriminately, the courtesan might be the mistress of just one man, or many, but a courtesan always chose her patrons, very often for her own pleasure as well as theirs. Her gifts of company and conversation as well as of erotic pleasure were only bestowed upon a favored few who paid fabulous – sometimes-ruinous – sums for them.

As the cosmopolitan world became literate and the press flourished, some courtesans learned how to write memoirs, and were not above sheer blackmail. Among the many journals of the *demi monde*, that of one notorious courtesan, Harriet Wilson, established the benchmark for utter outrageousness. She notified the public, via the current newspaper in London, that she was about to publish her memoirs, and would be willing to accept the 'tidy sum' of 200 pounds (roughly 10,000 pounds in today's market) from any of her patrons who wished to be 'excused' from her manuscript. Katie Hickman's lively book *Courtesans* contains a cartoon from the London Journal, circa 1885, in which several of Harriet's patrons crowd to her desk, cash in hand, including the famous Duke of Wellington himself, in full military garb![78]

While for the most part the popular courtesan entertained many suitors and friends in her lively salon and enjoyed unprecedented public attention, characteristically her life may well end in illness, poverty and abandonment. Rarely, but occasionally, she married an adoring

---

78 Hickman, *Courtesans*, Illustrations opposite 236.

wealthy suitor, and thereby established, over time, a respected place in society.

Hickman continues:

> Perhaps one of the definitions of a courtesan should be that she was a woman who dared to break the rules. The rules of sexual morality gave way at first, but in their wake fell other, perhaps more far-reaching barriers of class, society, and female propriety. Courtesans were shunned by 'respectable' society, and yet, despite itself, society - men and women alike, was fascinated by them. Courtesanry reached its apotheosis in nineteenth Century England and France, until Victorianism quelled it with a stricter code of family values.[79]

The early Greek Hetairae were precursors of the Courtesan, by nearly two thousand years. But both phenomena demonstrate, by their existence alone, the singular repression of the female throughout history, and the ability of some women to gain a measure of notoriety and prestige by virtue of their own talents. The shadow side of the courtesan can be measured many ways, but perhaps it lies, by today's standards, not so much in her sexual proclivities as in the narcissism of some, reflected in relentless hunger for notoriety and publicity of our high-visibility celebrity women. In place of the divine feminine figure, in our day we have our popular camera-hungry icons.

## Geisha

A comparable tradition in Japan was transformed by law between 1600 and 1750 to distinguish the phenomena known as 'elegant and educated Geisha' from common prostitution. At that time, special entertainment areas were set aside in the larger cities in order to separate women specifically trained in the arts of hospitality, languages, music, dance, tea service, and knowledgeable conversation from their more lowly and less talented sisters. The legislation was adopted, in part to provide the business establishments of these districts—restaurants, theatres, private as well as public party facilities, etc. with the benefit of the evolving Geisha charm and mystique. But the tradition of Geisha was originally geared toward providing sexual availability along with

---

79 Hickman, *Courtesans*, 24-25.

pleasurable entertainment, like the Hetaira women of ancient Greece. When, where and if, the Geisha were separated from the connotations of sexual availability is difficult to identify. As recently as the 1990's Arthur Golden's novel and the later film, *Memoirs of a Geisha*,[80] presents his protagonist, Sayuri, as a gifted artist with impeccable standards of taste and refinement. She is also the same woman whose virginity had been sold by her 'owner' when she was little more than a child. As a powerful geisha in Kyoto, her late evening appointments were never to be discussed, and the identity of her patrons kept secret until after death, either hers or theirs.

Only a few years later, G.G. Rowley's translation of *Autobiography of a Geisha*,[81] the painstakingly developed story of Sayo Masuda, tells the tale of an illegitimate peasant child sold into indenture when she was little more than a baby, to a Geisha house in a rural area. Her childhood is spent as a chore maid and servant to her 'older sisters.' She overcomes her condition by her own fierce courage enough to provide for her little brother, whom she finds after she escapes from the man who had 'bought her' from the Geisha house to be his property.

A third more recent document, *Geisha, A Life*, by Mineko Iwasaki,[82] published in 2002 presents a considerable contrast of Geisha life in the Gion Kobu district of Kyoto. Iwasaki records a far more glamorous and pristine story of her life of artistic and moral virtue. But she, too, becomes troubled by the system, and angry that so much of her hard work fills the pockets of others. The opening pages give her personal account of the contemporary Geisha life as a highly stylized art form, with no association whatever with the element of sexual availability. She does go to some length in insisting that her choices were voluntary.

In all three of these literary works, the shadow of a deep sense of furious injustice smolders, and breaks out in over-reactions, even violent rages, in unexpected places.

The primary task of a Geisha is to learn how to make guests feel welcome, entertain them, provide interesting conversation, preside

80 Arthur Golden, *Memoirs of A Geisha* (New York: Random House Vintage, 1999).
81 Sayo Masuda, *Autobiography of a Geisha*. Edited by G.G. Rowley (New York: Columbia University Press, 2003). (Note: Thomas Harper, of Waseda University, Tokyo, gave this memoir to Rowley.)
82 Mineko Iwasaki, *Geisha, a Life* (New York: Washington Square Press & Co., 2002), 5.

at social and religious celebrations, and bring color, grace and the ancient Japanese traditions of hospitality to each occasion for which she is hired to appear. The work is difficult, demanding, highly disciplined, and non-stop. The business is firmly controlled, and highly in-bred. The future of even the most elegant Geisha seems to be limited to the businesses that spawn the business itself.

Aspects of the Geisha life seem to be part of a vanishing world. Many may miss its colorful charm, but there are those who will also celebrate the possibility of a more independent life. Perhaps there is a way to keep the style, charm and tradition of earlier times alive, with a stronger protection and independence for the talented women involved.

In terms of Toni Wolff's definition of a HETAIRA, the Geisha qualifies because her primary ego investment is in the quality of the relationship with her partner, or partners. While Wolff's definition combines other qualities, we begin to wonder: What is a Contemporary HETAIRA?

As mentioned earlier, the present day HETAIRA types are often 'father's daughters,' who as children were more drawn to his activities and company than watching or emulating mother's world. She intuitively pleases him, and herself, by sharing his interests. Father in turn often favors this child with special attention and information, and spends time talking with her while sorting out his own ideas and plans. In the best scenario, he also helps her consider her own tastes, talents and interests, and to develop her own skills and opinions.

Laura, a woman of 50 years, is embarking on a new career. She is trying to figure out the dynamics of her own type:

## Narrative: Laura's Story

> I have a memory of when I was probably only three or four. I don't remember wanting to please my mother. I liked to get up in the morning and set the mirror up for my father in the kitchen so he could shave. And I got his cereal bowl out for him, and the milk, and his spoon. I remember intentionally thinking this is going to make him happy, and my mother can sleep, because she hated to get up.
>
> I remember doing a lot of things to make my father happy. He would smile and talk to me, spend time with me.

My mother used to do strange things for my father that I ended up doing for my first husband, like heating his socks and underwear on the register before she woke him up, so that he would feel comfortable getting dressed. She probably did teach me a lot about it, and then she got to a stage where she just wanted to sleep in.

I remember that my mother wrote notes to my dad. I didn't know how to write, so I know this was before I went to school. I just wanted to draw pictures for him so that I could put them in his pocket and he could find them during the day. And then he would come home and say, 'Oh, I got your note...'

I just watched my mother. I don't remember particularly wanting to please my mother. It was my dad I wanted to please. I know I was his favorite.

Well, the HETAIRA is definitely my type. I mean it has played itself out my entire life. It has been a very difficult type... It's really great finding all this information. It explains a lot of things for me. It's been very difficult, being married, and being a HETAIRA.'

Laura was never really conscious, as she moved along her path, that her ego goals (the choices she made) were centered primarily in the quality of relational life with a partner. This characteristic is indeed what Wolff termed as definitive in the HETAIRA type. As a small child, a major part of Laura's future was already in place and embedded in her unconscious. As in all four types, the HETAIRA also carries the possibility of a dangerous and self-defeating unconscious shadow component. If it is made conscious, there is a way to apprehend it, and guard against its possibilities for despair and defeat.

Psychologically, this level of father/daughter experience can be a double-edged sword. Although a fantasy incest relationship is common in little girl children, ('I'm going to marry Daddy when I grow up,') it can come perilously close to an actual incestuous relationship with the father, at least in the psychological sense, whereby either consciously or unconsciously, the young woman feels, 'There can never be another man for me that can compare with my wonderful Daddy.' And unconsciously, she may choose men that are apt to be 'less than' her own father. (Note: In this work, we are considering the normal range of relational development. In the worst scenarios, of course, the stories of abusive and exploitive parenting abound where parental attention moves into narcissism and perversity. Such stories are as close to us all as the next-door neighbors, but they are not the purview of this book.) In the best scenario, the father, as well as sharing his world with his daughter, takes a sincere interest in her own interests, her tastes and ideas within her own world, and encourages her. Fortunate is the daughter for whom this occurs.

On the other hand, within the natural healthy HETAIRA evolution and development, the girl's interest in pleasing the father helps her break away from the mother. In any case, she is unlikely to stay home after adolescence, directing her interest to other males, mentors, teachers and boyfriends, with whom she easily forms bonds. Whatever the means of upbringing, her first ego priority remains with the quality of her relationship with her male partner.


## The Barbie Phenomena

At what level do we associate Barbie with the HETAIRA archetype? A recent news item reported that 150,000 Barbie dolls are sold in America *per day*! Since she is so ubiquitous, of course she does have an impact on the culture. A look at the Barbie phenomena may help to establish the HETAIRA qualities therein. Most conspicuously, it is clear that Barbie's omnipresent preoccupation with that she wears is axiomatic. The art of self-adornment for children is as ancient and as innocent as the first chain of dandelions decorating a three-year-old, and seems to continue in most of us all of our lives, to some degree. Certainly both Courtesans and Geisha were famous for their clothing styles. Meniko Iwasaki reported that she weighed ninety pounds, and her full evening costume as a Geisha weighed an additional forty!

M.G. Lord, in her book *Forever Barbie*, comments on the long-lasting fascination of the public with the famous doll, whose creation was actually inspired and designed to recreate a European play-boy toy of easy virtue called Lilli:

> Barbie was knocked off from the *Bild* Lilli doll, a lascivious plaything for men that was based on a postwar comic character in the *Bild Zeitung*, a downscale German newspaper similar to America's *National Enquirer*. The doll, principally sold in tobacco shops, was marketed as a sort of three-dimensional pin-up. In her cartoon incarnation, Lilli was not merely a doxie, she was a German doxie — an ice blond, pixie-nosed specimen, of an Aryan ideal — who may have

known hardship during the war, but as long as there were men with checkbooks, was not going to suffer again.[83]

Lord goes on to say that Ruth Handler, who invented Barbie, 'Took Lilli, ... described as a 'hooker or an actress between performances,' and re-cast her as the "wholesome All-American girl."[84]

## Narrative: Pam's Story

> My mom raised my three sisters, and me and there was never enough money, and sometimes not even enough food. I never had a Barbie doll. But I had a cheaper version, called Madge.
>
> I had a friend whose mother made, and bought, many Barbie clothes, gorgeous little outfits, and my friend probably felt sorry for my Madge doll, and me, so she gave some of the pretty doll clothes to me.
>
> And so I had a box full of Barbie things! Well, one day my friend's mother came over. She stood on the front porch, and demanded that I return the Barbie clothes. So I went upstairs to get them. My mom must have been at work.
>
> Up in my room I quickly tied strings to them, long strings, maybe yarn, and called to her from an upstairs window and hollered, 'Here they are!' So the mother came to the edge of the porch, and I angled the clothes on strings, through my upstairs window. And when she would reach for them, I would just yank them back up.
>
> I'm not sure how it all ended. I guess she just got mad and went home. But I kept the doll clothes a long time, even though they didn't fit Madge very well. It felt to me like *I just had to have them!*

How does Barbie reflect the juvenile quality of HETAIRA?

Barbie wants more than anything to be admired by all, and ultimately to attract the most popular boy friend and live for grown up parties, games, etc. Barbie's social life, (her popularity) is her essential goal, which she seems to achieve by the varieties of outfits she dons. And it is all very natural in a child's life, up to a point. It is sort of like the life of the butterfly, nestled in her cocoon of dreams, and in some sense, rehearsing how to fly. But also, as she grows older, she learns how to maneuver how to be admired, not only among the cutest, but also how to be the best, Barbie. The down side is that in this sense, she may not

83 M.G. Lord, *Forever Barbie* (New York: Walker Press and Co., 2004), 7-8.
84 Lord, *Forever Barbie*, 9.

be an individual at all, but a competitive little manikin, herself doll-like, and it is in that manner that we understand something of the pre-adolescent and adolescent HETAIRA in all of us. She is totally innocent, up to that point, and later, poisonous if she succeeds, thereby sabotaging her own natural ageing and maturity, where she would ideally be reaching for other kinds of validation. For Barbie is apt to be a relentless competitor, and some of the spiteful rage we read about in the Geisha tales seems to smolder within her persona of relentless and highly competitive cute sexiness. (Check out the 'mean girls' syndrome.)

It would be tragic, indeed, to be caught in the Barbie phase forever, and unworthy of the great HETAIRAE of history. But we do acknowledge the phenomena as an important stage in the lives of girl children. Yet, left without a maturing character of her own, she may well become the humorless and gorgeous trophy wife, omnipresent on the television soaps, and/or remain in the idolatry of celebrity worship. From little girl Barbie play, our child goes to junior high and high school, and may experience her first flush of power when boys begin to notice her. For some young women, that becomes the only 'power' they ever know. If she remains in this stage at age eighty, whereby her goals are still conforming to peer pressure and clothes, she remains the adolescent girl, at least psychologically, who has never grown up. Sadly, she has little actual self-hood out of which to negotiate her own mature personal happiness. Perhaps we can recognize how 'Barbieism' might influence the shadow possibilities inherent in the lives of the HETAIRA type. One would hope that the 'Forever Barbie' woman remains more of a case of arrested psychological development than of any great cultural descriptor.

Lord maintains that Barbie's appeal lies in the fact that the doll signifies the Great Mother archetype, a 'space-age fertility goddess.' We do not agree. We think she represents the archetype of the Kore, the eternal youthful girl who dreams over the narcissus flower. She hovers always between daughterhood and motherhood herself, without much of a chance at self-hood, although she is well endowed with the 'outfits' of countless professional personae, a substitute for credentials, degrees, or actually working at difficult tasks. There has been a rumor that a 'Mommy' Barbie is being developed, but it is certainly late in coming. Perhaps that is because Barbie, as an archetype, can't really grow up; by her very nature she must stay forever the young girl. Whatever Barbie's appeal to the younger set, she does seem to be imperishable, and like all archetypes, she remains somewhere in all of us.

Not all future HETAIRA women start off as caught in the Barbie phase of juvenile attitudes, by any means, although there is good evidence of it in some of the sexual games that bombard us, relentlessly, via the media. We also see her in exploitive sex shops and in the Playboy Bunny icons strong in the 60s and 70s, as well in some of the reports of teenage 'friends-with-privileges' and 'hook up' behavior. Barbie has a lively competitor in the American Girl dolls, also somewhat politicized, as was Barbie, early on. And on the opposite end of the profitable doll kingdom, the Brats dolls are rapidly becoming competitive in the market.

A cursory review of the current material on teenage sexual behavior as reported in the press and in such work as Sabrina Weill's book *The Real Truth About Teens and Sex*, signals a relatively new era, in which there are several issues for consideration:

* There is a considerable shift going on among young teens in which sex is considered more playful and less personal. Sex 'just happens,' for the most part, as is reflected in the reports.

* There seems to be even less free and truthful discussion between parents and teenagers about sexual issues than ever before, according to Weill.

* There is a counter movement whereby teens take abstinence vows 'until marriage' and confine their social lives to their own in-crowd that conforms to this principle. Often heavy petting is allowed, but not intercourse. Oral sex is common, but rarely reciprocal.

* The impact of the internet has added to the list of options on the subject that can be informative, dangerous, helpful or hurtful. Internet availability spreads the feelings, habits and fantasies of teenagers in rapid waves, and reaches remote distances with unfiltered information and images, fostering inevitable swift change.[85]

---

85  Sabrina Weill, *The Real Truth about Teens and Sex*, (New York: Berkley Perigee Publishing Co., 2005), 116-140.

How the general public reacts to these issues of sexuality among teen-agers is changing quickly, and will influence the cultural attitudes and behaviors of the future. The fears for parents are, as always, disease and premature pregnancy.

This delightful and poignant comedy-drama film presents the scenario of a young woman who seems to know how to tame and civilize the instinctual world of both the animal kingdom and the man she hopes to claim for herself:

## Film Study: *The Accidental Tourist*[86]

Macon Leary (William Hurt) and his wife Sara (Kathleen Turner) live in Baltimore, MD, where he writes practical 'guide books' for business travelers who do not want to leave the comforts of home, and, like him, strongly prefer foreign lands to have as few uncomfortable attributes as possible. Macon's own temperament and the reclusive pattern of his family of origin would never have prompted him to venture outside of his marriage, but he finds his world enlarged beyond all expecta-tions following the tragic death of their only son, randomly killed in a robbery. In a scenario well known to therapists treating some of the survivors of such devastating tragedy, Macon and Sara are not able to sustain any sort of comfort together, or even closeness. All they are able to do for each other is to reflect and intensify each other's pain. Sara decides to move out.

Gloomy Macon breaks his leg through an accident caused by Ed-ward, his late son's dog. He and Edward move back into his parental home still occupied by his siblings, who have taken to not answering the telephone. This is fine with Macon, although his editor is unhappy when he can't reach him. This is a good portrait of non-relational life.

The time comes for a business trip, with no advance warning. Ed-ward cannot stay with Sara. Macon takes Edward to a dog-sitting estab-lishment and finds Muriel. 'Muriel Pritchett...call me sometime. Just to talk.' (Geena Davis won an Academy Award for this role.) 'Talk?' says the startled Macon. Muriel soon tames the recalcitrant Edward. She suc-

---

86 *The Accidental Tourist*. 1988. See Film Index.

cessfully makes room in Macon's heart for herself, and also for his own new life.

Muriel owns her business. She is 'intelligent,' as she stresses to Macon. Undeterred by his stolid ways, she understands that he needs and wants in order to break out of his old patterns. She is relational, both to animals who understand her language, to Macon whom she comforts without words, and later to her friends who pitch in to care for her son Alexander, so she can go to Paris to find Macon. She teaches Macon to use words in a personal way. Muriel fulfills her true HETAIRA nature with Macon, and as a secondary benefit, Alexander her son finds a strong surrogate father and is spared Muriel's doting fussiness over his health.

How the HETAIRA archetype emerges in our lives remains the principal subject of the following chapters.

# Chapter 9

## Familiar Qualities Of The HETAIRA

### (Friend, Companion, Lover)

Toni Wolff's ideas:

- "A woman's spirit and sexuality are colored by psyche."

- "The HETAIRA is instinctively related to the personal psychology of the male."

- "The individual interests, inclinations, and possibly also the problems of the male are within her conscious field of vision."

- "She will convey to him the sense of (his) personal value quite apart from collective values, as her own development demands her to experience and realize an individual relationship in all its nuances and depths."

(Paraphrases): Psyche influences a woman's spirit and her sexuality. For HETAIRA, both her conscious and unconscious preferences require her to experience personal relationship in all its depth. She is in close contact with the male, and sensitized to his nature. It is her function to nurture the personal psychic life of the male and lead him to aspects of himself of his full potential. (Author's note: As well as her own.)[87]

As Toni Wolff portrays the HETAIRA at her best, she inspires the man in her life to his highest possible achievement. Unstated by Wolff, and a paradigm for our times, might be: And also at her best, she maintains her own identity, her own work, and her own creative self-hood as well. This is not easily accomplished, as we will see, and remains the ultimate challenge of the contemporary HETAIRA. Mutual self-nurture is, perhaps an unfamiliar piece here.

---

87 Wolff, "Structural Forms," 8.

It is necessary to note that all traces of the element of prostitution or a history of poverty, slavery or any other set of social factors related to prostitution are entirely absent from Wolff's choice of words — only the identification of the relationship as a first ego priority remains.

We have chosen three women from the early twentieth century who characterized HETAIRA at her most creative and productive best, as described above by Toni Wolff. Their lives span the era from 1861 to 1986, a period of powerful social changes in the relational lives of women and men. Arguably, there has never been, since the beginning of recorded history, such an earth-shaking set of developments for women within one century as occurred during that time period. Most notable are the serious changes wrought by the availability of reliable methods of birth control, and the growth of the concept of self-determination for both men and women, particularly in free countries.

While these women led dissimilar lives in many respects, they had more in common than a first glance might reveal. All three were European, but from very different cultural backgrounds. All three labored to self-actualize professionally as well as to be present to their partners who were among the most famous men of the twentieth century. All three contributed substantially to the ongoing creative lives of these men in significant ways, and also established their own reputations as professional women in their respective fields. They are exemplary for us in that sense. All three lived their childbearing years before fail-safe birth control methods were available. Their lives and work have influenced the current thinking about the HETAIRA archetype, and illustrate how modes of understanding the feminine spirit have evolved. They are Lou Andreas-Salomé, Toni Wolff, and Simone de Beauvoir.

## Lou Andreas-Salomé 1. Early Years

Lou Andreas-Salomé was not only immensely gifted as a writer, psychologist and observer of her twilight culture; she was the occasion and spur of genius in others. Nietzsche, Rilke, Freud and a host of important contemporaries were set alight or shadowed by her passage. Her *Memoirs* touch the nerve of modernity. "They are not at every point to be trusted. Which makes the game the more sparkling and strangely poignant." –(George Steiner)[88]

Aspiring students of dynamic psychiatry will inevitably come across a famous picture of the historic Weimar meeting in 1911, the third formal assembly of the Psychoanalytic Society. The assembled brilliance of minds set the stage for what is known in our culture as depth psychology. One immediately identifies the central figure of Sigmund Freud. But by far the most conspicuous face in the picture is that of a stunning woman in the first row. Her eyes are alert and strong; her tranquil face set off by soft hair waving naturally over a wide forehead; she has a sensuous mouth, and a loosely fitting fur draped over her shoulders. She is comfortable in her selfhood, and in her body. She is—Lou Andreas-Salomé.

Lou lived a life of principled and rational independence, made possible at first by a large inheritance. But it was not just her privileged family background that earned her the attention she gathered around her. It was her dynamic mind and spirited presence that later insured her continued welcome in the select circles of European intellectual life. She maintained a high standard of behavior and work for herself and never lost sight of her own passionate love of life, even though she lived through some grim times in history, separated by choice from her family and the land of her childhood.

Ljola (Lou) Salomé was born in 1861, the only daughter of a general officer in the inner circle of court life for Czar Nicholas I of Russia. She grew up in a sumptuous apartment across the street from the famous Winter Palace in St. Petersburg, and remembered enjoying long walks with her father as he ventured forth in the neighborhood wearing his distinguished uniform. She had five brothers, and was the youngest and only female child. Her father came from the Baltic region, of a French Huguenot family of strict Calvinist religious practice. General Salomé died in 1879, when Lou was seventeen or possibly eighteen years old. She was unquestionably the darling of the family, adored for her beauty, her sparkling mind, and her cheerful disposition. There was an admiring grandfather as well, who seemed to have spent a great deal of time trying to think of surprises to delight her, and from whom no request of hers was ever denied. Along with her five brothers, there

---

88 Lou Andreas-Salomé, *Looking Back Memoirs* (New York, NY: Paragon House, 1990). Steiner's remarks on Jacket.

were seven males, very early on, as her admiring audience, in regular attendance. That she was forever comfortable and energized in male company is of no surprise. Lou writes in her memoirs:

> Fraternal solidarity was so much a part of my experience within the family; as the youngest and only sister, it continued to have an influence upon my relationship to men throughout my life: regardless of how early or late I came to know a man, I always felt a brother was hidden within him.[89]

She inherited a goodly portion of the family wealth that sustained her as an independent woman and provided her the means to seek her own education and private studies, until the Russian Revolution and World War I depleted those resources. For the most part, she designed her own education. She chose her mentors as she needed them, remaining near those whose talents and intellect complimented her own.

What of her heart? Over her lifetime, there were many men. But in her memoirs, she put forth four names as remaining the most prominent and enduring: Gillot, Andreas, Rilke, and Freud. Her biographers and archivists list another name, Georg Ledebour, although she does not mention him by name in her memoirs. He is included in this brief study because it seemed his intervention into her life may have made a significant contribution to her maturity as a woman, and helped her develop her adult HETAIRA nature. (These relationships are identified and described in the chapters ahead.) She was not able to include 'the whole woman, body and soul,' until her thirties, even though by that time she had lived in an unconsummated marriage for several years. She was also already established as a successful writer, and was known throughout Europe as the woman who had turned down a famous proposal of marriage from the hugely popular scholar and author, Friedrich Nietzsche.

In the story of Lou's first romance with Hendrik Gillot one senses that for this young woman, ideas, knowledge, learning itself, was a palpable, even sensory experience. The seventeen-year-old girl found the discovery of her own intellectual abilities to be so exciting that she interpreted these encounters as of the ultimate value, bypassing completely her own immature sensuality. The man in question understood her exuberant highly spiritualized sexuality, coupled with her natural vivacity, as

---

89 Salomé, *Looking Back*, 22.

being 'in love.' This mistaken evaluation of her feelings remained an uncontested part of Lou's own blithe-spirited persona for several years, and sent many enraptured suitors away disappointed, sometimes furious, and at least one, (Paul Ree) probably suicidal. 'Union,' for her was something like a dynamic intellectual and spiritual intimacy, disconnected at least consciously, from her maturing body.

Lou's idea of sharing the world with the men in her life was her determined, highly intuitive instinct to seek deeply a full understanding of her male partners, their soul-level makeup, their dreams, their passions and their abilities. As a young woman, this was the moral principle that governed her associations with her male friends. The whole issue of sex itself remained in the shadow. For Lou, sex was an unacknowledged kingdom, until she was in her thirties.

Of Lou's mother little is said. She seemed to have kept to herself a great deal, and enjoyed reading. Late in her life, Lou wrote of her in her memoirs, "I did not have in Mama a natural friend."[90] Very early, as an off-shoot of the daily household religious observances, the little girl developed a super-sensitive private religious life, wherein God became her secret inner companion, to whom she would relate, every night, the private stories of her friends, her dreams, her pets, her daily child's world. She would fall asleep, comforted by the entity which her fruitful imagination gave her as 'God,' safe in his loving arms.

For her personal code of living and sense of responsibility, her faith ultimately became what we in our time would term as a belief in a higher power, a deep reverence for all living things, for creation itself, and a strong belief in her own need to remain capable of reverence. It did not include the doctrinal dogmatic of God, as taught by the church. When she reached the age of confirmation, she resolutely refused to participate, a matter that her family found very disturbing. However, she claimed high standards for herself in that she set her own expectations of work, study and determined independence. It also seems no surprise that her first love was with a distinguished clergyman, twenty-one years her senior, Hendrik Gillot. (See Chapter 3.)

While the information gathered from her memoirs and other accounts does not totally confirm what occurred with Georg Ledebour (Chapter Three), one can assume that he might have been the man who finally called her on her 'game' of distancing her consciousness from

90 Salomé, *Looking Back*, 159.

the sexual signals that innocently poured from her, thereby exposing this shadow part of her personality, so conspicuous to others, but unknown to herself. Her own sexuality was liberated and available by the time she met Rilke, the man for whom many would say her greatest contribution to the world was achieved.[91]

## Lou Andreas-Salomé 2. Rilke

When Lou Andreas-Salomé was thirty-six years old, her husband, Friedrich Carl Andreas, held a distinguished teaching position at the university in Berlin. By this time also she was an established writer who had published five books, including her famous biography of Nietzsche. She was vivacious, beautiful, exotic, and highly regarded in intellectual, academic, and literary circles, with an astonishing number of famous friends and acquaintances throughout Europe. Rumors established her as femme fatale. In the spring of 1887 she visited her friend of long standing, Frieda von Bulow in Munich.

Rainer Maria Rilke was at that time an aspiring young writer in Munich, and sixteen years Lou's junior. He had read many of her published articles and books, and wrote to her anonymously, sending some of his poetry, to the 'famous and gracious Lou Salomé.' They began a correspondence and met shortly at a tea. The meeting must have been electric; something of the young man's mind and sensitivity reached Lou's intuitive tracking of the emerging soul of true genius.

Rilke had always dreamed of a love that could consume him, help him heal the wounds of his convoluted experiences with his own mother, and provide the light of insight into his own direction. This is exactly what happened for him with Lou. "They soon became lovers, and spent time at Frieda's summer home in Wolfratshausen. Lou returned in the fall to Berlin, and Rilke followed soon after. He was a regular visitor in the small home Lou shared with her husband."[92]

As Lou grew to know Rilke, she understood something of his need to belong to the earth in ways that she herself had taken for granted, as a part of her childhood, 'the straightforward spiritual connections that

---

91 Salomé, *Looking Back*, 1-40.
92 H.F. Peters, *Rainer Maria Rilke: Masks and the Man* (New York, NY: Gordian Press, 1977), 41-43.

Russia exemplified, which seemed to rise from the very earth.'[93] They began to plan their first trip to Russia, which occurred in the spring 1899, Andreas with them. This trip was, for Rilke, the establishment of an entirely new plateau of perceiving God through nature, through the faith that he experienced in the Russian peasants, and the great religious celebration at Easter in Moscow. Interestingly, Lou, who had unequivocally disconnected herself from the idea of the existence of a dogmatic concept of the divine, had instinctively retained what it was of the natural world whereby Rilke could establish his own religious grounding:

> In the thousands praying in Moscow's chapels and shrines before their private icons: the twofold gospel that God is the abyss of which 'everything' is the surface, and that most men, if not all, are brethren. It is an old gospel, but it was wonderfully invigorating to the young poet's life and art. In the spirit of piety he opened his heart to humble things from then on, cooked under the conviction that he stood in relation not to a small group of literati, not a passing epoch, but to all mankind.[94]

The second Russian trip occurred six months later, May to August 1990. Lou prepared Rilke by seeing to it that he spoke the language fluently, and could express himself to those he met as well as understand what it was that he was experiencing, that which was somehow unavailable to him in Europe. Andreas did not accompany them this time. This journey covered far-out regions of Russia. They visited sacred shrines; the nineteen domes of St. Sophia, they crossed the Ukraine and the Volga, and ended at St. Petersburg.

The Russian journeys marked the most significant part of their time together. Lou writes of this time as when she was 'as his wife, for three years'; the first marriage of man, woman, body and soul, for her as well as for him, and her instinctive understanding of his need for the spiritual security which her own childhood had provided her. Had he made the trips to Russia alone, it would have been just another journey, cold and foreign. Lou recorded words in her memoir about that important trip:

93 Salomé, *Looking Back*, 39-43.
94 Salomé, *Looking Back*, 40.

It seemed as if wherever we were, we were meeting one and the same man, as if he came from the nearest village regardless of whether he had a standard Russian nose, or that of a Tartar. This unity... came from an openness and spirituality in the Russian face, as if the basic humanity we all share found eloquent expression there. It was like learning something new and different about yourself from someone you just met, and loving him. That inevitably had a decisive effect on Rainer, given his constant search for the most profound wellsprings of the human condition, providing him with the images with which he eventually became God's hymnist [...] The impulse to the work he was yet to create emerged from that realm for Rainer. God himself was always the object of his art.[95]

They parted soon after, with an agreement that he would not contact her except if his life were in danger. However, they continued their relationship for years from a distance, and occasionally met for brief periods. Both commented upon how quickly and easily they slipped into a rich comfort zone, when once again in each other's presence. Lou must have known she could never give this man her entire life without the loss of her own autonomy. And that this was what he needed and could not refrain from claiming. They continued to write to each other in a correspondence that does Wolff's choice of the word HETAIRA proud, in that Lou continued to unlock the best elements in Rilke's world for him and for his work. In Lou's memoirs, Rilke was the only one she wrote of using the word 'love' directly.

Less than a year after his return from the second Russian trip, Rilke was married to sculptress Clara Westhoff. They had a daughter, Ruth. With overpowering financial worries, they moved to Paris, where Rilke became Auguste Rodin's secretary for a period of time. Lou remained supportive of Rilke whenever he called upon her. In 1902, Rilke found himself in despair over the impossibility of his marriage. He felt himself overcome with the grief of the world, and it was to Lou that he turned. She responded by writing, "You are the poet of the poor and the oppressed."[96] His biographer Norbert Fuerst validated that Rilke was elated with her letter, and that the one person Rilke needed the most to hear from at that time was Lou.

---

95  Salomé, *Looking Back*, 73.
96  Norbert Fuerst, *Phases of Rilke* (New York, NY: Haskell House Publishers, 1971), 21.

In her memoirs written years later, Lou speaks of this enduring love:

> If I was your wife for years, it was because you were the first truly real person in my life, body and man indivisibly one, unquestionably a fact of life itself. I could have confessed to you word for word what you said in declaring your love: 'You alone are real.' Thus we were a couple even before we had become friends...[97]

In her letters over the years, Lou wrote to Rilke with love and a great tenderness, but she also often wrote not so much as a peer, lover and HETAIRA muse, but as an older (AMAZON) advisor. The correspondence shares much of the Freudian training of her later life. In her work *You Alone are Real to Me*[98] Lou is, indeed, a loving ex-lover, but also she realized retrospectively that she had become an insightful and mature psychotherapist. In the introduction to this book, her translator Angela von der Lippe commented on this element of the combination of Lou as a thirty-six-year-old woman in love, and the maturity of a professional woman in her 60's, the heart of Lou as HETAIRA is clearly expressed in giving him her serious undivided attention as her primary goal for however long she was able to manage it, *without loosing her own selfhood*. She truly understood his soul, helped him get a glimpse his own depth, and functioned spiritually and artistically, thereby inspiring his own commitment to his work. Her HETAIRA relationships, after Rilke, continued during her lifetime with several professional men of notoriety, and are addressed in further chapters.

## Toni Wolff 1. Early Years

Toni Wolff was herself a HETAIRA, by her own definition of the word. She writes of this type out of her own experience over many years as companion, friend, trusted colleague, confidante, *femme inspiratrice* and for a period of time, mistress to Carl Jung. Her early years, much like Lou's, were spared financial burdens. She was the first child of wealthy Swiss parents. Her father Konrad Arnold Wolff was a successful merchant who had lived in Japan for twenty years prior to his marriage, and had established a substantial importing business in the mercantile

---

97 Salomé, *You Alone are Real to Me*, 3-24.
98 Salomé, *You Alone are Real to Me*, 3-24.

field. He returned to Switzerland at age forty-two, ready for his arranged marriage to Anna Elizabeth Stutz and intent on raising a family. He was considered a sensitive compassionate man, completely devoted to his family. Jung's biographer Deirdre Bair describes: "They lived in the cantons of St. Galen and Argau briefly before finally moving to the stately *Jugenstil* mansion on Freiestrasse in Zürich, complete with well-tended gardens, an extensive library, lush tapestries, paintings, and rich fabrics of uncommon beauty."[99]

Toni was born in 1888, followed by two sisters, Erna and Susanne, each child two years younger than her predecessor. Reportedly, the girls enjoyed every advantage. They were presented with all the accouterments of culture suitable for young women in their time — music, sports, and whatever creative pursuits interested them. Toni was her father's favorite, and the two delighted in each other's company. She was a thoughtful young person who enjoyed spending long hours with him in his private library, and he was a willing provider of information regarding whatever interested her. As she matured, her interests in philosophy, mythology, poetry and comparative religions became prominent, which were interests he also shared. He encouraged her intellectual curiosity.

All three girls attended elementary and secondary girls schools in Zürich, and were sent to finishing schools in French Switzerland to prepare them to become efficient mistresses of sizeable households with incumbent social responsibilities. Toni wanted also to attend the University of Zürich, and was disappointed that her parents did not favor that manner of education for a young woman of her social position. She was encouraged to take course work there if she wished, but not to matriculate in a formal degree program. Herr Wolff believed that a university education was fine for women who did not have significant dowries and may need to prepare themselves to earn their own livings, but this was not the case for his daughters. To comfort her, Herr Wolff sent her back to Geneva 'for more courses in fine home making.'[100] She was also encouraged to spend six months in England to learn the language, and entreated not to burden herself with feelings of being inconsequential in the world, but to enjoy her girlhood. [101]

99 Deirdre Bair, *Jung: A Biography* (New York, NY: Little Brown and Co., 2003), 196-197.
100 Bair, *Jung: A Biography*, 196-197.
101 Bair, *Jung: A Biography*, 198.

After her time in England, Toni did attend classes at the university, where she formed friendships with people from a variety of backgrounds and contrasting circumstances. While she enjoyed socializing among them and visiting their preferred haunts, she never invited them to her own home. Among these friends was a serious young man from a background similar to hers named William Wolfensberger, [102] who was headed for a career as a writer, plans of which met with his father's approval. But when William decided to pursue ordination as a protestant minister, siding with the liberal socialist element of the Reformed Church, his father removed his financial support entirely. Toni was enamored, and thought William was courageous in his determination to support himself on the small stipends he was able to earn by tutoring other students. She saw his commitment to his calling as admirable, and his life style romantic. It was clear that she wanted to share it. William, however, was a determined ascetic and felt he needed to accept a distant parish call, and go on alone. Toni was disappointed at his rejection. This very sadness coincided with the sudden intrusion of her father's fatal illness.

Herr Wolff died unexpectedly in 1909, an event that altered the course of Toni's life in profound ways. The young woman fell into a deep depression. Her despair was severe enough to worry her mother; she had remained despondent and without appetite for life for several months. Finally Frau Wolff decided to seek psychological help for her daughter. She had learned of Dr. Jung's practice through friends, and brought Toni to him for treatment. Jung was thirty-five when he met Toni, and she was barely twenty-one.

The work went slowly at first. Gradually, Jung discovered the extent of the young woman's interest and background in classical mythology and philosophy, and he began to share with her the development of his own theoretical framework. Toni herself was slowly awakened from her illness by becoming interested in the evolving psychology of Dr. Carl Jung. Here the projections may have blossomed in Jung's private office in his home on Seestrasse in Küsnacht. Her sessions surely reminded her of the long hours spent with her father in the seclusion of the Herrenzimmer on Freiestrasse in Zürich as she was growing up.

In August of 1911, Jung wrote a letter to Freud announcing that he would be bringing several guests with him to the Third Psychoanalyti-

102 Bair, *Jung: A Biography*,197.

cal Congress at Weimar in September, among them 'a new discovery of mine, Frl. Antonia [sic] Wolff, a remarkable intellect with an excellent feeling for religion and philosophy....'[103]

## Toni Wolff 2. Jung

Toni's own analysis lasted three years. These years were pivotal for Jung as well. His conflicts with Freud had begun to be openly known, and he was struggling with his own issues of disagreement with the man who had been his inspiration, and whose work, *The Interpretation Of Dreams*, had made such an impact on the entire 'marginal field of psychiatry' which he had chosen as his specialization. His own family was rapidly expanding. In 1914 Jung's wife Emma gave birth to their last child, there now being five, the eldest born in 1904. Jung experienced his own carefully planned and dangerous 'Confrontation with the Unconscious,' with Toni standing by as his confidante, and serving as his analyst as well. It is thought that sometime during the year 1914, their intimate relationship became generally known.

As Toni matured, she maintained a steadfast support for Jung's work, gradually becoming a lay analyst with a full practice in Zürich. She took on the important role of President of the Psychology Club, the organization of his followers and students, which ultimately established the C.G. Jung Institute of Zürich.

Years later, when Toni had become a powerful analyst in her own right who served the Jungian community in distinctly influential ways, she had worked out the dynamics of herself as an HETAIRA, and brought this concept into her work with her analysands.

Because of the highly personal relationship between Toni and Jung, and the great respect each held for Emma, they themselves did not write about their arrangement. The two did nothing to keep it secret, however, except that they simply did not talk about it, and they agreed to destroy all of their personal correspondence. In Jung's work *Memories, Dreams, Reflections,* he does not refer to her personally. But he added two paragraphs after her death, late in his life, writing in January of 1959 from his retreat at Bollingen, in which he presents his statement of faith as well as of the mystifying experiences of human love:

---

103 *Freud-Jung Letters,* 439-444.

## Jung on Eros

> At this point the fact forces itself on my attention that be-
> side the field of reflection there is another equally broad if
> not broader area in which rational understanding and ra-
> tional modes of representation find scarcely anything they
> are able to grasp. This is the realm of Eros. In my medical
> experience as well as in my own life I have again and again
> been faced with the mystery of love and have never been
> able to explain what it is. Like Job, I had to 'lay my hand in
> my mouth. I have spoken once, and I will not answer.'(Job
> 40:4f)
>
> Here is the greatest and smallest, the remotest and the
> nearest, the highest and lowest, and we cannot discuss one
> side of it without also discussing the other. No language is
> adequate to this paradox. Whatever one can say, no words
> express the whole. To speak of partial aspects is always too
> much or too little, for only the whole is meaningful. Love
> 'bears all things' and 'endures all things' (I Cor.13: 7).
>
> These words say all there is to be said; nothing can be
> added to them."[104]

A part of Toni's HETAIRA story also suggests the need for some understanding of Jung's wife, Emma. Deirdre Bair offers her description of
Emma during this early period:

> Emma undoubtedly resented Toni's personal relationship
> with Carl, but she equally resented his growing intellectual
> dependence on her because family demands severely lim-
> ited her time with her husband. By the time he came down
> to breakfast in the mornings, she was seeing the children
> off to school. While this relationship was never easy to as-
> similate for Emma, their children or the rapidly growing
> community of Jung's students and analysands in Zürich,
> somehow they all managed to coexist in a manner that was
> not only civil, but proved to be ultimately creative for all
> parties concerned. When Emma's responsibilities for rais-
> ing the family of five children subsided somewhat, she too
> became more deeply engaged in Jung's professional life. In
> time she became known as a respected analyst in her own
> right, and contributed significantly to the growing corpus

---

104 C.G. Jung, *Memories, Dreams, Reflections*, 353-354.

of printed matter that developed into the still-multiplying Jungian canon of studies. At one point, Emma and Toni had a joint analytical experience with Carl Meier.[105]

Author's Note: With the exception of the first full year after her marriage, Emma was probably pregnant or most likely nursing for ten years straight, during which time she delivered five children. – (Molton, Sikes).

Jung's close friend Laurens van der Post reported: "In the end, Emma was generous enough to testify: I will always be grateful to Toni for doing for my husband what neither I nor anyone could have done for him at a most critical time."[106]

Toni Wolff ultimately defined and described the HETAIRA archetype as she experienced it over the years. Further study of this dynamic relationship is explored in the following chapters.

## Simone de Beauvoir 1. Early Years

This remarkable woman, often cited as the mother of the twentieth century feminist movement, also conducted her private life in the HETAIRA mode, during her fifty some year relationship with Jean-Paul Sartre. Their union was one of dynamic interaction, and a primary indicator of her personal ego strength. Simone de Beauvoir was able early on to live her professional, spiritual and physical selfhood in the context of her relational life with Jean-Paul Sartre with a minimum of misgivings. They negotiated this relationship out of a model they both developed and agreed upon themselves. Unlike Toni, she had been able to prepare herself fully for professional life in acquiring her distinguished graduate credentials from the Sorbonne with a major in Philosophy. She was among the first women ever to have achieved this position.

Simone's family background vacillated somewhere between the bourgeoisie and the aristocratic. Her mother, Francoise, had been carefully brought up in a rich and provincial Catholic family from Verdun, and educated in a convent school, comfortably supported by Papa's career as a banker. Simone's father also had a heritage of wealth provided

105 Bair, *Jung: A Biography*, 249-250.
106 Laurens van der Post, *Jung and the Story of Our Time* (New York, NY: Vintage Books, 1975), 177.

by his grandfather's success as a tax inspector, who had acquired for the family, among other amenities, a country estate of 500 acres where Simone spent idyllic childhood summers with her sister enjoying the delights of nature before returning to Paris for school.

From the work of Axel Madsen, the following is adapted from a summary of her childhood, from de Beauvoir's *Memoirs of a Dutiful Daughter.*

Her father, Georges, was the youngest of three children, who had been denied the career of his choice, that of acting, and went to law school instead. But even though he passed the bar exam, he never chose to practice law. Instead, he took a position as secretary to a successful lawyer, which was tedious work, but allowed him the freedom to devote himself to amateur theatrical productions that were his deepest pleasure. Georges was able to assume the affectations of carefree entitlement characteristic of the leisure class 'more from a studied theatricality than an actual financial security' and led a carefree life of artistic and intellectual vitality while steadily eating away his inheritance.[107]

Simone and her younger sister Helene attended a convent school, at Mother's insistence. Mother devoted herself to the girls' education. She learned Latin and English in order to help them with their studies. She went with the girls to Mass each week, and Georges, never. Simone shared an intellectual liveliness with her father, and enjoyed his wit and charm.

Axel Madsen, biographer of Beauvoir's and Sartre's life together, gives a charming profile of Simone's relationship to both parents as a young girl, mentioning that her father grew more attentive as she grew up, taking pains with her writing, and often dictating from Victor Hugo. She considered him remarkable funny, astute, poetic, and socially brilliant. He treated her as a young adult, although sometimes impatient when she behaved in a childish manner. She reported that her mother was more tolerant when she behaved sometimes like a little girl. Yet she took any criticism from her father lightly, while her mother's criticism left her feeling desolate. At the onset of World War I, Georges was mobilized and had to leave the family for military service. He suffered two serious heart attacks, and was finally given a desk job until the war

---

107 Axel Madsen, *Hearts and Minds* (NewYork, NY: William R. Murrow and Company 1977). Quoting from Simone de Beauvoir *Memoirs of a Dutiful Daughter,* World Publishing, 1959), 16.

ended. But living on a soldier's pay forced the family to rearrange their life style, which they accomplished by moving to a smaller apartment, and doing without household help. Simone did well at school, and Georges, realizing that there would not be a sizeable dowry for her, encouraged her to pursue a Lycee education with the Sorbonne in mind, even though there were only two women known to have achieved the doctorate in philosophy at that time, which was Simone's choice as she matured.

## Simone de Beauvoir 2. Sartre

Simone met Jean-Paul Sartre at the Ecole Normale in Paris, where both were preparing for the qualifying examinations to provide them with teaching positions in literature and philosophy. In 1929, she was doing her teaching internship, and had among her fellow interns such colleagues as Maurice Merleau-Ponty and Claude Levi-Strauss, so the quality of discourse and humor must both be challenging and exciting for her.

Simone and Jean-Paul were introduced by one of his friends. They made an interesting duo. Simone, tall, willowy, and decidedly attractive; Jean-Paul short, square, decidedly homely, with the horned-rim owlish look of an intellectual, and an irresistible self-assurance. He loved her beauty and her quick mind. She loved that he was always thinking. And that he was so convinced that writing was the most important work in the world. He encouraged her to take her own writing seriously, which of course she did.

Early in their lives together, Simone and Jean-Paul decided not to marry, opposing the conventional forms of union. Sartre also posed that he might desire adjunct, 'lesser' relationships from time to time, maintaining that his needs for feminine variety had nothing to do, personally, with her. He simply preferred the company of women to that of men. At one point, when they had hoped to manage joint teaching appointments, Sartre proposed marriage, but Simone had refused on idealistic grounds, since neither of them really wanted to ally themselves with conventionality.

The contract which they ultimately designed, and under which they negotiated their relationship, included two main points. They would honestly tell each other in detail everything that happened, and they would keep no secrets from each other. He told her that 'the real world, that is what he lived in with her.'

Regardless of this private contract so bravely agreed upon, the partnership took a toll on Beauvoir emotionally. She feared over-dependence on a man who wanted multiple sexual relationships, and as their story evolved, it was clear that although she had agreed to this contract, it was not altogether comfortable for her. As for Sartre, jealousy of any kind was unknown to him.

In 1933 when he was teaching in Berlin and she in Paris, Simone first heard about his affair with Marie Gerard. After this, when Sartre was able to return to Paris to live, Simone reserved her independence within the committed relationship by traveling, or taking jobs outside Paris, when he was there with other women.

In time, de Beauvoir experienced intimate relationships with two other men as well, Nelson Algren (1947-51) and Claude Lanzmann (1952-69).[108]

A recent essay by Lewis Menard suggests that Simone's 'love affairs,' ostensibly with both men and women, were actually compensatory in nature, and that she was thereby merely confirming Sartre, and enabling him to continue in the classic sexist arrangement, by which the man sleeps around, and the woman nobly accepts the situation, on 'philosophical stilts.' Menard goes on to conclude:

> Beauvoir was formidable, but she was not made of ice. Though her affairs, for the most part, were love affairs, it is plain from almost every page she wrote that she would have given them all up if she could have had Sartre for herself alone.[109]

Somehow, after reading his comments, it is difficult not to agree, at least somewhat. However, the two prevailed, nonetheless.

Other dimensions of their relationship began to flourish. They began to exchange their written work with each other, critique each other's writing freely and fully, and found a rewarding depth as this quality of their life together deepened. In 1939 Europe became unstable, and finally erupted into WW II when the British and French declared war.

---

108 Madson, *Hearts and Minds*, 176.
109 Lewis Menard, "Stand By Your Man" *New York Times Magazine*, September 26, 2005, 146.

Sartre was inducted, and did his military service tending a weather station. In May, the Luftwaffe struck, and the German army crossed the borders of Holland, Belgium and Luxembourg.

After he was released from service, Beauvoir and Sartre lived through the occupation of Paris as many Parisians did, scrounging for food, combining their skimpy resources with friends, and trying to keep out of the way of the suspicious Vichy government. Simone had always maneuvered to remain as free from domestic duties as possible, but in 1943, she took to feeding her friends in her room-with-kitchen at the Hotel Louisianne, and living, for the most part, on sauerkraut and turnips. She began to take stock of the difficulties, deceptive advantages, traps and obstacles that most women encounter in marriage. She would write in *Prime Of Life* among her first reflections on the feminine condition, that she also felt how much they were both diminished and enriched by this experience.

The years after the war had all the world talking about Existentialism, and reading the works of Sartre, his young friend Albert Camus and Simone de Beauvoir. Along with fame came money, which Sartre considered a moral problem. He never took money seriously. He gave it away. A more troubling presence in Simone's life was Delores V, a young New Yorker whom Sartre met on his first trip to America. He had gone back a second time to be with her. He was in New York with her when Harry Truman announced Victory in Europe, May 7, 1945. Later, Simone wrote of this in the third volume of her autobiography, *Force of Circumstance*, re Delores:

> At present their attachment is mutual, and they planned to spend two or three months together every year. So be it. Separation held no terror for me. But he evoked the weeks spent with her in New York with so much cheerfulness that I became uneasy; so far I had supposed him to be attracted mainly by the romantic side of this adventure; suddenly I wondered if (she) were more important to him than I was. In a relationship that has lasted more than fifteen years, how much is a matter of habit? What kind of concession does it imply? The way he described Delores: she shared completely all his emotions, his irritations, and his desires. When they went out together she always wanted to stop or go the same instant as he, and I wondered if this meant

that Delores and Sartre were together at a depth that (I)
had never achieved with him.[110]

Simone is describing a part of the HETAIRA shadow known as the
'anima woman' sometimes called the femme inspiratrice, the woman
who (unconsciously but quickly) imagines, or responds intuitively, to
the man's inner anima, and becomes his ideal. It is a familiar phenomenon, especially among very young women. Toni Wolff was accused of
this by some of her critics among her Jungian colleagues. This behavior
is flattering and comforting to the man, who believes that somehow
he has met a soul mate. But it is apt to be a disaster for both people
involved. The woman, as yet, has no real sense of herself, and unconsciously becomes the man's ideal. It is enormously seductive behavior,
and ultimately confusing and disappointing for the man and exhaust-
ing for the woman.

As the years went on, Beauvoir revisited the question of whether it
was possible to reconcile fidelity and freedom. What was possible, or
not, regarding the life she had made with Sartre? She wrote, "There are
many couples who conclude more or less the same pact as Sartre and
myself; to maintain throughout all deviations from the main path, a
certain fidelity."[111]

Each of them continued to have affairs, as they aged, some of which
became somewhat macabre, at least by twenty-first century standards.
In June of 1956, when Sartre was over sixty, he met Arlette Elkaim, a
seventeen-year-old student preparing for the Ecole Normale. She was
the daughter of a Jewish Algerian merchant. She had written to Sartre
when her philosophy instructor had expressed some displeasure about
her 'Sartrian ethics' for a paper she was writing.

A girl of frail beauty and nervous intellect, Arlette soon became his
mistress and when, two years later, it was rumored that she was pregnant and Sartre was ready to marry her, she nearly caused an unthink-
able rift between Sartre and Simone. The possibility of marriage to the
now twenty-year-old Arlette was more than Simone could take. She expressed this to friends at the height of the crisis, but they didn't altogether agree. Before the war, when Sartre had proposed marriage to her,
she had said No, and now was in no position to cry foul.

---

110 Madson, *Hearts and Minds*, 99.
111 Simone de Beauvoir, *A Farewell to Sartre* (New York, NY: Pantheon, 1984),
    14.

Eight years later, Sartre asked a court to allow him to adopt Arlette, and did so, thereby making her his daughter.[112]

The years of Sartre's blindness and final illness were spent in de Beauvoir's apartment, and required the cooperative help of both Arlette and Simone to keep him comfortable and entertained.

A similar legal process occurred later in Simone's life: Sylvie le Bond de Beauvoir was adopted by Simone before her death, and later became the executrix of her estate. In the same manner, Arlette Elkaim Sartre took over legal supervision of Sartre's estate after his death.

In 1972, Simone wrote an essay on the truth of ageing, *The Coming of Age* (NY: G.P. Putnam), in which she mentions the work of a distinguished older woman, none other than Lou Andreas-Salomé:

> ...the remarkable woman whom Nietzsche and Rilke had loved, who at fifty became Freud's friend and Freud himself, cancer-ridden and writing totally fresh works in his late seventies and dying at eighty – after having undergone thirty–three cancer operations during the last sixteen years of his life. Her final judgment is severe.[113]

Madsen concludes:

> *The Second Sex*, which gave Simone lasting fame, seems dated today. But her conclusion that men and women must recognize each other as peers remains, not so much a social manifesto as a challenge for private relational lives.[114]

In the light of the positive and familiar aspects of HETAIRA discussed above, how do we understand personal growth for the HETAIRA?

As the Toni Wolff style of HETAIRA woman evolves conceptually in the reader, it becomes clear that the maturing process of the HETAIRA, of course, has stages of child, young woman and adult, as with all four types. Her more specific self-knowledge will occur as she matures, and as she begins to reflect on the choices she has made, and why she has made them. This introspective process takes some real soul searching on her part. It is a process that is apt to develop most fully in the second half of life. It is important that she do this self-examination without debilitating guilt, negative self-judgment, or defensiveness. If she dis-

---

112 Madsen, *Hearts and Minds*, 27.
113 Madsen, *Hearts and Minds* quoting Beauvoir, *Coming of Age*, 271.
114 Madsen, *Hearts and Minds* quoting Beauvoir, *The Second Sex*,182.

covers that indeed, she has strong HETAIRA tendencies, then it is wise for her also to develop other areas of her nature that perhaps have been left fallow, and to accomplish some important self-nurture. She may even have projected the responsibility for her happiness on her partner or partners. It may take a mature HETAIRA a while to understand that she alone is responsible for her own happiness and for making her life productive and interesting.

In so doing, it becomes clear that her HETAIRA nature as a young woman in love is most conscious of all that her lover is. As she matures, she begins to understand all that he is not. Her own maturity next requires that she ceases trying to reform him to suit her, and begins to evaluate and stimulate all that he longs to accomplish and is still capable of becoming. This process is also her own inner work, which requires serious self-reflection. In wisdom, she directs herself to both. In the best scenario, this is a mutual progression, with committed and reciprocal efforts of both the lover and the beloved.

# Chapter 10

## Less Familiar (Shadow) Possibilities Of HETAIRA

Toni Wolff says:

- "For the man, the relationship is usually less conscious, and less important. For the Hetaira it is decisive. In this lie both the significance and the danger of the Hetaira."

- "Everything else – social security, position, etc. is unimportant."

(Paraphrases): The shadow side of the male is open to the HETAIRA, as is also his unconscious creativity. If she idolizes him, she may affect him enough to loose his sense of the realities of his life. She may bring him to a point where he, for instance, gives up his profession to become a 'creative artist' and/or divorce his wife, feeling that the Hetaira understands him better than his wife, etc. If she insists on an illusion or some nonsense and thus becomes a temptress, she is more Circe than Calypso.[115]

Regarding the mythological names of Circe and Calypso as they apply to the HETAIRA type: Circe is one manifestation of the HETAIRA shadow, which captivates, enchants, and renders her victim-lover unconscious, thus he is unable to fulfill normal challenges of life outside her realm. He is in this sense, captive of her charm. Calypso, the free woman, on the other hand, restores, protects, nurtures the lover and sends him off into the world, refreshed. (It is still *her* island. She is not diminished by what service she has freely rendered.)[116] When considering the HETAIRA shadow, it is necessary for us to work from more than one perspective. In the personal realm, it is important to consider the changes in our culture regarding women since Wolff wrote. One issue has to do with the politicizing of feminism, which was originally

115 Wolff, "Structural Forms," 6-7.
116 Edith Hamilton, *Mythology* (New York: Little Brown and Co, Mentor, 1969), 204-205.

intended as a summons for all women to self-awareness, and a recap of the basic issues regarding fairness of the centuries-old tradition of patriarchy. Once the issue is politicized, then its value to the least self-aware among us is lost. It all becomes too political, and consequently 'personal.' It is no longer what happens under a patriarchal system. It is about *me*, *my* father, *my* husband, *my* boyfriend, *my* children, *my* boss.

In the archetypal or more universal sense we are challenged to think and behave in a manner that may be contrary to conventional wisdom. For example, MOTHER is for the most part considered by collective society as 'good,' and romantic liaisons (HETAIRA) in or outside marriage as 'dangerous' or 'less good,' or for many, downright 'bad.' If we begin to see the basic ego positions of the four types as essentially *different* rather than *good* or *bad,* a paradigm shift begins to take place. A more objective attitude develops. Both MOTHER and HETAIRA have lesser-known darker aspects that can become counter-productive to creative living, safety, health and freedom of all the individuals concerned. Both what we have idealized and what we have demonized in others, require a strong dose of reality. The tendency to make automatic judgments into categories of 'good' or 'bad' may need to be tempered somewhat.

In a study of Wolff's work on HETAIRA in this section, it is also help-ful to review the archetypal theory of anima/animus that provides the underpinning of her conceptual framework.

## Archetypes in Brief

1. Archetypes are ideas or experiences that are common to all people. They live in the psyche of everyone. They are neither negatively nor positively charged in themselves (Example: The idea of 'home' or 'mother' or 'child' or 'law' exists in all people.) These are universals. Everybody has them. All archetypes are in all of us to some degree, as part of our innate human structure. The personal experience with each archetype is of course very different, but the 'ideas' remain.

2. Each human has an internal counter-sexual archetypal structure within the psyche, which is usually only partly conscious. For the man, the counter-sexual feminine internal image is called the 'anima.' She is his ideal. When he falls in love this unconscious ideal is projected on his partner and she becomes more perfect

than human to him. When he discovers that she is less than his ideal, that is, less than his unconscious ideal of perfect, it is a serious moment for them both. In the best scenario, he learns the difference between imperfect yet still genuine human love, and his own boyish romantic idealism. In many, maybe most, cases he is incapable of learning this, and keeps on looking.

According to Jung's ideas:

In the woman the same thing happens as she deals with her inner animus. When she projects her inner masculine, the animus, on a living male, eventually she discovers he is less than perfect. If she does not learn how to love herself and her man in the midst of all the imperfections they manifest as human beings, her unconscious inner animus becomes judgmental, bossy, and essentially disconnected. She becomes oblivious to those around her and isolated in her lofty opinions.[117]

The process, in Wolff's therapeutic model, is to bring this ideal into consciousness. Toni Wolff explains this issue by stating that a woman may (unconsciously or consciously) project her inner animus unto a man who's faith in himself and what he can can produce is in need of encouragement, and be of great help to him with her assistance. In the same manner, a man can project some ideal of perfection on a woman and create for himself a sort of *femme inspiritrice*. While this can work for a while, ultimately it ends in disappointment and what Wolff calls *destructive consequences*.[118]

## The HETAIRA and Sex

Even though Toni Wolff does not discuss sex openly, it remains a fundamental part of the way HETAIRA has always been characterized. How a woman perceives herself as a sexual being capable of giving and receiving human love needs to be identified first on a continuum of maturity, as well as its actual long-term significance. Just where is sex a real issue, as the HETAIRA develops in our twenty first century?

How might the HETAIRA view the non-personal sexual world of the prostitute? The narcissism of the Barbie Doll celebrity world? The hype of salacious media advertising? Or the oft-reported Helen Gurley Brown

---

117 C.G. Jung, "Anima and Animus" general information.
118 Wolff, "Structural Forms," 6.

sexual 'ideal'? In none of the other types is the question of sex more conspicuously identified. Even as we make our advances in sexual research,
literature, medicine, art and cultural awareness, still, sex remains the
pivotal underpinning of how humans unite. Sometimes they marry,
sometimes un-marry and re-marry, remain celibate or monogamous,
or remain 'free' and available to a number of options. Sooner or later
we realize that satisfying adult human intimacy is broader than sex,
and more inclusive of the other elements, which such women as Lou
Andreas-Salomé, Toni Wolff and Simone de Beauvoir tried to reconcile.
However sexual issues are understood, it seems impossible that they be
casually ignored, or, as Lou finally discovered, 'forever sublimated.'

## Lou Andreas-Salomé 3. The 'Teaser' as Shadow

### Henry Gillot

The most popular clergyman in St. Petersburg around 1889-90 was one
Heinrich Adolph Gillot, who held services at the Dutch Reform chapel
attached to the Dutch embassy. He was an intellectual who often based
his sermons on the classics as well as Biblical themes. He was a handsome man, who wore his flowing hair like Franz Liszt, and added to
his genuine attractiveness, he was tutor to the Czar's children. A friend
invited her to visit a church service.

At the tender age of seventeen, Lou was completely smitten. She immediately wrote him a letter requesting an audience with him to discuss
matters 'having nothing to do with religion.' This encounter was the
source material of her first novel, *Ruth*. She began making regular secret
visits to Gillot's study. He was also a scholar, and Lou became indebted
to him for a major introduction to her own natural abilities in logic,
classics, languages, and her first direct, uninhibited experience dealing
with intellectual problems and issues. She was thoroughly excited and
stimulated by her own ability to reason like a true scholar, in rapid-
fire brilliant exchange. Both teacher and pupil were delighted, and the
meetings in his study continued. Somewhere just before or during this
time, Lou's own beloved father died. And at Gillot's suggestion, Lou saw
fit to confide the thrilling experiences she was having with him...to her
mother. Rilke's biographer describes this event:

The inevitable confrontation occurred between the general's widow and her daughter's tutor, which culminated in Mother's accusation, 'You are going to be responsible for what happens to my daughter!' And his response, 'I *want* to be responsible for what happens to this child.'

As in Pygmalion, the tutor was on the verge of falling in love with his own creation.[119]

He was a married man, forty-one years old, and helplessly considering a drastic divorce. He had teenaged daughters of his own. A divorce would have been a scandalous blow, and the end of his career. But the hardest blow of all for him came from Lou herself, who claimed to be 'thunderstruck,' at his declaration of love, even though once she had 'fallen in a swoon while sitting in his lap.' Had there been no encouragement on her part to lead him to believe in her physical familiarity as an intimation of her intentions? According to Lou, none whatever. For her, their 'intimacy' was of an intellectual and spiritual dimension entirely. Anything beyond that was completely, and naively, out of the question for her. It must be remembered that she was only seventeen, and had never been surrounded by older men who misunderstood her exuberant affection.

However, Gillot returned to the Netherlands, but remained her tutor and friend for her lifetime, from a distance. It was decided that Lou would go to Switzerland to study, accompanied by her mother. Gillot arranged for Lou's examination to be confirmed in the Christian faith, a requirement of the Russian government without which she would not be permitted to travel out of the country. Gillot conducted the examination.

The man had a slow recovery from the entire experience of his involvement with this astonishing young woman, with the warm heart and attractive body of a girl, keen mind of a genuine scholar, and a vital exuberance. Still, it was he that gave her the name 'Lou,' finding the endearing Russian name Ljola, or Lola, too difficult to pronounce. This was doubtless a helpful contribution to her later notoriety in Europe.

Biographers point out that General Salomé died in time to be spared learning about his daughter's first love affair. The details of his death

---

119 Wolfgang Leppmann, *Rilke: A Life* (New York: International Publishing Corporation, 1984), 70.

are unclear, but this event could not have helped but add psychological impetus to Lou's infatuation with Gillot.

This similar scenario occurred several times thereafter, whereby Lou withdrew herself when confronted with a man's confession of his impassioned love. This idealism of hers happened later when she was twenty-one with philosopher Paul Rée, perhaps with his close friend Friedrich Nietzsche, and later with her own husband, Friedrich Carl Andreas.[120] Her 'love' for each of them had its own particular story, but the fact remained that for at least the first thirty years of her life, Lou kept her sexual self at a distance even from her own consciousness. The truth of the sexual nature of the men she admired was also completely absent in her own awareness. It was isolated, kept separate from her intellectual, spiritual, and emotional manner of loving, while she held these values in the esteemed state of ecstatic idealism. Her own sexuality remained an undiscovered country for some time.

The shadow is that of naiveté, the sort of residual juvenile behavior we encounter in teenagers, little more than children, who insist upon dressing in provocative clothing in public, and then are completely astonished when approached in a specific manner for sex by men or boys who misunderstand their signals. Such encounters, to say the least, can be very dangerous for them.

## Georg Ledebour

After Lou's marriage (and prior to her relationship with Rilke,) her arrangements with successive lovers began to be legendary. Early, perhaps first, among them was a liaison with Georg Ledebour, a Social Democrat editor in Berlin. In her memoirs she writes of him as someone whom both she and Andreas thought to be interesting and attractive, and who became her friend. However, at one point, when he first knew her and was totally engrossed in their preliminary exchanges, he became noticeably angry. Upon discovering that this exciting woman was married, and probably also deeply engaged in stimulating, inviting and vivacious dialog with him, Ledebour became furious with her, and demanded to be told why she did not wear a wedding ring. She laughingly replied that she and Andreas had forgotten to obtain rings before their wedding, and had decided to just leave it that way. Ledebour an-

---

120 Salomé, *Looking Back*, 73.

nounced to her that she must. And when he declared his love for her, he told her that she was not a woman, she was a girl. The statement thoroughly upset her, possibly because she realized she shared some of these same confusing feelings herself. It is interesting to speculate that this man might well have been the un-named one of whom she wrote, in her later life, as sharing an adult sexual attraction. She wrote that in this case, not only is there a distinctly higher profound fondness included, but also the desire and ability to relinquish one's individual being. But she mentioned no names.

And, regarding her earlier experiences: "Those years, in common sense soon lay behind me due to my decisive meeting with the man who threw open the gateway to Life, leaving me more in a state of boyish readiness than feminine acquiescence."[121]

Ledebour had probably called her bluff regarding her own shadow, the part of her that was determined to remain deeply, even personally, vivaciously, engaged in male relationships within her own boundaries of intellectual and spiritual exchange. She wrote of feeling very confused and troubled by the fact that she might actually be...falling in love.

Perhaps because of extenuating circumstances and realizing their brief relationship was endangering the lives of others, they agreed not see each other for a year. There is no record of what transpired with Ledebour after that. But Lou was ready for a fuller experience by the time she met Rilke in 1897.

## Toni Wolff as 'Impersonal'

One shadow possibility for the HETAIRA has to do with her reticence in forming close associations with women. Toni was little understood by the cadre of Jung's women supporters, and others within the psychological club, where she served as president for sixteen years. She had few women friends, and few knew her personally.

---

121 Salomé, *Looking Back*, 214-215. Identified by Archivist Ernst Pfeiffer, 130-131.

## Interview: Ingaret van der Post

The following is an excerpt from an interview conducted on March 8, 1970 by Gene F. Nameche with Ingaret van der Post,[122] the wife of the well-known friend of Carl Jung, journalist Laurens van der Post. Ingaret van der Post was an analysand of Dr. Meier, and at his suggestion, she worked for a period of six to eight months with Toni Wolff. In this piece, Toni is working in a highly impersonal style with her analysand, which is common analytic practice. However, it is clear that this was certainly very comfortable for the discrete and formal Miss Wolff, and helps us understand how her manner of relating was carried, particularly with women. Nameche's notes indicate that Ingaret van der Post spoke of herself as one who was actively involved in the training program at the Jung Institute.

INTERVIEWER: You spoke of when you first went to Zürich, working with Toni Wolff. How would you describe Toni Wolff at that time?

IVDP: At that point, the thing that struck me was—she was an aristocrat. She had this beautifully boned face and figure, which, for the Swiss, is rather unusual. Her hair was sort of white and gray and piled high, and she looked like a prophetess, like a commanding and mythological figure, and she actually was a very wellborn person. She was also a very well-dressed woman. She took great care of her clothes. She had a very elegant figure. All these things were, I felt, a part of herself, really. I was very impressed by this because a number of psychiatrists, as you know, get into this inner world, and they neglect both their manners and their clothes and all the outer things—the personal values. But Toni Wolff had these; she was a woman who was very highly developed in this aspect, and this struck me very much. I thought it was very important. I admired and respected this. I am not sure that she liked me very much. I don't know. I don't think that I would have said that there was a great rapport between us, as a matter of fact. It is, I think, much more difficult to work with somebody your own

---

122 Ingaret van der Post Interview conducted by G.F. Nameche, March 28, 1970, translated by Renate Rosing (Boston: C.G. Jung Oral History/Bibliographical Archive, Rare Books and Special Collections, F.A. Countway Library of Harvard Medical School).

sex. Anyway, for me, it was more difficult. I think for her, it was also more difficult. We were both people who, in a sense, knew more about men than we did about our own sex—we were more interested, possibly. Perhaps I was just too green, or too naïve. She was such an experienced and remarkable woman that I think I must have really looked like a schoolgirl to her. Also, I do think that she was perhaps more ill in herself than anyone knew even at this time.

INT: Had the arthritis that she suffered with begun then?

IVDP: I think, she didn't say anything about it. She was a very remarkable woman.

INT: Did she speak to you about herself at all?

IVDP: No, never.

INT: I understand that she was very reserved.

IVDP: I'm certain that she would never have spoken to me about herself. It was just a purely working basis. No, she was very impersonal in that way. I remember once, I think my husband gave her his book, which had been a 'Book Society' choice, *Venture Into The Interior.* I remember her saying, "Thank you so much for that book. I skipped through it. I didn't have much time." I was simply staggered because I thought, well!

INT: Such a rude thing to say!

IVDP: Such an extraordinary thing to say to an artist—that you skipped through his book. I was amazed, but my husband didn't seem to mind. There again, this question of rapport, I think, was important. This was a strange remark to make and I was horrified! It was all right with my husband. That was the important point. He didn't seem to mind it, and he is very sensitive about these things. All artists are. He was a tremendous admirer of hers.

INT: He was?

IVDP: Yes, tremendous. I think she could almost have said anything. I think she is perhaps the only person in the world who could have said that. This was a part of the Zürich thing. You said things that you never forgot, and I expect it still is, too.

INT: But you found Toni Wolff as a rather distant and remote person?

IVDP: To me she was, although I don't think she really was; to me she was. We worked together, and she was businesslike, but I didn't feel that I made any impression on her, really. But then perhaps this was a good thing. I was there to do a job, and I think perhaps – this is always a very difficult point – this question between involvement and non-involvement between an analyst and a patient. I think that had I been a sick person, which in a sense I wasn't, then I'm sure it would have been a very different thing. One was there to study with her. And study we did.

Some aloofness may well be the outer mask of a natural shyness. Toni Wolff's shadow of being 'impersonal' seems to have been more conspicuous to women than to men. Many years later Dr. Gerhard Adler of London had this to say about Toni's aloofness while speaking of her in eulogy at her funeral:

> As the strongest impression on me from beginning to end, the ceaseless goodness, kindness and a capacity for self-sacrifice remain. For many people, as I know well, this side was concealed or only found after difficult detours. For with the kindness and deep understanding of humanity went a sharply different side. This sharpness was, however, in reality, nothing other than the self-protection of an endlessly differentiated person. Never again have I encountered this blend of real pride and deep humility in one person. Moreover this same woman could show bewitching charm and fascinating femininity, which melted bitterness and superficial severity. She did not yield herself easily in human relations. But once the ice was broken, there was no legitimate demand or request to which she did not respond with a full and unforgettable self-sacrifice. To each of her relations she stood with such truth and constancy, that it is no wonder that hundreds of people world-wide depended on this woman as a criterion in their own course of life, as the enduring inspiration to a noble solution of their troubles in life, and as the truest friend, to whom an appeal never went unheard.[123]

---

123 Gerhard Adler, "Toni Wolff Eulogy" presented at her funeral March 25, 1953. St. Peter Church, Zürich. Translated by Thomas Willard.

## Simone de Beauvoir 4. Generalizations

As Simone de Beauvoir matured, she began to understand some of her own sheltered upbringing, and her penchant for making generalizations regarding her experience with her students and even her friends. For example, Madsen cites that one point in her early teaching philosophy (1938), she made a general statement to an eighteen-year-old student in class that completely disregarded the reality of the life her student was living:

> One day, when she (Olga D.) asked (S de B) what it really meant to be a Jew, Simone replied with absolute certainly, "Nothing. Nothing at all. There are no such things as Jews. Only human beings." Long afterward I would tell her what an impression she had created by marching into her Polish friends' room and announcing, "My friends, none of you exist! My philosophy teacher has told me so." As Simone would admit, she and Sartre were sometimes deplorably prone to abstractions.[124]

## Shadow Pictures

## Yoko Ono and John Lennon

A Collective Report

Vera John-Steiner, in her book, *Creative Collaboration* (see Chapter 4), includes mention of some difficult collaborative relationships. For our purposes, we have touched upon this famous relationship, because this tragically brief but very public duo seemed to experience some initial challenges worthy of mention.

While much has been written about this relationship, Wolff's words describing Circe, and Jung's identifying the 'animus hound' seems to have some relevance here. It is rumored that their relationship was such that John found it important, if not urgently necessary, to include Yoko in all the issues and efforts of his professional music world, all rehearsals, all recording sessions, all performances. According to some reports, he gave her absolute veto power on his work, even insisting that she

124 Madsen, *Hearts and Minds*, 26.

'sing' according to her own ideas of what that meant. The results of that have been strongly debated, depending on what critic or fan is commenting. But it is clear that John's free access to what had been his own creative genius took a decided turn as their early marriage progressed. Somehow perhaps his own ego strength might have been compromised. That he deeply respected her elite education and taste among the cognoscenti of the art world, and her social status as the daughter of privilege, is understandable. That he may have felt the pangs of his own background, and eagerly reached for her more sophisticated experience and sense of entitlement is still open to conjecture. But some truth remains that she also bestowed upon him the elegance of her own taste as well as her own self image. How this might have played out over the years of his and her natural development in marriage will never be known, but at some point rather than freely stimulating each other's best creative energy in their separate fields, the relationship seemed to become needlessly competitive and subject to each one venturing into the partner's chosen profession in a manner that seemed, at least for a time, counter-productive. To feel 'less than' or 'more than,' the partner is to fail to see the truth of one's self. Nevertheless, she still remains a noteworthy figure in today's world and will probably always hold a celebrity profile in history.

## The Anima Woman: A Marilyn Monroe Legend

A personal friend of Marilyn Monroe, who was out shopping with her in New York one day, recalls that no one seemed to notice who she was. When they got into a cab, the friend said something like, 'Gee. Come on. Be MARILYN!'

Monroe shrugged, said "OK," and taking a deep breath, the ethos of MARILYN slipped over her like a shimmering gown.

She leaned forward and spoke to the cab driver in the MARILYN voice, that famous 'little me' half whisper. The cab driver knew immediately who she was, and nearly drove the cab off the street.

(The source for this story remains apocryphal.)

For poor Marilyn, the final confusion of her personal selfhood with her magic public persona made it increasingly difficult for her to claim her own separate and private reality. Whether the 'legend' above actually happened or not, it describes how an *anima woman*, (mentioned earlier) might well behave. The Anima Woman is the familiar HETAIRA who intuits, either consciously or unconsciously, the male's ideal woman, and becomes her. She usually manages to protect herself from knowing that this is exactly what she is doing, but if she does understand it, then she also knows how to enjoy the fun of her flirtations, and when to back off and become real. That this can be a self–aggrandizing shadow is clear. It signals that some women who have not figured out how to become themselves, which is indeed a difficult process, will become encompassed by a psychological mandate to live, or take on, another persona. It is apt to be …the 'ideal woman' of the current man. Or, for the professional, the collective image of ideal. This was Marilyn's great gift, and she became an icon with it. But it seems to have failed to assist her in having a truly gratifying personal life.

## The Loss of Self-hood: Camille Claudel

More dangerous still than the juvenile tease shadow or the highly charged anima woman is the HETAIRA who looses her own personal creative life entirely, having allowed herself to be emotionally, spiritually and intellectually devoured by her partner. Such was the life of Camille Claudel, the beautiful and talented young sculptress who became mistress to Auguste Rodin when she was a young woman. After some time, when he refused to divorce his wife and marry her, she became subject to a fatal alcoholism, and spent thirty tragic years in private hospitals, unable to rescue her own promising talent from her outrage at her former lover. She never allowed herself to own her own talent, apart from him. For Camille, Rodin represented a super-human strength, larger than her own life. She represents the issue Toni Wolff's notes mentioned, in that she had no real understanding of where the relationship was in *his* life, but could only factor it through her own wounded perspective. By the loss of her sense of self, she had unconsciously awarded Rodin the position of God in her psyche, and thereby granted him full permission to destroy her own ability to recover from her grief. Abject misery was, for her, a choice, which placed all the blame externally for her own lack of faith in her self.[125]

One of the most tragic and difficult areas of personal growth for the HETAIRA is in neglecting to separate her personal responsibility for her own talents from the powerful influences of her partner, be they positive or negative in nature. This requires a strong ego intentionality, which many talented women have not been able to cultivate. The ego must be strong enough to support the talent.

It is not uncommon for the immature HETAIRA to take on the identity of her partner, particularly if he is prominent. She becomes, not herself; she is 'the football captain's girl' or 'the senator's wife' or 'the commissioner's girl friend.' The loss of this projected identity can be extremely painful. Her ego strength is compromised. It is highly possible for women to live in a free society with all the advantages of talent, opportunity and choice, and still remain psychologically bound, unconsciously, to the will of the male world. This sort of unconscious bondage need not be an inevitable HETAIRA shadow. But if it is indeed her situation, then the woman is unable to remain in creative mutual relationship, and at the same time, peacefully negotiate her own needs with a sensitive and loving partner. If they are not peers, there is an unconscious one-downsmanship, and true friendship or balanced partnership is barely possible. At least, not for long.

Becoming conscious of some of her shadow possibilities can help the HETAIRA type, over time, to find the self assurance she needs in her own life.

---

125 Anne Delbée, *Camille Claudel* (San Francisco: Mercury House, 1992).

# Chapter 11

## Of HETAIRA and Some Career Thoughts

Toni Wolff wrote:

- "The security offered by marriage or a profession is of vital necessity to a woman."[126]

It is clear that the talented HETAIRA will not want for opportunity to do well in a profession. By nature of her basic interests, she may find her way to one that involves men, reaches their interests and needs, and also encourages their appreciation of the feminine world. One example is the fertile field of advertising, and the omnipresent use of feminine symbols. Other opportunities are virtually limitless. There are unexpected HETAIRA attitudes and proclivities in a vast number of professions.

Jungian Analyst Robert Johnson gives a sterling example of this. He was familiar with Wolff's work, and wrote about a HETAIRA teacher who helped him when he was a lonely young man, with his artificial leg, who wanted to learn to play the pipe organ:

### A Single HETAIRA

One week the organist at our church was out sick, and an assistant took his place. Her name was Ethel Rand. We had never met before, and I approached this stranger with my usual awkward shyness, finally sputtering out that I was interested in learning to play the organ and did she think it was possible?

'Well, I don't know why not; at least we could try,' she replied. I began taking lessons with her the following week.

Miss Rand was a spinster who taught piano and organ lessons as well as served as the assistant musical director at

---

126 Wolff, "Structural Forms," 7.

the church. She was in her early sixties when we met and still lived with her aging mother. Of English ancestry, she maintained a charming accent that added to her intrigue. She was theatrical and showy, she wore bright colors and dramatic clothing, and when Ethel spoke, she made sweeping dramatic gestures with her hands; she would come into a room and take control of it. This was just what I needed at that time, and though I didn't know any terminology for her type, she was a perfect HETAIRA woman. This little-known Greek word is the only term I know for that rare woman who can be companion to a man, never a sexual partner, not a wife, but one who provides grace and charm that men value highly. In the literature of ancient Greece one hears descriptions of a famous HETAIRA woman in Athens who had the respect and delight of the highest society of that noble city. We have no word for this quality now – indeed, we hardly recognize that capacity in a woman – so I have to look to the ancient world to describe Ethel Rand. [127]

While it is interesting to review a few professional venues of some notoriously famous HETAIRA women in the past, most of them had also integrated their strong AMAZON qualities as well. We are grateful for the offerings of 'Famous Females' website for this resource:[128]

## In A Lighter Vein

_'Mata Hari'_: 'M'Greet' (Margaretha Gertruida Zelle, 1876-1917.) Dutch dancer and spy in German service during World War I. A dancer in Paris, she joined the German secret service in 1907, and during the war she betrayed important military secrets confided in her by the many high allied officers who were on intimate terms with her. In 1917 she was arrested, convicted and executed by the French, even though she had also agreed to spy for the French, and named several high ranking German officers from whom she was able to gather information. Actually, she spied for both sides.

_'La Malinche'_: an Indian woman who helped the enemy. She lived from 1495 to 1540, was sold to the Tabasco Indians near Vera Cruz, and eventually went to work washing and cooking for the personal use of

127 Robert A. Johnson, _Balancing Heaven and Earth_ (San Francisco: Harper San Francisco, 1998), 25.
128 www.famous-women.com

the conquistador Alonzo Hernandez. She became his advisor for dealing with the Indian tribes, and helped Hernandez to conquer Mexico
City. She was baptized and called Donna Maria. In 1524 she married
a Spanish nobleman, Juan Jamarillo. Her wedding present: two towns
and a large piece of land.

## The Performing Arts

The arts of music, dance and theater have always been a haven of sorts
for the woman whose primary ego investment is in being admired
by men, whether for professional or personal reasons. Katie Hickman
points out that her HETAIRA presentation is not necessarily her profession, but an aspect of it. In former times, the HETAIRA was and is still
in the Geisha tradition, that of an entertainer, both for individuals and
for community occasions.

> The entertainment frequently was highly creative. For in-
> stance in Greece, female *and* male (Hetairo) were engaged
> for acrobatics, plays, gossip, poetry readings, and sexual di-
> version. The famous Hetaira, Aspasia of Miletus, mentioned
> in the Introduction, was a teacher of rhetoric. Her pupils
> included Socrates and Pericles, who were drawn to her be-
> cause she was *sophe* (wise) and *politike* (politically astute).
> In surviving examples of her speeches, she combines *Eros*
> (sensuality) and *arête* (artistry).[129] The young Sarah Bern-
> hardt was able to transcend the established social codes for
> courtesans, and was a welcome guest, by virtue of her tal-
> ent and fame, in the distinguished homes of Europe. Such
> an achievement seems natural in our day, but this was very
> complex for Bernhardt because she was raised during an
> era when all women stage performers were also considered
> to be sexual libertarians, in the courtesan tradition.[130]

## Creative and Collaborative Dynamics

Of interesting relevance to the HETAIRA type is the work of Vera John-
Steiner in her book *Creative Collaboration*.[131] She presents the position

---

129 Hickman, *Courtesans*, 13.
130 Hickman, *Courtesans*, 26-27.
131 Vera John-Steiner, *Creative Collaboration* (Oxford, UK: Oxford University
   Press, 2000).

beginning to be understood in vastly growing circles: that in many professions, particularly those devoted to creative work in the arts, sciences, teaching and education, that, rather than thriving on solitude alone, the creative process is clearly enhanced by the reflection, renewal, and trust inherent in human relational cooperation.

We would like to present the idea of creative collaboration as we work on the issues related to HETAIRA creative life. John-Steiner cites some of the relational duos that lived several ways together, and we have added to her listings with some HETAIRA headings and names we have selected as well:

Long-term creative and collaborative marriage: Georgia O'Keeffe and Alfred Stieglitz, Will and Ariel Durant, Jessica Tandy and Hume Cronyn, Pierre and Marie Curie, Joan Didion and John Dunne, Anne Jackson and Eli Wallach, Diego Rivera and Frida Kahlo, Carlo Ponti and Sophia Loren, Mel Brooks and Anne Bancroft, Pamela and Averell Harriman, Paul Newman and Joanne Woodward, Senator Tom and Jane Dodd, Robert Venturi and Denise Scott Brown.

Long-term creative and collaborative relationships outside of marriage: Jean-Paul Sartre and Simone de Beauvoir, Katharine Hepburn and Spencer Tracey, Carl Jung and Toni Wolff, Martha Graham and Eric Hawkins.

Short-term relationships with dynamic creative energy for both partners: Anais Nin and Henry Miller, Ted Hughes and Sylvia Plath, Lou Andreas-Salomé and Rainer Maria Rilke.

John-Steiner explores and illustrates how this concept is carried through the study of several collaborative relational experiences. Particularly applicable to the HETAIRA profile are those related to intense personal relational adult life. For example, Anais Nin made a career out of writing extraordinary erotica. She herself, famous for her collaborative and highly creative liaison with writer Henry Miller, succeeded in making her relational life with Miller also a contributing factor to her own creative professional life. Their stories move the model of the HETAIRA profile into challenging dimensions. By delving into complex collaborations, we can begin to understand how the mutual self-nurture of creative and collaborative relational life provides many advantages for both participants such as growth of ego strength (self-esteem), and the ability to take risks via the mutual support conducive to imaginative risk-taking. Both of these elements are of primary importance.

In Toni Wolff's rarefied definition of the HETAIRA type, partners must be peers, which means they share a balanced degree of interests, intellect, talent and energy for life. This does not necessarily mean that they have reached the same degree of professional competence, but that they are both engaged to a comparable degree in their development. In our examples, it is clear that Andreas-Salomé taught Rilke something invaluable. Jung taught Wolff, and later she taught him; and Will Durant taught his wife Ariel so that together they became esteemed historians. Secondly, seeking mutual professional interests has become increasingly important as more and more women seek out professional lives in the working world.

Creative collaboration is not a guarantee, however, of long-term relational life by any means. Problems arise, jealousy can be a factor, people experience different phases of growth and stagnation all the time, and rarely in tandem with their mates. But the idea of relational life as a sound-contributing factor for fostering and nurturing mutual creative lives provides a fresh perspective on the manner in which we understand an important dimension and vitality of the HETAIRA experience.

## A View of the Three Women as Professionals

### Lou Andreas-Salomé 5. Writer, Psychotherapist

Lou was an established professional writer before she met Rilke, and several years his senior. It was as a writer that she continued to be known and achieved her prominence. She had published her book on Nietzsche in 1894, and several other well-received works. If one considers the sudden universal and highly overwhelming vogue of Nietzsche in the eighteen nineties, one can realize what it must have been for struggling young Rilke, in May of 1887, a man with little more than hope of becoming a renowned writer. To be accepted and validated by the woman who had rejected the marriage proposal of the author of

*Zarathustra* must have been a help to him, and a bolster for his self esteem at some level.

We have seen her in full bloom as a prototype of Wolff's model by the manner in which she was able to assist Rilke to develop his broader understanding of himself as a poet. And it is through her later collegial association with Freud that another dimension of her own world blossomed into a creative usefulness, for Freud as well as herself. It was as a talented psychotherapist that she supported herself during her later years in Kongsberg in 1923-1937, after two wars had devastated Europe. It was through her later association and friendship with Freud that another dimension of her own world as HETAIRA blossomed into mutually creative usefulness in their collegial friendship and they became close personal friends as well.

## Toni Wolff 4. Professional Colleague, Analyst, Scholar, Teacher, and Writer

Toni Wolff's sister Susanne was married to Dr. Hans Trüb, who was also a noted psychiatrist and had a close association with Jung. She speaks from a position of close personal experience regarding Toni's relationship as assistant to Jung, in an interview conducted by Frau Renate Rosing and G.F. Nameche nearly twenty years after Toni's death. Both of the Trübs attended the early meetings of the Psychological Club over which Toni presided, and were deeply involved in the early development of Jung's work. Susanne spoke of Toni as follows: "While Jung was working on the collective unconscious, my sister Toni was so important for him. She had an understanding for it. She, perhaps, was able to encourage him, and so gave him the faith (in himself.)"[132]

Toni's work as one of the founders and later president of the Psychological Club assisted in the establishment of the long term and thriving international C.G. Jung Institute of Zürich. Dr. Carl Meier spoke of this as part of his eulogy delivered at her funeral, March 25, 1953:

> In 1915, Toni Wolff became a member of a committee for
> the establishment of the Psychological Club of Zürich. As

132 Susanne Trüb, Interview by G.F. Nameche, (Boston, MA: C.G. Jung Oral History/ Bibliographical Archive, F.A. Countway Collection, Harvard Medical School Library).

a member, she took leadership in the club's creation, and in 1917 she served as chief officer of the club's board of directors.

From 1928 to 1945, she was reconfirmed as President, year after year, and a fact, which by itself shows what unshakable confidence she inspired. The idea of a C.G. Jung Institute had long been an imperative. No one was better able than she to lay the groundwork for this great experiment. She was on a committee of three with Professor Jung that did the main work, and the Jung Institute thus stands on her shoulders. I shall never forget the regal selflessness and self-understanding, the incomparable wisdom and knowledge and skill, with which she set herself to the task.

Not only her students but all who knew her talents as a healer, all who had the fortune to benefit in some way from her art, who came to understand (what cannot otherwise be known) of Toni Wolff's service at the Club and Institute... give thanks for her clandestine work, her knowledge of the sanctity of the personality, her absolute trustworthiness, her complete discretion, her sweetness and bitterness, her courage and her reticence, her winning Eros and focused Logos, her maternal and her virginal qualities—in a word, the great paradox of her integrated personality.[133]

Regarding Dr. Meier's comments, additional validation in print by Jung's biographer Ronald Hayman also gives substantial credit to Wolff as a contributing intellect and peer in the development of Jung's famous typologies:

Toni was a woman of formidable ability. She was responsible for the most important parts in his (Jung's) books. I (Meier) know from the two of them that many parts of the Types are due to her insistence on clarifying this or that... She could be a hard taskmaster. But alongside the reading, (Jung's extensive studies on his work in Psychological Types), Toni's work was pivotal.[134]

---

133 Carl Meier's Eulogy at Toni Wolff's funeral, March 25, 1953, St. Peter Church, Zürich. Translated by Thomas Willard.
134 Ronald Hayman, *A Life of Jung* (New York: W.W. Norton, 2001, quoting Carl Meier), 218-219.

Jungian scholar Sonu Shamdasani in his work *Jung and the Making of Modern Psychology*, summarized this effort as follows:

> Toni Wolff was instrumental in introducing the functions of intuition and sensation, and finally intuition was dealt with critically by Emil Medtner. According to Franz Jung, they met on a regular basis with a sort of committee consisting of Emil Medtner, Toni Wolff, Adolf Keller and some theologians, which worked together in the preparation of *Psychological Types*, particularly focusing on the issue of terminology.[135]

Dr. Joseph Henderson writes of her as a professional in his introduction to Irene Champernowne's book, *A Memoir of Toni Wolff*, wherein he compares these two women. He mentions that Champernowne was at one time an analysand of Toni's, and later an esteemed friend who was with Toni on the last full day of her life. In his expression of the esteem with which Toni's work as an analyst and teacher was regarded, Henderson said:

> In the late 1940s and early 50s, Irene Champernowne found what she needed from Jung's assistant in Zürich, Fräulein Antonia Wolff, commonly known as Toni. She was a reserved, aristocratic and very private individual in the strongest possible contrast to Irene Champernowne with her warm, democratic, outgoing personality. In a relationship that began as a strictly analytical association, with Toni Wolff as analyst and Irene as analysand, many difficulties in communication had to be overcome. Eventually their common dedication to the study of Jung's psychology brought about a mutual personal regard, and one can see from this memoir how they finally became friends. This was no ordinary friendship, however; they were, one might say, friends of the spirit.
>
> As a friend and colleague of Toni Wolff (and an analysand briefly on two occasions) I have often wished that something of her very personal dedication to the welfare of her analysands could be described. The present account gives a much more intimate and poignant picture of

---

135 Sonu Shamdasani, *Jung and the Making of Modern Psychology* (New York: Cambridge University Press, 2003), 68-69, 94.

this than anything I could have imagined would ever come to light.[136]

In all of this, her most powerful experience as an analyst is perhaps best described by her service to Jung as his own analyst during his seminal voluntary descent into the unconscious. This unique journey was the precursor of a singular process, which ultimately became an inherent component of Jung's psychology for those in pursuit of transformation, or passage into new mid-life perspectives. It is the encounter by which one becomes finally acclimated to who he or she actually is. This experience is described in several places in the Jungian corpus.

Laurens van der Post, well-known journalist and friend of Jung's spoke of the significant role of Toni Wolff as Hetaira, and as colleague and friend of Jung in his work, *Jung and the Story of Our Time*. Laurens van der Post himself added this tribute to her, following a description of her work, which articulates her well-deserved position in Jung's life:

> She herself seems to me clearly to have been an inspired Hetaira, and one cannot read what she has written on this type without experiencing it as being flame and flicker of her inmost self. In this essay and others she was to make her own contribution to analytical psychology. When I first met her, I remember thinking in the primitive way natural to me, that these were eyes capable of seeing in the dark.[137]

## Simone de Beauvoir 5. Writer, Editor, Critic, Companion

De Beauvoir's description of 'thinking together' with Sartre, her life-long collaborator, has qualities that are both intimate and convincing. She wrote of people reporting that each of them listens to the other with great attention, and yet very carefully criticized and validated each other's thoughts, and seemed to think along the same lines. She felt that they had a 'common store of memories,' and could finish each other's sentences sometimes. She often found their minds traveling

136 Irene Champernowne, *A Memoir of Toni Wolff*. Foreword by Joseph Henderson (Los Angeles: C.G. Jung Society, 1980), 2-3.
137 Hayman, *A Life of Jung*, 16.

along the same inner path, and arriving at similar conclusions at the same time.[138]

Beauvoir was a copious keeper of journals and records of their life together, and also those periods when they were living with other people while still remaining in their 'primary relationship' with each other. Biographer Axel Madsen wrote that they 'treasured their equality as well as their freedom.' But toward the end of their lives together, Sartre spoke of her effect on him as a professional writer, and how much they needed each other, in a rare personal interview in 1965: Vera John-Steiner quotes him regarding 'the gift of confidence': "I quote Jean-Paul Sartre saying to Simone de Beauvoir, 'You did me a great service. You gave me a confidence in myself that I shouldn't have had alone.'"[139]

Madsen writes that even after Sartre's death, de Beauvoir carried Sartre's belief in her: He even gave her full permission to edit his fiction work, which he sent to her while he was in prison camp and she was in Paris and during World War II.[140]

Their admiration for each other's work and their professional compatibility was mutually creative, for over fifty years. It never really faltered. That the relationship was problematic at times is clear. But they found a way to make it work for them. As colleagues and creative collaborators, their partnership was indisputable.

---

138 John-Steiner, *Creative Collaboration*, 200.
139 John-Steiner, *Creative Collaboration*, 200.
140 Madsen, *Hearts and Minds*, 91.

# Chapter 12

## Of Men and HETAIRA

Toni Wolff wrote:

- "The function of the Hetaira is to awaken the individual psychic life of the male and to lead him through and beyond his male responsibilities toward the formation of a total personality."

- "Usually this development becomes the task of the second half of life, after the social position has been successfully established."

(Paraphrases): Instinctively, her interest is directed toward the personal contents of relational life in herself and in the male as well. Her function is to help him discover and share the hopes, dreams, ambitions, talents and possibilities in his nature, and bring these from hazy awareness to consciousness. She can help him accomplish more than he sees in himself as a responsible man. This is not without danger to him and her as well.[141]

## Homage: Mary Magdalene

It might be said that the ultimate HETAIRA of the Christian world was none other than the woman who was closest to Jesus, Mary of Magdala. Her name has been radicalized, praised, reviled, slandered, canonized, and turned into a feminist icon with equally passionate rhetoric, so much so that she becomes, for women, the archetypal container of all great opposites. In this sense, she is the opposite of the mother. Yet in the biblical text, she and the mother of Jesus are often mentioned together with no conspicuous rancor between them. That she was also at one time condemned as a prostitute by the church is an historical fact, later officially refuted.

---

141 Wolff, "Structural Forms," 7.

So much has been told and written about her that the representations, conjectures, acclamations and declamations seem superfluous. It is both the biblical Mary Magdalene of scripture, and the historic Mary of Magdala that effect our understanding of the HETAIRA archetype, since she was known as the 'Companion' as mentioned in Wolff's description, and also carries a strong portion of her adjacent types, AMAZON and MEDIAL WOMAN. Whoever she was, as an associate of Jesus whom he loved, the story and conjectures regarding this powerful, intelligent and loyal woman will always be of immense interest to the world. There are many who consider her an extension of the divine feminine figures of ancient times, and still lay flowers at shrines erected in her honor. In this sense, it is appropriate for us to do homage to her in our writing of this section on HETAIRA and Men.

## Lou Andreas-Salomé 6. Rée and Nietzsche

In Lou's second year at the University of Zürich where she was taking some courses, she was barely twenty years old. Some problems arose with her health, and she was told to seek a warmer climate. A letter of introduction to the notable woman of letters and progressive ideas, Malvida von Meyersburg in Rome, established the setting for her forthcoming meeting with Paul Rée, (mentioned in the Introduction Section III) and later Friedrich Nietzsche. Lou liked to walk in the moonlight with the brilliant philosopher Paul Rée. She shared with him her ideal of how she thought she would like to conduct her life. She would prefer to live in an apartment or house for students, both male and female, who would study, talk and learn together. Separate bedrooms. Later, Lou and Paul Ree set up an arrangement of this sort. Soon he proposed marriage, and was declined. But the close friendship and casual living arrangements remained. Soon Nietzsche showed up, one of Ree's closest friends, and they established a temporary three-person household. Nietzsche immediately fell in love with Lou, and shortly, also proposed marriage. At the time, he wrote, "I found no more gifted or reflective spirit...Lou is by far the smartest person I ever knew."[142] Then later he described her as "sharp-sighted as an eagle and courageous as a lion, yet, in spite of it all, a very childlike girl."[143] She was the first, and last,

142 Leppmann, *Rilke: A Life*, quoting *Breife an Peter Gaste*, Leipzig, 1914), 70.
143 Leppmann, *Rilke: A Life*, 73.

woman with whom Nietzsche had led a personal, highly spiritual and intellectual exchange, except for his sister Elizabeth. He suffered deeply at Lou's refusal, and some say he never recovered.

Lou and Ree had five years of close friendship with each other. She wrote in her memoirs of what it meant to try to really try to understand him. Ree had begun a tentative study of medicine, and they moved to Berlin. Her commitment to Ree was to remain close as friends, and to seek true understanding of each other's inner lives.

## Andreas

In time Lou actually married Friedrich Carl Andreas, a professor of oriental languages at the University of Berlin. He was a man twenty years her senior, brilliant, gentle, and idolized by his students. Henri Gillot performed the marriage at his church in the Netherlands, where Lou had been confirmed. One of Lou's conditions under which she agreed to the marriage was that her relationship with Ree be allowed to continue.

Contrasting comments explaining the stories of this unique marriage have emerged, some written by Lou herself. Professor Andreas had proposed many times, and she had remained uncertain. On the evening before their engagement was finally settled, Andreas calmly plunged a dagger into his own chest in front of her, just missing his heart. She rushed from the house to find a doctor. The wound was serious, but he recovered. Perhaps under the threat of his possible suicide, the marriage was agreed upon. The intellectual and spiritual bond between them was very strong, and she wrote about him with enormous respect and insight into his inner world.

Union was theirs, on many levels, save the one which most characteristically typifies marriage. Lou never told Ree about her refusal to consummate her marriage with Andreas. She felt that this would have humiliated Ree.[144]

She recalled another episode, after the marriage. She was sleeping on a couch, and was awakened by a strange noise. Apparently Andreas had attempted to 'conquer' her while she slept. She woke up to find that she was trying to strangle him. The noise was his throat rattle. Lou Andreas-Salomé wrote:

---

144 Salomé, *Looking Back*, 127.

> That wasn't the only time we stood at death's door, fin-
> ished with life, perplexed, having set our family affairs in
> order. We were both filled with the same perplexity and
> despair. Of course these were hours, moments, far differ-
> ent from the rest of our experience. We were bound by
> so many common inclinations and instincts. In general,
> it seems to me, the value of this (meaning sex) is over-
> estimated. Of course it builds bridges, gives pleasure, and
> leads to shared work, but just as often it simply glosses over
> personal differences and disparities, rather than allowing
> people to see one another clearly and thus draw together
> even more profoundly.[145]

In contrast, it is clear that theirs was a dynamic relationship of a highly
committed character, wherein she struggled to know the inner workings of this quiet and profoundly gifted thinker, a man somewhat
adrift, torn by the callings of two cultures, the European achievement-
oriented mind set, and the contrasting 'timeless tranquility of Persian
philosophy and life style.' But she seemed not to have had even the
faintest inkling that Andreas, or any of the men she had befriended at
that time, felt very differently about sex than she did. One lovely entry
in her memoirs marks the importance that her relationship with Andreas held in her life. A still powerful tenderness lies within these lines
written about Andreas many years after he died at the age of 85:

> He remained so full of life after many years, with such a
> good and joyous heart, so capable of both anger and ten-
> derness - walking with an animal's caution he awakened
> the blackbirds with a few notes in imitation of their song.
> They replied softly, falling into sweet conversation, as did
> the rooster in the hen house, who having fallen asleep, was
> awakened by his call, and seized by ambition, tried to out-
> crow the stranger.[146]

Back in the early years in Berlin, Ree finally left,'... thrown completely
off course,' and they separated. He left a little note, folded around a
picture of her as a child, which he had treasured. It read, "Have mercy.
Don't look for me."[147] He never married. No longer a young man, he
studied medicine and eventually became a doctor, serving the poor in
his familial estate lands in West Prussia. Sometime later, he was killed

---

145 Leppmann, *Rilke: A Life*, 71.
146 Salomé, *Looking Back*, 123.
147 Salomé, *Looking Back*, 55.

in an automobile accident in the Alps. Biographers wrote that the situation suggested suicide.[148]

As a mature person, Lou's efforts, among her selected male partners, were to follow and participate in their elements of genius, and/or their great intellectual passion. Her own passion was to probe, with a skillful intuition, the inner workings of the minds, souls, fantasies and dreams of her partners. In so doing she gave them her close and highly valuable attention. Ideally, as with Rilke, this stimulated great strides in their own creativity. One can see, in her history, her emerging professional competence as a talented psychotherapist.

## Freud

Several years later, as a woman of forty years, and after Ledebour, Rilke and other liaisons, Lou met Sigmund Freud and participated in his inner circle. Her relationship with Freud began in 1911 at the Weimar conference, and lasted until her death in 1937. During this long association, some of the familiar aspects of the HETAIRA, particularly that of friend and confidante are recorded in her memoirs, their correspondence, and among his biographers.

Lou came to Weimar with Dr. Paul Carl Bjerre of Stockholm, one of her many admirers. When she first approached Freud about wanting to study psychoanalysis with him, he laughed amiably, and suggested that she go home first and pursue background studies for six months. She did so. Biographer Peter Gay wrote about these early episodes as follows:

> Far more than a pliant female playing a supporting role to genius, she was a productive woman of letters in her own right, endowed with a prolific if eccentric intelligence, and no less impressive gift for absorbing new ideas. Karl Abraham, who came to know her in Berlin in the spring of 1912, told Freud that he had never encountered such a comprehension of psychoanalysis as that of Lou Andreas-Salomé.[149]

---

148 Leppmann, *Rilke: A Life*, 74.
149 Peter Gay, *Freud: A Life for Our Time* (New York: W.W. Norton, 1988), 616.

She came back to Vienna in the fall of 1912, and was invited by Freud to attend his Wednesday private seminar and later the Saturday/Sunday colloquium of his closest associates and students. She became a disciple and then a serious student. Freud first spoke of her as 'a woman of dangerous intelligence.'[150]

Later, more seriously, he described her as one whose interests are really purely intellectual in nature. When Lou inquired as to whether she could undertake a training analysis with him, she was told that there was no difference between a training analysis and one conducted with a person who was suffering from psychological illness. And so as an analysand, she underwent that rigorous experience. She wrote of it 'in general' in her memoirs:

> It is with good reason that depth psychology requires that someone who wishes to become an analyst should first have submitted himself to the demands of its methodology, to the brutal honesty of an investigation into his own psychic makeup. The intellectual excavation, which is to be undertaken on the living subject, achieves its goals in research and in therapy — only through active involvement.[151]

Their relationship over the years was close to being familial, sometimes paternal, often collegial, and yet distinctly personal. They were known to travel together occasionally, she often visited in his home, and at Freud's request, she became a close and beloved confidante and mentor for his daughter Anna. She wrote and published several articles on the concepts of psychoanalysis, and established her own career as a lay analyst in Goettingen, when Andreas left his university position in Berlin to accept a new appointment there. She often sought Freud's advice and counsel as well as participating in the ongoing critique of his work on the wider stage of international affairs.

There was a spiritual bond of sorts between them as well as an intellectual compatibility. On a personal level, their exchanges were affectionate. In her later life when finances became difficult for her in the beleaguered Germany of the 1920's, Freud regularly sent her money in substantial amounts, which she felt free to accept. The subject of sublimation often was brought forward in Lou's memoirs, and one gathers

---

150 Gay, *Freud: A Life for Our Time*, 192.
151 Salomé, *Looking Back*, 98.

that her work with Freud assisted her not only as a potential analyst, but also in the development of her own adult sexuality, which must have been made clearer to her. Freud considered himself to be 'safely beyond Eros, and engaged in the delivery of world-shaking development in the area of psychiatry and psychology.'[152]

At the time of her death, Freud remarked to his friend Arnold Zweig, "I was very fond of her, strange to say, without a trace of sexual attraction."[153] Lou was five years his senior in age. Freud outlived her by a little more than a year.

In what manner, then, do we describe Freud's impact on her life, and hers on his, as that of HETAIRA? Arguably, because of the quality of the correspondence they conducted over the years, the energy with which she undertook the mastery of his exacting methods, and unqualified regard each felt for the other, as both professional colleagues, and warm human beings with mutual goals and interests. It was a deep and mutually valuable relationship.

## The Sweetbitter Journey

### Toni Wolff

Lacking clear references, we may imagine that a change in Toni's attitude came only after the journey of her long relationship with her analyst, mentor, colleague, friend, companion and former lover, C.G. Jung. At some point, she must have struggled with the phenomena of a love affair that became an echo – barely whispering what it had been. Or perhaps had never been, at least in the same measure for Jung as it had been for her.

David Hart, a classroom student and former analysand of Toni Wolff, sheds some light on how she managed her own personal despair, at least at one point in her healing process:

> ...I was in a small discussion group that Miss Wolff held in German with several of the trainees. We were concentrating on the nature and meaning of analytic work, and one of the Swiss members, a man, asked her, 'Is not the great therapeutic agent in analysis - love?' [...] She laughed him

---

152 Gay, *Freud: A Life for Our Time*, Information.
153 Gay, *Freud: A Life for Our Time*, 616.

> to scorn. She quoted with sarcasm the great poem of Schiller's, 'An die Freude' ('Ode To Joy'). [...] Miss Wolff found it ridiculously sentimental, just like the notion that love had anything to do with psychological healing. Most telling of all, she thereby revealed that this absurd sentimentality was, in her opinion, what love was all about. I could not comprehend the full impact of her outburst.[154]

Mr. Hart knew her as his teacher. He described her as dressing mostly in black, her language and thoughts precise and intelligent, and coming forth from a disciplined mind. He mentioned that she sat very erect in her teacher's chair.

> Another side of her nature would reveal itself for me when she smiled. This smile was broad, warm, and disarming, and it rendered her initial appearance of severity completely untrue. Here shown forth what I immediately felt was the real person – one who was sensitive, vulnerable, and deeply connected to those around her.[155]

In addition to his seat in her classes, she was his analyst for a number of months until she suggested that he work with a male analyst to round out his experience to a worldlier informed stance. Hart wrote that only later did he become aware of the disappointment and disillusionment Toni Wolff probably suffered in the course of the years of her relationship with Jung.

So much of the story of Toni Wolff and Jung, has to do with the whole nature of the transference issue, a tricky evolving concept, not substantially understood for a long time. It is still a subject for serious study and discussion. In our day, working with transference has become central in the analytic or depth therapy process. What's love got to do with it? Everything.

---

154 David Hart, "Toni Wolff and The First Jung Institute" (Los Angeles: Psychological Perspectives #31, Spring-Summer, C.G. Jung Institute of Los Angeles, 1995), 75.
155 Hart, "Toni Wolff and The First Jung Institute," 74.

# Chapter 13

## Of Children and HETAIRA

Toni Wolff wrote:

- "The HETAIRA is instinctively related to the personal psychology ... of her children if she is married."

- "A conventional married woman who is unaware of her HETAIRA nature or who has repressed it, will without fail make secret loves of her sons and girl friends of her daughters, thus binding them exactly the same way as does the MOTHER who is unconscious of her own nature."[156]

According to our interviews with HETAIRA women, they often bear children, and in general the children seem to develop with no more or less difficulty than children of the other types. There is no reason to criticize the HETAIRA type as incapable of managing motherhood adequately, should she choose to do so. Her becoming a mother may not be her highest priority, but the results are not necessarily subject to more problems.

## Lou Andreas-Salomé on Motherhood

Andreas-Salomé tried to explain her decision about not wanting to have children early in her memoirs. In it, she seems to be pleading a case that she herself has some trouble understanding.

It is as if the choice regarding this issue were coming from a vague and partially unconscious place:

> There can be no doubt that the failure to experience motherhood bars a person from the most valuable part of being a woman. I remember how astonished someone once was when in a long discussion of similar matters in my later years, I confessed, 'Do you know, I never dared to bring a child into the world?'

---

156 Wolff, "Structural Forms," 5-7.

> How other young women came to terms with the prob-
> lems of love and life in those years, I only know in scat-
> tered cases. Even then my attitude is a bit different than
> their acquiescence. But that wasn't the only reason. In
> their youthful optimism, other girls my age still tended to
> view everything they longed and hoped for in the rosiest
> of hues. But I lacked something necessary for such opti-
> mism — or perhaps I knew too much: some sort of ancient
> knowledge must have impressed itself upon my basic tem-
> perament like an immovable stone beneath my foot.[157]

As for so many women, the decision to bear children or not to do so is
made primarily in the depths of the unconscious, and for a variety of
reasons, some of which may be entirely unknown. This seems to have
been the case with Lou Andreas-Salomé. One thing that is consistent
with the HETAIRA type, however, is that in choosing *not* to become a
mother, her initial relational priority (that of the quality of her relationship to her partner) will not be displaced by the demands of another
entity. Some HETAIRA women become mothers who view mothering as
a sort of creative project, or an outlet for some of their HETAIRA skills. If
the children sometimes feel displaced, as mother seems to prefer adult
male company to theirs, they are also spared the anxiety of feeling responsible for mother's happiness, and are thereby relieved of one of the
problems of some obsessive over-mothering.

## Narrative: Karen's Story

Karen felt that her mother's HETAIRA preferences influenced her own
life, but that her food problems had more to do with what she felt was
her mother's inauthentic behavior than with her type, as such.

> My Mother was most certainly a HETAIRA. Although she didn't
> have men friends outside her marriage, to my knowledge, she cer-
> tainly preferred her personal relationship to my father than that
> of my sister or me. Sometimes I think that the reasons I have such
> a hard time with my weight have to do with her. I used to hate to
> see her primping every night before he came home. She seemed so
> phony to me, always so sweet and agreeable with him, while for me
> she was distant, cross, and she rarely engaged with anything I did.

---

157 Salomé, *Looking Back*, 18-19.

I was partly scared of my Dad because he loudly disagreed with my opinions and wanted me to think his way. Even so, I really enjoyed, at some level, engaging him in controversies. At the same time, I was annoyed at mother for trying to control me into never arguing with him. While Dad's and my relationship was certainly contentious and noisy, I think sometimes that my mother was actually jealous of the time my father spent with me, and the arguments, and discussions we had.

## Single Parenting

The experience of children being raised primarily by one parent is a familiar one. The symbiotic bonds of co-dependence inherent in this situation may present the problem for the mother that Toni Wolff was suggesting. The mother who has no private personal physical/intimate adult life of her own may become over-involved in the life of her child in a manner that becomes problematic, particularly when the child enters puberty. In what manner does it occur, that she becomes a secret (unconscious) lover to her son, or an intimate, sometimes competitive 'girl friend' to her daughter?

If we consider the 'unlived life' of the woman whose own inherent HETAIRA has remained undeveloped, she may try to place the natural needs of the HETAIRA for intimate bonding into her relationship with her child. The result may appease the mother's hungry ego, but in the long run, it becomes problematic in that the child is burdened (unconsciously) with the woman's need for self-actualization through the child's achievements and attention. (See Compensatory Mothering, Part Two.)

## Film Study: *Postcards from the Edge*[158]

The plot explores the relationship of a pill-popping adult daughter Suzanne (Meryl Streep) and her fading movie queen mother who is a heavy wine drinker, Doris (Shirley MacLaine). They are enmeshed in a crippling co-dependency. Their story is revealed in a series of flashbacks for Suzanne who is being discharged from a rehab unit after she blacked out, and was dumped near death in an emergency room by the boy-friend-of-the-moment. The customary stomach pumping and

---

158 *Postcards from the Edge*. 1990. See Film Index.

group therapy treatment was accomplished, and because her insurance company will not cover her unless she follows their specifications, she is being released to the custody of her mother, with whom she has not lived for several years. Before she leaves the hospital, Dr. Feldman (Richard Dreyfus), who treated her when she was unconscious, sends her flowers, and mentions that he would like to see her, maybe, socially. She is flattered, but too unsteady to imagine dating yet, and misunderstands his invitation as 'checking up on her,' to see that she stays off the pills. In the car Mother is very solicitous about her daughter's recovery for about two minutes, when she begins talking about herself and all she has had to put up with regarding this sick daughter of hers, the 'only person in my whole life that I have ever truly loved.' Suzanne tries to re-enter her acting career, which is on the skids. Her self-esteem is doubly wounded when she overhears the costumer complaining that her upper legs have grown flabby, and she is 'over-the-hill' as a glamorous star.

In flashbacks and conversations with Mother, who holds and sips the ubiquitous glass of wine, several hard memories surface. When Suzanne brought her friends home during her high school years, her mother would perform for them; she would sing and dance, twirling her skirts high, (wearing no underwear.) Her mother had also started Suzanne on pills when she was age nine, to 'calm her down.' When Suzanne accuses her mother of these things, Doris protests, then pleads, that she just wanted to be her friend!

Doris also thinks Suzanne should be singing, preparing an album, which she feels to be Suzanne's best talent. But Suzanne doesn't have the strength for this, and feels bullied by her mother. Daughter tries to continue with the current film. She does poorly, can't seem to concentrate, and forgets her lines. At home, she starts picking up pills from Mother's medicine cabinet. A fatherly friend and director (Gene Hackman) gives her strong and kindly advice, and promises her a good role in a couple of months, when she 'gets away from her mother.'

The denouement occurs when Mother, well lubricated with successive drinking, has a wreck in her car, and lands in the hospital emergency room herself. Suzanne brings Mom her clothes, carefully applies makeup to her bruised face, and they talk more freely. Doris says that she was always jealous of her daughter's youth, beauty and talent. A patch-up of sorts occurs, and it is clear that there is a stronger and more honest bond developing. Some small promise of a decent relationship is in the air.

While this make over might be just a superficial 'cure' for both mother and daughter, there is a feeling of new life. The film concludes with Suzanne making a video recording, of *I'm Checkin' Out of this Heartbreak Hotel*. It is clear that Suzanne is well on her way to new energy for recovery.

## Toni Wolff 6. Narrative: Susanne Trüb

> Toni had no children, and there is no record of her personal thoughts on the matter. However, there are some interesting and somewhat relevant statements from her sister Susanne Trüb in an interview conducted after Toni's death:
>
> I am the youngest of the three sisters. Toni was my spiritual mother, and she owned the intellect in our family... (Our mother) was somewhat a child, a dear child, and surely admired her husband deeply, and adjusted herself totally. But (she was) not at all able to handle Toni. From her early years Toni was a difficult child. Toni should have been a boy. [159]

Susanne also mentioned that at the time of their mother's death, Toni took over some of the grandmother attributes for her sister's children.

Toni's colleague Barbara Hannah tells another story about Toni that may be relevant to this issue, possibly relating a touch of maternal instinct outside the care of Toni's clients:

> The war (WWII) revealed the most ardent patriotism in Toni Wolff. I always knew Switzerland mattered tremendously to her, but she was over fifty when the war broke out and I admit I was surprised that she put her time and her car voluntarily and unstintingly in the service of the *Frauendilfsdienst*. She was already threatened by arthritis and the rough life was anything but good for her, but she spared herself nothing. She was in the motorized section and of course had to sleep in dormitories, often under cold and uncomfortable conditions.

---

159 Susanne Trüb, Interview with G.F. Nameche, 1970.

> Edward Bossard, a mutual friend of Toni's and mine, de-
> scribed how he had been a young colleague of Toni's father
> in Japan, told me that he knew her commanding officer
> and he had told him that Toni was the most valuable as-
> set her unit possessed: not because she was a good driver,
> in fact she was seldom allowed to drive a car. But because
> she had such a marvelous influence on her much younger
> companions. She could inspire them to work as no one
> else could and never countenanced any relaxation until
> the last job was done. She never spared herself, in spite of
> her much greater age and increasing arthritis, and her ex-
> ample worked miracles in her environment.[160]

While this might be considered as an example of Wolff's partially evolved maternal instinct, her motives were admittedly *impersonal* in nature. Her impact, however commendable, speaks arguably more for her ardent patriotism under duress than for a natural maternal inclination.

## Simone de Beauvoir 6. Abortion and Adoptive Parenting

Madsen relates the story of de Beauvoir and the abortion issue, which places her squarely and openly in opposition to having children her self. In 1938, Sartre was writing a novel, *Road to Freedom* whose hero was a man named Mathieu. At one point in the story, Mathieu was struggling to find enough money for an illegal abortion. This subject was not unfamiliar to both Sartre and Simone.

It was decades before she, along with a hundred other prominent French women, would say so publicly. In a feminist campaign to change the country's abortion laws, twenty prominent Frenchwomen, including de Beauvoir, signed a public confession that they had had illegal abortions, and invited the French government to prosecute them. The government chose not to do so.[161]

However, both Sartre and Beauvoir became adoptive parents, each of adult children, during their later years; perhaps they were feeling the need of heirs. They were also famous for their extended family of close

---

160 Barbara Hannah, *Jung: His Life and Work* (New York : G.P. Putnam, Perigee Books, 1976), 274.
161 Madsen, *Hearts and Minds*, 267-270.

friends and young people whom they supported socially and very often, financially. They also fed and even housed many an impoverished
student.

# Chapter 14

## Of HETAIRA and Other Types

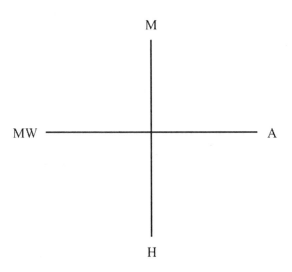

Toni Wolff Says:

- "A second form will assert itself from within. Thus, an impersonal one will join a personal form. If the second form is not integrated, the original one will be exaggerated and turn negative."

- "The immaturity of the third and fourth forms will require honesty and humility. Thus these experiences function to awaken the individual spiritually."

(Paraphrases): As the HETAIRA matures and comes to terms with her own nature, she will begin to explore other parts of herself. Her adjacent types are the AMAZON and the MEDIAL WOMAN. The fourth and most difficult for her is the MOTHER, which will require some spiritual depth of character to assimilate."[162]

---

162 Wolff, "Structural Forms," 4.

If she is an extravert, her AMAZON qualities will quickly develop, or may perhaps have done so early on. It is possible that she has known pieces of her AMAZON self along with her HETAIRA propensities. She may have related to groups, learned to rely on the marketability of her talents, and taken up the responsibilities of some self-discipline, which her natural leadership will require.

If she is an introvert, her MEDIAL capacities may be more prominent, as she already feels most comfortable in an inward mindset. The integration of the fourth type, the MOTHER, whereby the ego position accommodates the nurturing of someone other than the lover, seems to evolve slowly, even painfully, if at all. Rachel Fitzgerald describes the following experience of the introverted HETAIRA succinctly:

> Each form's maturation process influences the development of other archetypal expressions of relationship. When a woman finds change terrifying, she may be gripped by the perception of an inner emptiness. She is like a motherless child dependent on the generosity of others. Experiencing the seeming inertia of the material world of the mother indicates being unable to tolerate peaceful contemplation of The Other (the reciprocal party, other than the lover.) She flies into frenetic activity or distracts herself with comforts.[163]

Fitzgerald points out that a full understanding of how this process works, and why the opposite form is so difficult to integrate, rests in the woman's understanding of the importance of all four types as being valid expressions of the feminine psyche. The personal learning and new self-confidence she gains in exploring the adjacent types gradually prepares her to venture further into the opposite realm.[164]

One way to 'observe' the integration of the other forms would be to speculate on what progress in this direction was actually accomplished by the three unquestionably HETAIRA women we chose to follow through this section.

---

163 Rachel Fitzgerald, "Toni Wolff's Vision of Archetypal Femininity, © 2001, www.caplocator.com/interest-areas/Wolff'sVision.html. (Website now dismantled).

164 General information. See Rachel Fitzgerald's book: *She Moves in Circles*, Xlibris 2010.

## Lou Andreas-Salomé 7.

HETAIRA she was, thereby managing her choices exactly as she intended, and learning along the way. It does not seem that she suffered
much, if at all, regarding her HETAIRA life style, yet surely there must
have been times, particularly with her own mother, when these choices
were painful. Her sense of her inner selfhood was profound enough so
that she knew that even her beloved Rilke depleted her energy beyond
her ability to maintain the relationship without loosing herself. As a
HETAIRA, in her later life she kept her sexual involvement on a less
personal plane, and enjoyed several partners, being careful to see to it
that even though her choices were men of prominence and interesting in themselves, they were probably not her full peers, and therefore
somehow expendable. Her tendencies, for her later relationships, were
to choose younger men, and be the one who determined the duration
of the relationships involved. Her AMAZON qualities were well underway even as a very young woman, and she excelled brilliantly in her
scholastic efforts. As a therapist in her later life, she was probably able
to integrate through her extraverted intuition some MEDIAL moments,
and one might imagine, also some sense of the necessity of genuine
nurture of her patients. A lovely section in her memoirs illustrates some
MEDIAL tendencies early in her life, where she was responding to some
inner truth that defied her own reasoning:

> (In Paris) I made many new acquaintances, and was struck
> by many things, which I would not have missed for the
> world; but then the hour would come in which someone
> or something seemed to call me in the night. I've never
> been able to figure out rationally why or when it happened
> each time- regardless of how much I was enjoying my sur-
> roundings, open to them, body and soul. Something ar-
> rived uninvited in their place and was impatient to go...
> - surprising myself and everyone else, leaving secretly,
> without saying goodbye. And I arrived just as quietly,
> without sending word, in the middle of the night. I left
> my suitcases in the railroad station, and walked along the
> quiet path across the dark fields into the village. This walk
> was beautiful and strange. Although I could see little, I felt
> autumn in the falling leaves and in the stormy wind, and
> I was glad; in Paris it had still been 'summer.' Everyone in
> the village was asleep; only the bright lamp my husband
> used to illuminate the books in the tall cases still burned. I

could see his head clearly from the street. The door was on the latch, as always, and I stepped inside quietly. We didn't sleep that night. When it began to get light outside, I made a fire in the kitchen, polished the sooty lamp, and slipped away into the woods. Thick morning fog still hung in the trees, and a spotted doe glided silently through the pines. I pulled off my stockings and shoes, which you can't do in Paris, and was very happy.[165]

In reading this passage without further knowledge of Lou's life, it would seem incongruous that this marriage could have remained unconsummated. Yet it did, sustained by an indomitable silent truth. Lou had to protect her inner world.

MOTHER remained the conspicuously unknown factor for Lou. Except, that at 'self nurture,' she seemed to have done a good job of mothering herself remarkably well. Perhaps it was this quality that made her such an attractive friend and confidante of Dr. Freud. Except for Rilke, it seems she did not risk her physical sexual being with the men she genuinely and deeply loved at a soul level. It is clear that her sense of her own vulnerability had to be carefully guarded.

## Toni Wolff 7.

Toni's sister Susanne once remarked that Toni really only came alive when she was with Jung.[166] This was her life, her work, her passion and her essence. That he relied, over time, on her intellectually, spiritually and for a period sexually underscores how her perspective evolved.

She developed her AMAZON work independently, and probably at Jung's bidding, perhaps when the physical intimacy part of their creative collaboration had run its course. There is an early film of her, a sequence where she is seen typing at a manuscript furiously, in which she is 'getting down' to the actual AMAZON tasks of translating her own thinking into a form that the world could use. Also, she learned to take on the full responsibility for the distinctly AMAZON task of managing the Psychological Club, which, as mentioned, provided the foundation from which the world-famous C.G. Jung Institute of Zürich was created.

---

165 Salomé, *Looking Back,* 62-63.
166 Trüb, Interview with G.F. Nameche, 1970.

Helena Henderson, as a young woman seeking consultation with Wolff, spoke of her MEDIAL quality:

> She had many changeable looks, as many intuitives do, and could sometimes look beautiful and sometimes quite plain. Her extraordinary brilliant eyes, mystic's eyes, were always expressive. To me she fitted perfectly the 'medium' type of her own writing.[167]

As a MEDIAL WOMAN, we know that during Jung's perilous journey into the unconscious Toni stood as sentinel for him between the two worlds of the conscious and the unconscious, helping him as a mediator of those two worlds, thereby protecting his sanity. In this particular phase of their relationship, she who understood the value of this experience through her personal history with the process, was able to function as his analyst. Barbara Hannah writes that she was not proficient in the 'active imagination' part of doing therapy until tutored in this work by Barbara Hannah herself. This technique, considered by some to be a MEDIAL skill, is a prominent component of the standard analytical process, and may not have been completely integrated into the training procedure at the time of Jung's inner journey. In any event, there is also a definite MEDIAL quality in the report of her analysand Irene Champernowne, who later became her friend. Joseph Henderson mentions this issue in the foreword to her book: 'She mediated Jung's mind and intuitive ideas directly, for she had been part of their creation from the unconscious.'[168]

It is possible that Toni, who was a profound and rational thinker, felt uncomfortable about the MEDIAL world and may even have been somewhat afraid of it, as are many resolute thinkers.

## Simone de Beauvoir 7.

She is of course caught up in the HETAIRA mode entirely with Sartre first, which remained concurrent, then with Algren, then Lanzmann and then at the end once again, Sartre exclusively, when she conducted a solicitous nurturing role for him until his death.

---

167 Helena Henderson, *C.G. Jung, Emma Jung, Toni Wolff, A Collection of Remembrances* (San Francisco: C.G. Jung Institute of San Francisco, 1980), 203.

168 Irene Champernowne, *A Memoir of Toni Wolff*. Introduction by Joseph Henderson (San Francisco: C.G. Jung Institute of San Francisco, 1980).

However, even before she had become involved in her graduate studies at the Sorbonne, she was engaged in an extensive, well motivated and driven AMAZON world, which she attempted to reconcile in her writing with what was then perceived to be the nature of feminism. One might say that a significant part of her life was spent reconciling those two positions, that of HETAIRA and AMAZON, both in her public and her private domains. Her early ventures into adept AMAZON achievement may have been related to Sartre's constant encouragement and their collaborative careers. There is little evidence of any attempts on her part to explore either the MOTHER or the MEDIAL WOMAN perspectives.

## Book, Film and Television Studies

### *Charms for the Easy Life*[169]

This television adaptation of Kaye Gibbon's novel presents the worlds of three contrasting types within one family of women, and encompasses three generations as well. Miss Charlie Kate is a strong self-appointed extraverted AMAZON country 'doctor' who conducts a thriving medical practice out of her own natural talents, without a formal medical education. She had married her first love, had a child, and began to see patients at her house. Her husband could not stand watching her 'get good at what she loves other than him,' and runs off with another lady. Charlie Kate still keeps his old jackets in the closet, and goes to stand quietly with them in moments of sentimentality. He shows up years later and wants reconciliation. She equivocates. It only takes her two days to figure out that this momentary lapse of tumbling into an undeveloped HETAIRA mode was not for her, and returns to her practice, her life, and her management of her daughter's and granddaughter's lives.

Her daughter Sophia (Mimi Rogers) seems to have strong HETAIRA inclinations. She had turned down the suitor her mother had picked out for her, and married a man with a similar character as the father she never knew. She spends her time mostly at the movies. She faints at the sight of the more basic side of her mother's medical practice, is of no help in it, and settles into longing for a good man. She finally lands one after many years of dreaming. The third female, Margaret, (Susan

---

169 *Charms for the Easy Life*. 2002. See Film Index.

May Pratt) is a charming bookish high school girl who loves helping her grandmother with her practice, and seems destined to go off to college, where, as valedictorian of her high school class, she has managed to secure entrance and scholarships. She falters, however, in her choice of colleges, over which her mother and grandmother are in ferocious disagreement. At this juncture, because she is not yet able yet to take sides against either Mother or Grandmother, she decides that she isn't yet ready to leave home. Later, however, it is clear that she will go on to finish both college and medical school. At this point, she is actually the nurturing one of the story, the MOTHER. Her AMAZON part is suggested, and her own HETAIRA self blooms as she falls in love with a highly appropriate patient in a military hospital where she is volunteering as a letter writer for wounded soldiers.

Both Charlie Kate and Sophia had preliminary struggles with the HETAIRA part of their personalities. Charlie Kate gave up. Sophia finally mastered it with help, and young Margaret, it appears, will manage this just fine, and then go on to her AMAZON/MOTHER world. Less prominent in this film is the MEDIAL capacity, except perhaps in the entire reliance of Charlie Kate on a powerful and probably somewhat non-rational, thoroughly natural and intuitive penchant for healing.


Sometimes unknown or unacknowledged qualities of the HETAIRA develop through her relationship with the man she supports, often before he realizes her importance in his life. Such is the case of Matty Crompton and William Adamson in *Angels and Insects*. The film is based on the novella, *Morpho Eugenia* by A.S. Byatt

## Film Study: *Angels and Insects*[170]

During the Victorian era, William Adamson (Mark Rylance), a dark, handsome and penniless naturalist, has been offered refuge at the expansive English Manor household by his patron, Sir Harald Alabaster (Jeremy Kemp). After barely surviving a shipwreck where most of William's collection of specimens gathered along the Amazon River has been lost, he is soon to be enmeshed in a strategic plan of Lady Gertrude Alabaster, (Annette Badland) the rotund Queen Bee of Bredely Hall, and mother to a score or more of clamoring offspring. She has

---

170 *Angels and Insects*. 1995. See Film Index.

her eye on the unknowing William as a possible match for her daughter Eugenia (Patsy Kensit), the beautiful and melancholy oldest daughter, whose fiancée has recently suffered death by suicide. The reason for Lady Alabaster's hurried match making is that her second daughter Rowena wishes to marry soon also, and it is socially unsuitable for a second daughter to marry before her sister. Lady Alabaster's plans are launched during a sumptuous ball given at the Manor. Edgar, the surly eldest son of the family, has loaned William suitable attire for the evening, and William watches Eugenia dancing solemnly with her brother Edgar. William is already smitten by this gorgeous young woman, and wishes he had the courage to ask her to dance. Lady Alabaster insists that he must dance. Thus fortified, William cuts in by tapping Edgar's shoulder, and dances off with the glorious girl. Soon, however, for no apparent reason, she rushes off in tears, leaving William astonished and abandoned on the middle of the dance floor.

Sir Harald employs William to catalogue his own vast collection of specimens, and a courtship is soon underway. William cannot believe his good luck, and shortly there is a lavish double wedding, in spite of brother Edgar's taunts of disapproval. Eugenia's temperament is a bit of a mystery to William; she is warm and loving one moment, and strangely distant the next. However, William hopes that this will all smooth out after the wedding. In fact, he finds his bride to be alternately playful and energetic in bed. However, as soon as she suspects her first pregnancy, she becomes curiously detached. The door between her bedroom and his adjoining one is perfunctorily closed against him.

In addition to his other duties with Sir Harald's collection, William takes on assisting in the natural science studies of the cadre of young children in the manor household, at Lady Alabaster's request, although he longs to return to his own work of collecting, classifying and writing about the insect world. Also assisting in the educational tasks of the children is Matty Crompton (Kristin Scott Thomas), an impoverished relative of the Alabasters, who makes herself useful in the household. The slim and quiet Matty shares William's lively interest in the natural sciences, and is herself a secret writer of talent and resourcefulness.

Soon Eugenia produces twin girls; there is a brief reprieve for William in her good graces. But following the tradition of her mother's indefatigable fertility, Eugenia quickly becomes pregnant again, whereupon William's isolation is reinstated. Sadly, William realizes that if Eugenia has a private inner world, he will not be invited to share it.

The natural science studies continue, and Matty shares her fanciful and intelligent written work with William, who encourages her writing, and engages her helpful commentary in his own written work. Soon they evolve a mutual writing project, and William begins to notice Matty's subtle fragrance and slim wrists.

In three short years, Eugenia produces two sets of golden-haired twin girls and one towhead son.

There is a foxhunt. A servant overtakes William who is riding-to-hounds, and tells him that he is needed back at Bredely Hall. He returns to the quiet house, and hears giggling behind Eugenia's locked bedroom door. He bursts in through the second door from his own bedroom, and finds his wife in bed with her brother Edgar. Furious, he throws Edgar out, and confronts his wife. She tells him, haltingly, that this has been going on for many years. When her former fiancée had accidentally discovered the liaison, he killed himself rather than face the issue. When William demands to know if it is possible that their children are all actually Edgar's, she agrees that it is… possible. Sobbing, she asks William what he will do. William replies that he doesn't know yet, but that he is sure that he will not kill himself. And he adds that if he told the story, there is no one to tell who would not suffer in the telling.

Matty leads William to her room the next evening and quietly reveals that she has made arrangements. Their books have been sent to a publisher who has agreed to terms, so there is money available for them, and she has booked passage for two on a ship bound for Rio in a month's time. There is a tender and surprised true surrender to each other, and to a new life for them.

They are seen leaving Bredely Hall together by the early stagecoach, the next morning.

While the story has its own dramatic conflicts, the world of Matty and William almost perfectly describes the HETAIRA story of which Toni Wolff both speaks and exemplifies herself. HETAIRA stimulates and fertilizes the innermost life of the male partner, and he in turn brings forth her own creative life.

# Section Two

# The Impersonally Related Archetypes

## The AMAZON

### and

## The MEDIAL WOMAN

# AMAZON

## A Random Scroll

Bella Abuzz . . . Abigail Adams . . . Madeleine Albright . . . Maya Angelou . . . Artemis/Diana . . . Atalanta . . . Athena . . . Ethel Barrymore . . . Boudicca of Britain . . . Camilla, in Virgil's *Aeneid* . . . Mary Cassatt . . . Margaret Corbin . . . Catherine the Great . . . Madame Chiang Kai-shek . . . Coco Chanel . . . Hillary Clinton . . . Isadora Duncan . . . Eleanor of Aquitaine . . . Queen Elizabeth I Of England . . . Dianne Feinstein . . . Gael . . . Katharine Graham . . . Doris Kearns Goodwin . . . Hermione in Rowland's *Harry Potter* . . . Katharine Hepburn . . . Hippolyta/Antiope . . . Lena Horne . . . Jean Houston . . . Edith Mae Irby . . . Barbara Jordan . . . the Biblical Judith . . . Judge Judy . . . Jackie Joiner Smith . . . Charlie Kate in Gibbons' *Charms For The Easy Life* . . . Lindgren's **Pippi Longstocking** . . . Clare Boothe Luce...Margaret Mead . . . Golda Meier . . . Andrea Mitchell . . . Madame Nehru . . . Annie Oakley . . . Scarlet O'Hara in Mitchell's *Gone With The Wind* . . . Sandra Day O'Connor . . . Camille Paglia . . . Christine de Pizan . . . Emma Peel in TV series *The Avengers* . . . Penthesileia . . . Ludmila Pavlichenko . . . Ayn Rand . . . Major Marie Rossi . . . Condoleezza Rice . . . Eleanor Roosevelt . . . Bessie Smith . . . Sacagawea . . . Gloria Steinem . . . Martha Stewart . . . Margaret Thatcher . . . Belladonna Took, in Tolkien's *The Hobbit* . . . Queen Victoria . . . Oprah Winfrey . . .

"I know I have the body of a weak and feeble woman, but I have the heart and stomach of a king, and a King of England too"
—Elizabeth I of England, 1588[171]

---

171 "Spoken to her troops at Tilbury, 1588 on the eve of the invasion of the Spanish Armada, and wearing the full body armor of a cavalry officer." www. Britannia.com/history/monarchs.

# Chapter 15

## An Overview of AMAZON

Stories of AMAZON women have threaded a path through mythology and history for thousands of years. They have always epitomized the part of womankind that stands independent of the male, yet is also characterized by the masculine spirit of adventure, courage and conquest. The AMAZON is indefatigable, rational, specific in detail, and relentless in her drive to achieve her own goals. The myths surrounding her in western culture have changed over the centuries. However, she still retains these fundamental psychological characteristics, as she evolved from the mythological realm to that of a particular type of historically recognizable human female. She ventures, always, a little beyond the accepted norms of her culture, yet she is superbly attuned to the realm of public life where her contributions are legion. Her energy and tenacity are unmistakable.

## Where does the word Amazon come from?

Early Greeks were fascinated with the tribes of warrior women known as Amazons, and the mythologies must have begun a long time before Homer wrote about them, somewhere in the ninth century B.C. Stories of these ferocious women are recorded by at least fourteen other writers from 400 B.C. until the conquest of Rome in the first century, A.D.[172]

Wolff mentions that the name AMAZON, like the name HETAIRA, is so closely linked with history that maybe those terms are misleading. But she also mentioned that finding better terms that are also actually linked to a woman's personality and growth and recognizable to the culture as well, is difficult.[173]

The earliest tales of Amazon lore, reaching back in historic legend before the Trojan War, carry three distinct characteristics. The first was

172 Funk and Wagnalls, *Standard Dictionary of Folklore, Mythology and Legend* (New York: Harper and Row, 1984), 42.
173 Wolff, "Structural Forms," 8.

their passionate love of freedom and their antipathy toward men. Ae-schylus (450 B.C.) called them 'the warring Amazons. Men haters.' Sec-ondly, the battlefield was their professional preoccupation. Their skill in battle was formidable, and they were often sought to join in the warfare of other tribes. Their battles brought them their wealth, which was largely in horseflesh. They raised horses, trained them, befriended them, and sometimes traded them for goods. A third theme that flowed through their legends, that of eroticism, follows in their wake. For ex-ample, Achilles was said to have slain the Amazon Queen Penthesileia in battle, (1193 B.C.) yet he wept over her dead body at her beauty, her fierce courage, and the feelings of admiration and love, which they evoked in him.

Amazons reportedly came from the Caucasus region near the Black Sea. Their capitol was Themyscira. Because their stories are scattered among so many texts over a long period of time, a general summary traces how Amazons were known in antiquity, from the writings of Homer, Strabo, Herodotus, Diodorus, Diodorus Siculus, and Plutarch.

The early Amazons fought on horseback, and wielded at first spears and axes, then later bows and arrows, all of which they used with great skill. They had little or no interest in gold. In battle, they wore short tu-nics and leather shielding for their legs and arms. Of great importance were their massive shields, which protected them in battle, and could serve as small bivouac shelters at night. Most of the painted images of Amazons portrayed on ancient terra cotta pottery depict them with chalk-white arms and faces, whereas the males are more apt to be out-lined in black, but maintain the color of the pottery itself as the color of their skin. The motif of 'the wounded Amazon' was a favorite theme, repeated throughout classical history and art.

Among the earliest writings were the tales that Amazons waged war while they were still virgins. It was said that an Amazon woman had to kill at least three warriors before she was allowed to leave the battlefield life and become sexually active. These women scalped their victims with impunity, yet were also known to meet and mate periodically with men from other tribes. When the resulting offspring were born, the male children were either returned to the father warriors, or disfigured so that they could not fight, and used as slaves. The women were said to have cauterized the right breasts of their female babies so they would grow up to fight with their weapons unhindered. Herodotus (600 B.C.)

was the first to write about the life of the Amazons in a manner that depicted them as sexually active women. He recorded the tale of the Amazons and the Scythians, their fabled worst enemies. It is said that some of them paired up and married. But the wives would not return to the home of the Scythian warriors, and insisted that they would only live with them in a state of equality, in 'a different place.' So, according to Herodotus, they went to live in a 'mythical land' that established a way of life whereby neither partner was dominant and they fought together as comrades at arms, as well as partners in marriage. Perhaps this tale provides the study of the contemporary AMAZON with a challenge that speaks in a timely manner, since men and women have been looking for that mythical society ever since.

At the forefront in the Amazon literature is the Theseus legend. Theseus, cousin to Hercules, was given the task of obtaining the jeweled girdle from the Amazon Queen Hippolyta (some call her Antiope). Legend has it that he kidnapped her from the Caucasus region and swept her away to his home in Athens. The Amazons were furious, and began to plan for war. After Hippolyta had given birth to her son Hippolytus in Athens, the Amazon warrior women marshaled an enormous army of allies, both male and female, to ride and march with them to her rescue, a distance of several hundred miles. They reached the countryside surrounding Athens and camped outside the famous city where Theseus ruled and democracy was born. (And also, ostensibly, patriarchy.) A bloody siege took place that lasted several weeks. The result was that the Amazons were finally defeated, or so stoutly resisted that they retreated from the field, a depleted society never again seen in Attica.

Another tale reports that the Amazons were associated with Dionysus, God of wine, either as his allies or opponents. Those who are familiar with the tales of Dionysus will recall the droves of the Maenads, women who followed the god to the hills, and wildly celebrated him in orgiastic rituals which are somehow reminiscent of the bloody stories of cauterization and maiming that accompanied the earliest Greek Amazon tales. Warrior women who lived apart from men, however, are recorded in the histories and legends of numerous cultures, notably from India, Arabia, Ireland, England, Egypt, Syria, the Aleutian Islands, the South Pacific, and Brazil. Thus, the archetype is established as indigenous to the human psyche.[174]

---

174 *Standard Dictionary of Folklore, Mythology and Legend*, 28.

## Why These Stories?

Since the early tales are primarily mythological, we might wonder how and for what purpose they might have served Greek culture. William Blake Tyrrell, in the introductory statement to his book *Amazons: A Study of Athenian Myth Making*[175] offers an interesting way of thinking about these ancient myths. Tyrrell defines a myth as a story that explains something, generally a source of conflict or tension in a society. The myth provides a dramatic sequence. Tyrrell continues, suggesting that the Amazon myth is the exact opposite of what the ideal for women was in that society. The ideal for the male was the hero, who ruled, fought, went to war, and did glorious deeds. The ideal woman stayed home, tended her household, remained illiterate, and served in a custodial manner that maintained the male balance of power. In this sense, Dr. Tyrrell ponders the allegorical qualities of mythmaking and makes a point. But the ancient myths themselves reflect story beyond allegory, and in truth, there was an actual tribe of human women who bore the name AMAZON, and the history of their actual existence in both myth and history validates the archetype itself. Recent archeological findings substantiate the actual existence of Amazon culture. Such women did indeed live in ancient times, as did other warrior women who fought with or without their male counterparts near the Eurasian Steppes, Pokrovka, and the Black Sea region in general.

Within the span of time in which the Greek Amazon stories developed, these women were gradually presented less and less as 'men haters,' and other qualities began to emerge. Classics scholar Donna Edwards, in her thesis "Virgil's Camilla: Amazon, Hero or Woman?" describes this evolution:

> By the time of Virgil (70 B.C.) there was a narrowing of the Greek concept of the Amazons. There is no reference to married Amazons, or to treatment of men as slaves. The tradition by then was that Amazons were women who fought and rejected the idea of marriage. Virgil's Camilla presents an Amazon-like virgin woman warrior reminiscent of the Greek heroine Atalanta. She is a Valscian, (a tribe of agriculturally based inhabitants of territory desired by the Romans.) She led an army of both men and women troops in battle against the Romans. The Valscians were part of the

---

175 Wm. Blake Tyrrell, *Amazons: A Study of Athenian Myth Making* (Baltimore: Johns Hopkins University Press, 1984), 119.

non-Roman world that must be tamed before the Romans could establish their civilization. Camilla's right breast is neither cauterized nor removed, but laid bare in battle. Her father, a deposed warrior, did not raise her in matriarchy. However, she was dedicated in infancy to the virgin goddess Diana.[176]

Edwards also points out that Camilla died an inauspicious death, which, in the tradition of heroic myth, disqualifies her from being a bona fide hero. Tradition requires that another classic hero must kill a classic hero. Virgil wrote that while Camilla fought nobly against the Romans, she lost her concentration in battle for just one moment, when she was distracted by the colorful costume and plumage of an enemy, Chloreus. She becomes 'enflamed with the feminine sense of booty and spoils,' and is struck down by Arruns, who was not a hero of renown or fame. In Greek ancient tradition, in order to be historically called a 'hero', another 'hero' must deliver the fateful wound. The spear of Arruns enters her bare breast, delivering her fatal wound.

However else we see the classic Amazon in all her ferocious energy, she seems to be powerful, courageous, and ultimately doomed to some sort of tragic, even inglorious defeat. One assumes that this is exactly how the patriarchal cultures of civilized Greece and Rome wanted and needed her to be.

While we might find fault with Virgil's deciding what is, or is not, a 'feminine sense,' the story stands. It is up to us to define those ideas more clearly, and to celebrate the AMAZON type in her contemporary manifestation, as well as in the heroic traditions of the past.

## From Myth to Type

The following story relates the historically documented event during the Roman conquest of the British Isles, and takes place at about the same time as the story of Camilla as related in The Aeneid. This AMAZON woman now represents what we are thinking of as a type, rather than a member of a specific tribe, or a people with the particular cultural history of mythic Greece and/or Rome. Now she becomes universal, and human:

---

176 Donna Edwards, (Austin: University of Texas at Austin. Academic Thesis "Virgil's Camilla: Amazon, Hero or Woman?" 1990).

## Boudicca of Britain

Boudicca was an ancient British queen who lived in the year 60 A.D., and led a revolt against Roman rule. Her husband, Prasutagus, was king of the Iceni tribe and a region (now Norfolk) as a client under Roman occupation. When he died with no male heir, he had arranged to leave his private wealth to his two daughters under the protection of the Emperor Nero, trusting thereby to win imperial credibility for his family. Instead, the Romans annexed his kingdom, humiliated his family, spent his fortune, and were both rapacious and brutal. The historical account names the Roman philosopher and pseudo–moralist, Seneca, as instrumental in arousing the rage of the formidable Boudicca. Seneca's wealth was derived from property in Rome, and from various vineyards and estates elsewhere in the empire, (such as Britain). His profits went into usury. His actions in recalling his loans led to the rebellion of Boudicca. With Prasutagus no longer living, the Roman Procurator, (local authority of Rome at Iceni) refused to bestow on the wife and daughters their fathers rights and property, as was the Celtic custom of the times. This included all of the daughters' inheritance, which had been returned to Rome. Had the daughters been sons, they might have received at least some of their due, but it is doubtful that women were allowed to inherit land and property under Roman law at that time.

Boudicca became a living symbol of the eastern tribes and they rallied to her call to arms. Gerhard Herm includes a colorful description of her in his book *The Celts*. A literary portrait of her comes from the Roman historian Dio Cassius:

> Boudicca was tall, terrible to look on, and gifted with a powerful voice, and a flood of bright red hair that ran down to her knees; she wore a golden necklet made up of ornate pieces, a multicolored robe and over it a thick cloak held together by a brooch. She took up a long spear to cause dread in all who set eyes on her. Herm adds the images of her two daughters, similarly dressed, standing stalwart on either side of their ferocious mother.[177]

While the Provisional Governor of Iceni Suetonius Paulinus was absent from the region for a time, Boudicca raised a rebellion throughout East Anglia, gathering tribal support and troops, 200,000 strong, the chief

---

177 Gerhard Herm, *The Celts* (New York: St. Martin's Press, 1975), 212.

of whom were the Trinovantes of Essex. The insurgents burned Camulodunum (Colchester) Verulamium (St. Albans), the mart of Londinium (London) and several other military posts.

According to Tacitus, they massacred 70,000 Romans and pro–Roman Britons, and cut to pieces the Roman 9th Legion. The Roman general Paulinius finally met Boudicca's Britons at a point thought to be Fenny Stratford, on Walling Street. The night before the battle, it is said that Boudicca sent a rasher of hare to the Roman general for his dinner, in hope that by eating the timid rabbit, he might loose his courage to fight. The story has it that when finally faced with defeat, Boudicca either took poison, or died of shock. Her popular totem animal is, of course, the rabbit.

Centuries later, the following AMAZON story exemplifies almost perfectly what Wolff described as the AMAZON type, yet this twentieth Century woman would probably not have recognized herself as characteristic of anything like an archetype:

## Narrative: A Family AMAZON Story  (Told by Molton)

Velta Lane Hungerford, 1906-1993, Part I

> Velta was my husband's aunt. I met her only once, when we visited her near Macon, GA., in the 1960's. When we arrived at her trailer, we found her dressed in a comfortable caftan, her lovely auburn hair piled casually on top of her head. It curled loosely around the back of her neck from the afternoon heat. She was stirring a pot of what turned out to be a well-seasoned spaghetti sauce, and discussing business with someone on the phone at the same time. They were talking about peaches and railroad cars. She waved a spoon at us, and gestured for us to make ourselves at home in the small sitting area close by. I was excited, to finally meet the famous Velta. Here was the woman who could do anything, who had once announced herself as an Independent candidate for Governor of Georgia, and of whom my mother-in-law spoke with such pride.
>
> We had driven southward from Augusta to the little town of Gray, Georgia. On the way there my husband Warren spoke of her in the quiet voice he reserved for exceptional memories, and related that he was one of the three or four great women of his childhood.

Velta Louise Lane was born in 1906 at Griffin, GA, in Spalding County. Her father, James Alfred Lane, was a blacksmith and a carriage builder. He was a widower with three daughters when he met Rosilla Jane Harkness. His first wife had died in 1902 of typhoid fever when their youngest daughter, (Wilhelmina, my mother- in-law) was eight years old. After three years of grieving and trying to raise the girls while managing the blacksmith business, James Alfred courted 'Rosa' for just three weeks when she agreed to marry him. She took on the household, mothered the three girls warmly and well, and later produced little Velta who became the darling of the family.

Velta was a special child in every way. She was full of fun, beautiful and precocious, the delight of the entire household during her babyhood. When she started school she exhibited a sharp wit and a fine-tuned intelligence. These gifts were manifest in endless enterprises and projects while she was still in grade school. Family stories about her record that once, as a little girl, she took a flock of baby chicks from the barn, colored them in brilliant hues with food coloring, and carried them off in a wicker basket to market on the day before Easter Sunday. She sold each of them for twenty-five cents, and came home with a box full of quarters!

Another family story reported that often during her high school years she would prepare a shoebox full of extra sandwiches and cookies in the mornings before school and carry them with her. As the day wore on, she would sell them to her classmates and friends who were ready for snacks. These enterprises were not provoked by some crippling family poverty; while the family was certainly not wealthy, they were comfortable by the standards of the town. Velta simply enjoyed turning most any occasion into an opportunity to generate a little extra pin money, or as a means of supporting some of the pet projects that she enthusiastically espoused.

Along with her blossoming scholastic, social and fiduciary talents, Velta was known as a good organizer, which brought her a healthy measure of respect and popularity among her classmates. She always took the admiration of those around her as her natural legacy in the world. As the 'beloved child' in a family of admiring elders, she expected to be adored, helped and appreciated by everyone. And for the most part, she was. Some time after high school, Velta made it known that she wanted to go to nursing school, and that she wanted to do so at St. Elizabeth's Hospital in Washington, D.C. Her father did not approve of this, nor did other members of her family and friends, since higher education 'up north' was not a course often pursued by the young women of Griffin, GA. in those days. But she was adamant, and somehow won her case. By the mid 1920's, she was settled at St. Elizabeth's in the nation's capital.

During the years of Velta's training and her first job there, this historic mental hospital stood right at the seething core of a city in the throes of the great depression, and heading into the nervous pre World War II era. The sick, the desperate, the often forgotten remnants of humanity passed through those halls every day, fragmented by their illnesses and the powerful turmoil of their personal lives. The hospital served both young and old, all of whom were diagnosed primarily as suffering with various mental illnesses. Many of the patients remained there for most of their lives. As complex as this institution was, St. Elizabeth's still maintained a national reputation for innovative treatment in the fields of psychiatry, psychology and public health.

Velta's training at St. Elizabeth's was multifaceted. She was sent to Bellevue Hospital in New York City for additional maternity training, and her extensive experience in treating the aged was particularly important in her later years, since the specialized field of geriatrics was nonexistent at that time. After graduation she received her RN licensure, and continued to work in that milieu for ten or twelve years.

Eleanor Roosevelt articulated the *zeitgeist* of the time in Washington most clearly for many women during those years in her famous newspaper column, "One World." Her strong voice urged dedicated service to humanity, and captured the imaginations of a generation of young career women. Social service was the dominant value of the times, and something of a fierce mission to serve the underprivileged and downtrodden of the world had blossomed in Velta's spirit. Ready for a specialty in public health nursing, Velta was awarded a two-year contract to develop public health services in Georgia's rural Jones County, not too far from her family home. These special projects were funded by the federal government, largely in response to expanding public awareness of the plight of the poor in rural areas nationwide.

Velta settled back into a country society with her energy focused on public health issues. During her early rounds of assessing the needs of the poor of Jones County she organized clinics for visiting physicians to perform routine surgeries such as tonsillectomies and hernia repair. She developed vaccination programs, and later mounted a successful campaign to provide midwives access to supplies of silver nitrate so that the eyesight of newborn babies world be protected from the common scourge of infant blindness. In this work, 'Miss Lane' became a familiar strong figure moving in and out of the back roads of Jones County.

Before her two years of national funding were over, she met and fell in love with Joseph 'Mac' McWhorter Hungerford, a wealthy gentleman farmer and sportsman who also kept abreast of the political life of the county. She had not intended to remain in the area, but she and Mac were married. Their two daughters were born in 1940 and 1942.

She began to call herself 'Pat,' after an old high school nickname. She was curious about everything, and took an interest in knowing how Mac ran the farm he had inherited, one of the largest operations of its kind in the state. She learned the numerous variables and processes necessary for the cultivation, harvesting, packing, marketing and transporting the product of several thousand acres of peach trees. This was her first extensive business education, another important step in her unfolding future. She also looked after many of the health needs of families who worked on their farm, which numbered more than a hundred people.

'Pat' had become so familiar with Jones County that she decided to run for public office. She knew her public visibility among voters had grown by virtue of the work she enjoyed, and also because of her marriage to a prominent and popular figure. When the post of County Commissioner became available, she opted for the job, and ran in an open election for the post. To her credit, she defeated eleven men in the race, an unprecedented accomplishment for a woman at that time. This achievement won her statewide as well as some national recognition. Her major responsibilities on the Board of Commissioners were in the area of roads and revenue.

In 1949 Pat announced herself publicly as an Independent candidate for Governor of the state. While she knew that she didn't have a real chance at defeating the Democratic Party Talmadge machine, her announcement won her an even wider visibility as a courageous and competent woman of energy and vision. For a time, she enjoyed national attention from the press as a talented candidate for a gubernatorial race, a feat that was, if not unheard of, certainly very rare in the political world of the times. She withdrew her candidacy before the election, but she was satisfied that her name was now broadly known, should she decide to continue her political interests on a wider scale. She became Chairman of the Board of Commissioners of Jones County in 1951.

In December of that year, Mac died unexpectedly. Soon after that, Pat undertook the full supervision of the farm, which included the management of the workload for all the breadwinners who were dependent on the farm for their livelihood. She brought to that huge task the same enterprising curiosity and energy that she had brought to her earlier ventures, and the farm thrived under her leadership. In addition, she maintained her interest in public health work, and continued her term as Chairman of the Jones County Board of Commissioners. She was reelected to that position in 1953 by a wide margin.

In the late 50's, she acquired property adjacent to the farm and developed the first nursing home facility in the county. Within a decade, she owned and operated three such nursing facilities in the area, all under her skillful management. Years later, after her death, there was a merger with other facilities and the family association owned and managed twenty-seven nursing homes statewide.

Velta's daughter, Lynn Hungerford Nelson, herself a retired nurse and nursing home administrator, speaks of her mother in an interview as follows:

'I was never really sure, exactly, if Mother was so superior to other women, or if my own feelings about this were because she was my mother. But I did know that first of all, she was very, very bright. She could do anything. Play the piano... anything. She thought very quickly, unlike any woman I have known, regardless of education. For example, after taking on the management of the farm, Mother changed the major crop of the farm from peaches to pecans and later, cattle. These were sizable undertakings. She didn't bat an eye over it.

Later, the way she managed the nursing home business was really remarkable. Early on, she could have parlayed her unique management paradigm to the state level. But she preferred to keep it contained locally so that she could keep an eye on things and maintain quality control, because the nursing home business in general was developing very quickly. She was a natural business whiz. But she was not really interested in the amenities money could provide. She just liked the power which money generated that enabled her to do the things she wanted to do. Mother never made mistakes, or at least never admitted any. I remember her as being what we thought was egotistical. She certainly did just exactly what she wanted to do.'[178]

Molton continues:

Lynn and her husband Brick Nelson raised their four children on property adjoining that same log cabin where my husband had visited 'Aunt Velta' as a child. Warren had spent a week there in the springtime with his brother, when the hillside by the cabin was covered with a great field of blooming daffodils, spreading down to the sixty-five acre lake, which Velta and Mac had created by

---

178 Lynn Hungerford Nelson, Interview with Author Molton, 2004.

partly damming a lovely stream that flowed by their first cabin home. Warren was perhaps twelve years old that year. The daffodils are still there, and the lake, and the cabin. Three generations have lived, now, on the land that challenged Velta's energies, and amply provided for their way of life.

Mac and Velta "Pat," lie buried in a small private cemetery on the farm property, up on a quiet wooded hillside. There is another headstone up there marking the burial place of an earlier owner of the property, one Neiamiah Dunn, 17-- to 1821. Up there also are several small stone markers, unnamed, where slaves who probably lived and worked the farm were put to rest.

Through the example set by women such as Camilla and Boudicca, the AMAZON type can be seen as an historical and recognizable personage of the human race, and securely still existing, outside as well as within, the realm of myth and conjecture.

# Chapter 16

## Familiar Qualities of the AMAZON

Wolff relates many of the characteristics that were present in the earliest Amazon mythology:

- "Success and efficiency are her goals."

- "She is independent and self-contained."

- "Emphasis is placed upon her own personality development within the limits of the objective cultural values of our (her) time."

  (Paraphrases): She is independent of other people and of instinctive or psychic issues.[179]

Caroline Myss, herself a gifted MEDIAL WOMAN, describes the AMAZON archetype in her work, *Sacred Contracts*:

> Women have long been defenders of their families, and the Amazon tribe of Warrior Women has become legendary because of their ability to engage in fierce battle – even sacrificing part of their physique to facilitate warfare. Loyalty to the family and tribe is among the Amazon's notable characteristics along with nurturing their young and transmitting lessons of power and self-defense. In today's society, the Warrior Woman has emerged in her glory once again through women who liberate and protect others, especially women and children who need vocal and financial representation.[180]

---

179 Wolff, "Structural Forms," 8.
180 Caroline Myss, *Sacred Contracts* (New York: Harmony Books, 2001), 415.

## Film Study: *Tampopo*[181]

The Japanese comedy, Tampopo, mentioned in the introductory chapter, joyfully illustrates the positive AMAZON at work in a different culture. Westerners may consider, in this film, how the strict culture-bound status of women in Japan is in the process of relaxing. It is the presence of autonomy in the AMAZON type that is Tampopo's most definitive psychological characteristic. Juzo Itami's original comedy-satire concerns a widow, Tampopo (Nobuko Miyamoto), who embarks on a quest to make the best ramen noodles in Japan. She is determined, self-contained, and chooses her mentors carefully. Goro (Tsutomu Yamazaki), a John Wayne-style truck driver aids her in discovering and incorporating the particularities of her goal. "I didn't know a woman could do it! " he says. The film was given the unlikely dub as "The first Noodle Western," and parodies both the American Western and Japanese Samurai film genres.

One interesting story line in the film is Tampopo's young son, who obediently works to help his mother, and also carries on his own boyhood scuffles around the neighborhood gang of young boys. He does so with a good-natured inevitability, without Mother's interference, or even much of her notice. He, too, is remarkably self-contained.

The film characterizes the stellar devotion to detail and meticulous precision in AMAZON judgment. She is deliberate in finding her mentors and is also very specific about the smallest details as she moves toward her goals. While the audience expects the usual romance to occur, Tampopo seems not really interested, at least at this point in her story. She has another goal to accomplish. It is, unquestionably, her primary goal.

---

181 *Tampopo*. 1985, 1986. See Film Index.

# Chapter 17

## Less Familiar (Shadow) Possibilities Of AMAZON

### The 'Inferior' AMAZON

Wolff distinguishes between 'inferior' qualities, and the 'natural' shadow accompanying the true AMAZON form. The first, or lesser-known aspects, are preceded by what happens if a woman is not a true AMAZON by nature, in Wolff's parlance, but instead, makes an 'inferior' attempt at AMAZON behavior:

Wolff's *Inferior* AMAZON:

- "This woman may be driven by masculine protest, wants to be equal to her brother, will not recognize any outside authority or superiority. (She) Takes an attitude compensatory to her feelings of inferiority."[182]

    (Paraphrases): Socially she can become a social hyena, and at home a jealous fury. She takes little time for social life. Her relationships are mostly impersonal. She fights with exclusively male tactics: Power vs. Mediation. She is insensitive to the agendas of others.

These descriptions call for some clarification. When Wolff talks about the woman who is not operating out of her natural AMAZON characteristics, she implies that such a woman has a dominant antagonistic attitude as opposed to a healthy competitive stance. She seems to be gathering all of her motivational energy out of a repressed anger or even rage, the source of which remains unconscious to her, and can be projected on any convenient adversary. She overreacts to authority using the sharpness of the war weapon, or highly aggressive power moves rather than working out the necessary compromises, negotiations, and connectedness with others around her.

---

182 Wolff, "Structural Forms," 8.

While it is true that much splendid and liberating work can be fueled by a righteous indignation against corruption, social injustice, or painful effects of patriarchal thinking and practice, there is a fine line between creative energy launched to correct a social ill, and a generalized fury that is flagrantly waged against a particular sex, race, religious belief, custom or institution. The inferior AMAZON attacks, and must wage war, on whatever battlefield she can find. If she wins, soon she will need another battleground.

The source of her rage may well be a severe unconscious and unaddressed personal wound. In contrast to the 'true' AMAZON nature, the primary ego investment of the 'inferior' AMAZON is not located in impersonal collective consciousness, but is a suffering ego wound, caught in an unresolved and unexplored discretely personal history. It constitutes an over-reactive attitude of constant warfare, generalized and projected upon any available target. Her personal ego strength is diffused by the need for indiscriminate warfare. She may cast herself as a 'survivor,' but she may not ever happily flourish, because she requires the battlefield, even though the 'enemy' may change every day.

One way to spot the 'inferior' AMAZON in a group is by the manner in which she cuts people off. She can do so with one statement, delivered by her ex-cathedra, as if she were the ultimate and final authority on the matter at hand. She is proclaiming a rule that she thinks is infallible, but is actually just her own opinion. No further exchange is possible. When this happens, the room gets very quiet. The Jungian in the room will call this manner of behaving an 'animus attack.' The woman has lost her center, and is now unconnected with those present. She has become, for the moment, an inferior man, bullying others with her opinions.

In like manner, when this happens to a man in a room full of people, he will begin to sound whiney, critical, petulant and querulous. He is having an 'anima attack.' He has forgotten how to think logically, or to present the facts. He is swimming in feelings and can't figure out what the rules are. He, too, has lost his center. His awareness of those around him is diffused, and he has lost his connection with himself as well as others present. It is as if he has become, for that moment, an inferior woman. The loss of the relational principle is the prevailing symptom for both the man and the woman, at this juncture.

In contrast, Wolff identifies the shadow tendencies of the *Natural* AMA-
ZON:

- "Her personal complications are dealt with in a masculine
  way or repressed."

- "Patience or comprehension for anything still undeveloped is
  lacking, both in herself and others. Marriage and relationship
  are looked through the aspect of achievement, primarily her
  own."[183]

(Paraphrases): Her idea of human relationships may be mis-
used for business purposes.


The natural AMAZON works hard, and manages to stay connected and
in dialog, even with her adversaries, and focus her attention on her
own very specific goals. She can make necessary compromises, obtain
the experience she needs, and learn to understand the dynamics of
power in an impersonal manner. Such careful attention to detail has to
do with the true AMAZON nature, such as that exhibited by Elizabeth I,
or of many truly successful women in professional life.

A simplistic but still realistic manner of processing these ideas leads
to the conclusion that there are distinctly different ways of seeing life.
One helpful way of thinking about 'masculine' and 'feminine' in wom-
en has to do with the ideal that 'feminine' means, essentially, an ability
to remain connected with others, to hear as well as be heard, to see as
well as be seen, to be aware and in dialog with what is present. By the
same token, 'masculine' in women might be defined as the ability to
bring her goal-oriented ideas and talents to the world in a manner that
challenges her, and the world will reward. She likes and understands
the rules of the game, in how the outer world works.

A woman with this kind of strong masculine energy is one who has
that sort of goal-oriented outward sense of self, a typical AMAZON profile. But if she loses the ability to remain connected to those around her,
or the principles of basic civil exchange, then she loses something of
her essential feminine selfhood. She may become volatile and threatening in a manner that connotes aggressive power mongering rather than
healthy ambition and goal-oriented energy.

---

183 Wolff, "Structural Forms," 7.

Toni Wolff speaks of 'inferior' AMAZON behavior as 'not yet having crept out of shell of women's suffrage' — at the time of her writing, the women in Switzerland had not as yet gained the right to vote, and did not do so fully until 1971. Prior to that date, this issue characterized the entire struggle for equality between the sexes. Obtaining the vote certainly increased the options for women to achieve self-actualization. But the struggle for equality between the sexes still goes on, waged on other platforms.

A study on the varieties of AMAZON behavior is well presented in this film, based on the novel by Michael Crichton, which presents at least five different AMAZON-types, in various circumstances and stages of development:

## Film Study: *Disclosure*[184]

Tom Sanders (Michael Douglas) is an executive who heads a production division of a digital computer information corporation. As the film opens, Sanders, engaged in the busy morning confusion of weekday family life with his wife and young children, disregards a warning e-mail message on his home computer, and leaves for work. His main pre-occupation is an eager anticipation of receiving a promotion this day. There is a pending one hundred million dollar corporate merger. The president of the corporation is visiting the Seattle division where Tom works. When Tom arrives at his office, he is greeted with the chilling rumor that he might be out of a job! He shrugs it off, although visibly disturbed. He also hears that an old flame of his, Meredith Johnson, (Demi Moore) has arrived in his plant.

Actually, she is already eyeing his job, and has maneuvered herself into a favorable position with Tom's boss (Donald Sutherland). Meredith stages a seduction episode with Tom, which is really a calculated power move, and she fabricates a charge of sexual harassment to get him out of the company so she can take his job. One of Tom's technicians, Mark (Dennis Miller) describes her in mythological terms, as he shakes his head: 'It's like the old Amazon. Keep a few of us around for sperm, and kill off the rest.' A monologue of Meredith illustrates just about all of the 'inferior' AMAZON characteristics of which Wolff

184 *Disclosure.* 1994. See Film Index.

speaks. Succinctly, it appears to be a power-driven consuming rage. She says Tom 'broke my heart.' Somehow, one doubts it; wounded her pride, maybe. As her motives become more obvious, the shadow becomes more apparent. Meredith's sense of her own sexuality seems to be contaminated by her anger, which causes it to become depersonalized. Her speech continues, delivered in response to more and more astute questioning from the woman mediator, Barbara Murphy (Kate Williamson). Murphy has been brought in to review her accusation of Tom's sexual harassment. Meredith's anger surfaces, and it is void of any specific relational reference:

> You want to put me on trial here? Let's at least be honest about what it's for. I'm a sexually aggressive woman. I like it. Tom knew it and couldn't handle it. It's the same damned thing from the beginning of time. We lock it up, veil it, hide it, and throw away the key. We expect women to do a man's job, make a man's money, and then walk around with a parasol, lie down and let a man fuck us like it was still a hundred years ago. Well, no thanks.
> —Writer: Paul Attanasio

Had this speech been delivered to any astute therapist, a painful early personal history of sexual abuse and/or exploitation, having nothing to do with Tom personally, would be immediately suspected. Meredith's thinking on this issue is as self-serving and rigid as that of the most callous rapist.

For her, there is no middle ground between relational life and sexual aggression. Her rage is very clear, her illustration graphic. Also, her positive 'masculine' skills of clear headedness and careful problem solving were not as perfectly developed as she thought.

She made other errors in judgment regarding the particularities of the product she claimed to understand so thoroughly. She also misjudged the political realities of the corporation. She became, in the eyes of the audience, an inferior man. To the clinician, she is a seriously, possibly irrevocably wounded woman, and apt to be quite dangerous.

Meredith's energy is fueled by repressed rage, rather than a natural and healthy ambition. She exhibits what Toni Wolff described as the 'inferior attempt' of the genuine AMAZON. She is the creator and perpetrator of a deadly warfare, and sex is her weapon. She can no longer even be civil. Even in the struggle for power in the workplace, the decorum of civility must be maintained.

A 'natural' AMAZON portrait in the film balances Meredith's shortcomings in the character of Catherine Alvarez (Roma Maffia). She works as an attorney primarily in the field of sexual harassment, for both female and male clients. She demonstrates a powerful insight into the subtle issues of the case, and applies her well-trained logical mind skillfully. She meets Tom at a distinctly conscious, perceptive level, and informs him, candidly, 'Sexual harassment is not about sex. It is about power. A woman in power can be every bit as abusive as a man.'

Another touching portrait within the film is presented by the character Cindy Chang (Jacqueline Kim). We see in her a natural AMAZON still in training. Cindy is Tom's young secretary. She is fond of him, believes in his ability, and likes her job very much. In a moment of shared ebullience about a mutually completed work task early in the story, Tom swats her lightly, casually, on her buttock, as if she were a younger sister. She is uncomfortable with this, but does not yet have the experience, or poise to speak up firmly but non-aggressively. It is clear that had she done so Tom would probably have apologized, and learned the useful and important lesson. Timidly, Cindy brings the matter up during the mediation process when she is under questioning. Tom's apology is honestly offered, and accepted. Her brief cameo illustrates something of the developmental challenges of the AMAZON type. As she matures, she does not necessarily need a court case to get the respect she desires. Cindy Chang, for example, may be used to illustrate how young women sometimes relate to family members or schoolmates in a manner that is deferring and accepting of the male patriarchal model, instead of speaking up, without declaring war. She needs some self-awareness in order to enter the world of work, and develop some skills so that she need not remain uncomfortably compromised in working with male colleagues. There is scarcely any substitute for such skills, and one can understand how the AMAZON has been foremost of the types to achieve success in the predominantly male world of work. These skills, if not natural to the young woman, can be easily acquired, and need not necessarily be either uncomfortably confrontational or aggressive. The real skill lies in the manner in which the expression of discomfort is given. For some women it takes some gumption or ego strength when such episodes occur, to speak up, and say, calmly, firmly, not smiling but still pleasant, 'Don't do that. Okay?'

Of course, that is just a start. There are times when more drastic steps must be taken. But if a young woman has not learned how and when to set her own boundaries regarding her comfort zones at the office, she probably isn't ready to venture forth very far quite yet. This issue is not always a question of youth. Many women have never learned it, because it is apt to be contrary to the manner in which they were raised by their mothers and sisters as well as their fathers and brothers.

Two other brief AMAZON cameos contribute to the story: Mary Ann Hunter (Suzie Plakson), a hardworking engineer, and Barbara Murphy (Kate Williamson), is the skilled mediator already mentioned, who is the soul of an impartial judge, the exemplary 'Athena' of the tale.

The final winner of the promotion after the denouement at the office is not Tom. But he does keep his job, and earn back his rightful place in the future of the organization. There is another AMAZON woman whose presence in the story has been quietly but firmly defined, Stephanie Kaplan, (Rosemary Forsyth). She carries the day as a well-balanced, mature woman of warmth, relational connectedness, brains, talent and leadership. She is skillful in working behind the scenes. She understands the political realities of the office and works well within them without creating shipwreck. She, the natural AMAZON, wins the promotion to the vice presidential post.

This film, which is intended to explore issues related to reverse discrimination, does an artful job of identifying some of the subtleties of this important issue. Beyond that, the film amplifies a wide range of personalities inherent in the AMAZON archetype.

## More on Shadow and Self-Nurture

Two mythic themes from the ancient AMAZON stories provide metaphors for working with the specifically AMAZON need for self-nurture.

## 1. The Myth of Self-Mutilation

In the earlier tales of Amazon women there is the thread that reports the practice of breast cauterization, even of infants. Such violence is difficult for the modern mind to fathom other than as comparable to acts of primitive ritual commitment, to bloodletting as a symbol of solidarity in the face of battle. Three writers of ancient times, Diodorus, Strabo, and the early-unnamed writer who wrote *On Airs, Waters, and Places* in the fifth century B.C., recorded this phenomenon. So there must have been credible reasons why these reports survived the natural erosion of time. If we think about this as amplifying Tyrrell's theses, that 'the myth was necessary to accomplish an impression on the existing culture of the outcome of aberrant behavior,' then the stories certainly must have accomplished the task, by portraying the life of the AMAZON as a despicable and bloody affair. But if, indeed, the ancient Amazon stories have a truth to be acknowledged about the human spirit if only in a metaphoric sense, then mutilation of the body becomes an intrinsic part of the AMAZON shadow as an unconscious version of warfare.

The inferior AMAZON is challenged psychologically by refusing to take the body and its limitations as well as its strengths into respectful consideration. Self-nurture is primarily a mothering task, but still the AMAZON needs to understand that mutilation of the breast, the primal feeding place, indicates, at least metaphorically, a warning: The body must be understood as self. Physical embodiment is essential to the goals of the spirit of the true AMAZON.

The contemporary AMAZON may dissociate from her own physical and emotional needs. In fact, she can become seriously ill, addictive or accident-prone. This is the wound, the possible failure to honor one's own nurturance needs. Even though we live at a time when the zeitgeist for body workouts, exercise programs, diets, and expensive food supplements proliferate, the truth is that our culture is rife with problems for ambitious women in this arena. Addictions compensate temporarily where consciousness is lacking.

The AMAZON wants to excel; to be outstanding, to win the races, top the models, be the brightest, slimmest, strongest, fastest or wealthiest. If her ambition pushes her beyond her natural human limitation, she may compromise her body's instinctual integrity. AMAZON gets her fatal wound in the breast, as did Camilla.

- She will have to learn about patience with her physical and emotional limitations, and develop some substantial habits that protect her from her vulnerabilities. Her spirit may be indomitable, almost super human, but her body is not.

- She also needs genuine peers who are interesting and rewarding for her, and from whom she gathers ideas, pleasure, confirmation and validation.

- She needs to respond to her own feelings, and not expect all of her appreciation to come from the outside world and strangers. Such external accolades are apt to be short-lived and, by all reports, relentlessly fickle.

AMAZON behavior which is self-mutilating may take the form of the workaholic syndrome or other addictions whereby physical self-nurture and need for a satisfying relational life is overlooked and replaced with external goals and temporary consolations.

Wolff pointed out the warrior motivations of the inferior AMAZON are 'inferior' to the genuine ambition of the AMAZON achiever. If we asked Toni Wolff what the AMAZON needs to know, Wolff might, from her HETAIRA position of relational understanding, have replied, "*Stay connected. Make sense. Work fairly. Fight for justice with good will.*"

One might ask of the contemporary AMAZON type, who has worked to separate her personal rage in a conscious manner from her ambition, and is still energetically in pursuit of her own goals, how she might describe that developmental process.

The task of sorting out one's own inner world, a teeming mixture of conscious and unconscious material, is often the personal internal battleground. It is the hardest warfare of all. The pressure of it can be so unbearable that we may force it into external projections so that one bloody war after another leaves us only to repeating one bloody war after another.

## Drama Study: *The Eumenides* (The Furies.)[185]

In the *Oresteia* trilogy by Aeschylus written in circa 450 B.C., the question of raging feminine warfare is declared "unsolvable" by mere humans, and turned over to Athena, Goddess of Wisdom, to be decided. The hero of the story, Orestes, is tormented by 'The Furies,' (in Greek,

---

185 Aeschylus, *The Eumenides*, third play of *The Oresteia* cycle by BCE fourth century dramatist. Translated by Ted Hughes (New York: Farrar, Straus and Giroux, 1999), 152.

'The Eumenides'), a specter of wretched female hags who attack him mercilessly, and without reprieve. Ted Hughes, in his contemporary translation of this epic, describes these ghastly forces as:

> ...Strange sleeping creatures, like rags of soot that hang in chimneys like bats, but wingless, each of their faces a mess of weeping ulcers. Their bodies exhale a stench like maggoty corpses. Who are they? What are they? Some other kind, inhuman.[186]

The reason for the Furies' attack on Orestes is justified, they believe, because Orestes murdered his mother, Clytemnestra. In the world of 'The Furies,' the worst crime a human being can commit is matricide, and the perpetrator must die. To the modern reader, they also represent the enraged and dethroned voice of the feminine authority within the godhead, the ancient ones, who have been overturned by the evolving patriarchy wherein the voice of Zeus and Apollo supersede all other voices ruling the earth. The problem lies in the fact that Orestes was commanded to murder his own mother, Clytemnestra, by none other than Apollo, because Clytemnestra murdered Orestes' father, Agamemnon, when he returned home from the Trojan War. Apollo has called upon Orestes to vindicate his father's murder, in the 'new' order of the hierarchy of the gods, Zeus and Apollo. So the human is caught between the masculine principle of obedience, and the feminine rage for the crime of matricide. Orestes comes as a supplicant to the temple of Athena, after a long and tortured period of suffering and ritual cleansing. The furies will not leave him, no matter how deeply he repents.

By offering her 'Holy Persuasion,'[187] Athena, in the court of justice, addresses the howling Furies respectfully, and asks them what it would take to leave Orestes in peace.

In effect she is told that what the Furies want is their just place in the city. They want their rage against all who violate the feminine to be included in public life and religious life, in a respectful manner. They want to be respected for their pain, for their upheaval, for the lack of honor, which the new male-dominated democracy has inflicted upon them. 'Give us our name,' they demand.

---

186 Aeschylus, *The Eumenides,*152-3.
187 Aeschylus, *The Eumenides*, 176, 179.

Athena listens, and responds. 'Let me be just,'[188] she says. 'Let me remember the fair tongue of reason. I know you. And I know what men say of you.' Appeased, the Furies subside, when Athena offers them honor, and their rightful place in the ceremonies and sacrifices of worship in the city. Their rage is a legitimate part of the history of the human race. 'No family shall flourish without your favor,' she says. And to the assembled citizens, Athena announces that she welcomes to Athens these terrible powers, the implacable, the unappeasable goddesses, and the powers of darkness that have risen from the earth to watch over the ways of humans. The one who angers them lives in misery, until an acknowledgment is made of the source of the original problem. Attention is required. An apology must be made.

Orestes, the contrite suppliant, is granted his freedom from the torment of the Furies.

Athena, patron goddess of the city, justice and law, brings peace to the Furies, which provides us with a metaphor for calming the troubled minds of wild and enraged AMAZON wounding:

> Noble ladies, I beseech you, suspend your anger
> Till you have heard me speak.
> You shall sit on thrones of dignity.[189]

## Name the Source of Your Fury

The message for the 'inferior' AMAZON is to name the source of the personal 'fury' that torments her, bring it to consciousness, and work out her inner personal story. That is, to let it become conscious, respected, and given justice in her psyche. This task requires more than just acknowledgment of old wounds. It requires an understanding of how those wounds still function, in her everyday life, and what her projections of them might be. It requires a respectful and careful reliving of old trauma, and delivering the unacknowledged anger in some form to its original target, where it belongs. These wounds can be healed. Once free of them, she can proceed to fulfill her ambition.

---

188 Aeschylus, *The Oresteia*, "The Eumenides", translated by Philip Vellacott. (New York, NY: Penguin Putnam, 1959), 176.
189 Aeschylus, *The Oresteia*, "The Eumenides", translated by Ted Hughes. 197.

As it is in the macrocosm of collective consciousness, so is it in the inner world of psyche. Once again, when the AMAZON is operating solely out of unconscious 'furies,' her targets are legion. It is a wise and powerful AMAZON who tames her own fury not by will power, but by conscious respect for her own inner pain, and finding someone or some way to help her with knowledgeable compassion.

# Chapter 18

## AMAZON and Some Career Thoughts

Toni Wolff wrote:

- "Our present time offers the widest scope to the AMAZON. ... It is this form most frequently found in the limelight in public life."[190]

  (Paraphrases): Bravery and Physical adventure, travel, and sports are of this type, along with the highest levels of participation in business, politics, and every level of public life. Of special interest is the AMAZON who works at maintaining family life while pursuing AMAZON professional interests as well.

For the AMAZON, the truth is that in a free society today there is not much that she can't do. The sky's the limit. Ms. AMAZON flies, floats, bungee jumps and trains for astronaut duty. She conducts dangerous and highly skilled operations in many professions; she serves as a commanding officer in the armed forces; she runs for high public office; she manages her career, volunteer work and busy household simultaneously; she competes in sporting events, and drives the school bus; she pastors large church congregations, delivers packages, presides on the bench in courtrooms, performs microsurgery, and commands a space shuttle.

She also often makes futile choices for unconscious reasons, subverts her own progress, blames others for her mistakes, and gets caught in her over confidence regarding the options available to her. In choosing her career, she just might confuse 'Can I do this?' with 'Should I do this?' or 'Do I really want to do this?' Of course these same pitfalls occur for men as well as women, in career decision-making.

Rather than posing a seminar on Wolff and Careers For Women, the writers put together some cameos of clinical experience for the consideration of readers:

---

190 Wolff, "Structural Forms," 7.

## Bird's Eye View: Various AMAZONS In Distress

### Jo

She holds down an important job as manager of a sizable staff. She works long hours, and has made a rapid rise to her present position. She is an attractive woman, who takes good care of her appearance. On weekends she is inclined to sleep a great deal, and understands that she is depressed. She has a few woman friends. But she prefers to remain 'in control.' By that she means that she will personally initiate when they meet, and what they do together. She does not want to be expected to mix with her friends' family members or their other friends. She did not date in high school or college, because she felt so intimidated by her severely troubled family life. She is, for the most part, in touch with her siblings on a tenuous basis, all of whom live a considerable distance from her.

Jo has a sizable number of cats. She cares for them with great devotion. She is inclined to perceive some of her encounters with her employees, or her superiors, in a manner that is highly personal and over reactive. She needs to understand that having no family or close relationships of her own, she reacts to her professional associates as if they were her personal family. She realizes that some of the deep anger she feels is overreaction, and that her real anger lies with her painfully abusive family history. She labors to come to terms with this, and tries to develop a more active social life of her own. It is hard. But she is aware that if she is not able to develop her own personal private life, she may compromise her effectiveness as a professional. Depression erodes her energy.

### June

June went all the way through medical school, and discovered she really didn't like being available to people who were ill. In fact, sick people made her angry, and she found she distinctly disliked them. This was the career that her father wanted! She endured her work for fifteen years before she decided that what she really liked, and wanted to do, was to raise horses. Fortunately, in time she was able to make the change.

## Phyllis

Phyllis found her work as an attorney to be 'deadly boring.' While she liked her persona as an attorney, she discovered she wanted to be more closely involved with other people, and settled finally on a teaching career. She remained in the legal field, but mastered a specialization that interested her more than practicing law, which qualified her to teach on a law school faculty.

## Eudela

She finds herself nearly fifty years old, she is a past CEO, past director of charities, past expert in liturgical music, past trainer of voice, past psychotherapist, and is currently in Europe studying languages. She has been involved in several careers, and considers herself as being 'the other side of a difficult life.' When she graduated from college, she didn't have a single plan. The slate was clean and enormous. Had she had only one talent, she thinks the decision would have been easy. It was extremely difficult for her to choose from so many options.

She describes her current fellow students as really 'just kids, 20 somethings,' from Sweden, Japan, England, and South America. When any topic comes up, she knows something about it. They wonder at that, but she tells them that when they are her age, they will have had some experience, too. But it reminds her of back home, where many people couldn't believe that she would again just drop a career to go on an adventure. She doesn't get it. It is natural and easy. Like so many other things she has done in her life, her difficulty is in understanding and relating to people who think that the things she does are so difficult. 'She can't believe it.'

Her issues seem to have been confusing to her, so she projects the problem she faces regarding finding a satisfactory career outwardly, on others. Her dissatisfaction about others 'not getting it,' that she 'cant believe,' really describes herself. She is also unhappy and disappointed that she has not found a suitable partner to be there when she goes home. She struggles with the shame of a restless loneliness.

# Chapter 19

## Of Men and AMAZON

Toni Wolff writes:

- "The AMAZON is independent of the male because her development is not based on psychological relationship to him."

- "Relationship with a man is through a role of being a competitor or comrade who makes no personal demands, [ ] who deserves to be taken seriously, who incites his energies and inspires his best ambitions."[191]

(Paraphrases): The status of her married partner means little. She wants to earn her own laurels. Her energy may evoke admiration and attraction within the male. She is customarily efficient and successful. Her family members may be her employees.

The earlier myths present the Amazon woman as the intrepid warrior, who wages battle with fierce determination against primarily male adversaries. Yet she still joins with the male in clandestine meetings for procreation; one would hope, also for the experience of hungry and maybe even tender sex.

Included in Chapter Two was the tale of the Amazons and the Scythians, recorded by Herodotus somewhere around 600 B.C. You will recall that the Scythians were the Amazon's most powerful and omnipresent adversaries. When the Amazons challenged the Scythians, the men sent a troop of warriors with orders to camp near the Amazons but not to fight. They were instructed by their commanders on each side to send out one warrior champion to meet one worthy adversary. The pair met at night, and decided to make love. The next night, so the story goes, each one brought a friend, and on it went for many days and nights, until the Scythians and the Amazons agreed to become married. However, the Amazons refused to return with the Scythians to their homeland,

191 Wolff, "Structural Forms," 8.

and prevailed upon their husbands to 'move to a new place.' Herodotus speculates that they moved off to a 'mythological haven' where men and women lived together in equality.

One senses that Herodotus, some 2500 years ago, knew at some deep and profound level that this concept needed to be articulated to the world. It remains known today, as perhaps an illusive oasis somewhere in the desert of our mass marital drought. Somehow, the AMAZON, with her male lover beside her even if only in conjecture, can imagine a state of total equality with men, an inner space, both within the mind and also within a collective social system!

What is there in the Amazon myth, which invites the discovery and cultivation of that land? And is the AMAZON archetype to be a major custodial keeper of the charge, to find and explore it? We have already looked at the evolution of the AMAZON archetype as it became less and less bloody over history, and evolved from mythological tradition to that of mortal women. The AMAZON archetype described by Toni Wolff is that of a female today who has the same characteristics of ego strength focused on collective consciousness as did her Amazon predecessors. As we have seen, Wolff is very clear, in her delineation of 'inferior' and 'natural' AMAZON initiative that certain distinctions are made regarding her self-nurture. At the same time, the natural AMAZON is challenged to apply her own energy and curiosity to discovering how to enter freely into the admittedly vulnerable position of adult intimate relational life without loosing her autonomy, her freedom and her sense of self.

This juncture in mythological history occurred when Theseus, the greatest hero and ruler of Athens, carried off Hippolyta, queen of the Amazons, centuries ago when Athens was first settled. The story relates that after she had given birth to his son Hippolytus, her Amazon sisters rode to Athens to liberate Hippolyta from her captor. Well, perhaps Hippolyta didn't seem so terribly eager to be liberated from her certainly more domestic new life. One might postulate that she had found a mate that was her genuine peer in strength, ability, brainpower, and psychic energy. We don't know. Or she may have been held captive, or slain. For whatever reason, the ranks of warrior women in all their glory who rode to battle, either with men as comrades or as adversaries, all but disappeared from history, with the exception of a very few. But their mythology remained as a way of describing a heroic, and ongoing struggle.

The remarkable stories of the Amazons lived on and on. For example, 2500 years later, Shakespeare chose the legendary marriage of Hippolyta and Theseus as the backdrop for a major play about the ambiguities and magical mix-ups of matrimony, in *A Midsummer Night's Dream*. Shakespeare's customary way of managing marital or premarital difficulties in his work is that the spicy woman is ultimately tamed and brought under the control of her strong and benevolent husband or father. This was, after all, 16th century England. But it was also an England with an unmarried AMAZON regent, who was not about to be conquered, or tamed. The unspoken question, for our purpose, is 'What might a workable romantic relationship plan for an AMAZON be?'

* * *

The reason for the choice of this play in order to try to locate a connection between the AMAZON archetype and the tottering institution of marriage is not because it solves the massive questions, but because it amplifies them. The issues of courtship and marriage, with all the complications, plottings, enchantments, irrationality, family upsets, games and confusion have combined with the Bard's genius to make this comic fantasy a timeless delight. The subject matter has never paled.

## Drama Study: *A Midsummer Night's Dream*[192]

by William Shakespeare

Shakespeare dedicated *A Midsummer Night's Dream* to Queen Elizabeth I, who was most likely present for its first performance in the spring of 1595. Her prestige and patronage were essential to him and must certainly have affected his choice of themes. The subject of how his literal AMAZON queen might become married, and to whom, was a smoldering political issue at the time all across Europe, a matter on which many a career of statesmanship ascended, or ultimately collapsed.

---

192 William Shakespeare, *A Midsummer Night's Dream,* (New American Library, Penguin Putnam, Signet, New York, 1998).

This play was commissioned to be an epithalamium, written to celebrate the marriage of an aristocratic couple, and intended to be presented during the festivities preceding the ceremony. He used the names of Amazon lore to establish a setting of both classic and mythic scope in a celebration of 'matrimony,' or 'the peaceful solution of lovers' conflicts.' He borrowed from ancient Greece the names Theseus, the leader of Athens, and Hippolyta, the Queen of the Amazons, who are to be wed. All sorts of opposites are collected in one magic woodland. The faerie kingdom mingles with humans, the peasants with the nobles, the old with the young, the lovers with the scoffers, performers with the audience, the dreamers with the more lively ones. All are destined to participate on the magic night of the summer solstice. The festivities go on for many hours. Magic spells are incanted, mixed identities abound, and no one is safe from trickery and mischief. Everything turns upside down in the scuffle. Some of the pairing up is recast, all the silliness of temporary infatuation is made clear, the instinctual forces join with those of order, natural partners finally find one another, and the jumble of opposites eventually culminates in a peaceable truce. At least, for a time.

W.H. Auden points out that in the last speech of the play wherein Puck extends the blessings of the faerie kingdom to the bride and groom, the point is made that our dreams and desires about marriage are so confounding that:

> Perhaps they can best be examined through the metaphor of delusionary love juice, the mood of a celebrative occasion, and the intervention of forces of nature other than human, all under a summer moon.[193]

There are actually six different couples involved in the story: the ultra-noble mythical bride and groom, two sets of young upper middle-class lovers, two other-than-mortals, and one tragic pair of ancients, during a 'play within the play.' The latter perish of parental tyranny as Pyramus and Thisbe are delivered to the audience by the Bucolics in hilarious satire. Underlying all six pairs is the smoldering possibility of tragedy and disaster, its truth made tolerable by its comic mixture of pleasure, confusion, blindness and magic.

---

193 W.H. Auden, "A Midsummer Night's Dream," *Lectures on Shakespeare*, ed. Arthur Kirsch, Princeton University Press, Princeton, NJ. 2004, 54.

As blithe as this mixture seems to be, however, Harold Bloom's essay on the play points out that still, when we celebrate marriage, there is 'a clear division here, between past and future, as in all marriages. Let it be said, we are dividing the history of our lives.'[194] It is actually no comic matter, as Bloom also points out. In fact it is so serious that perhaps we bear it best... in satire.

How does this challenge the AMAZON, and why might the AMAZON type be appropriately suited to cope with the ambiguities regarding adult relational life, including children, intimate friendships, and men? Wolff's earlier ideas regarding familiar characteristics of the AMAZON remain relevant: (repeated and paraphrased):

> Alone among the four types she is independent of the male because her development is not based on a psychological relationship to him.

> Relationship with a man is through a role of being competitive, or (that of a) comrade and rival who makes no personal demands; a competitor who deserves to be taken seriously, who incites his energies and inspires his best ambitions, healthy competition or comradeship. (Paraphrased.)

Add to the fact that the playing field between male and female is now more than ever on level ground, the energy for life is apt to be comparable. The chances of a successful outcome are perhaps better than they have ever been. And is there not something about having a 'worthy opponent' or 'partnership,' which offers some advantage, from the start? What about shared professional ventures? What about learning to cope with painful jealousies? What about that matter of 'need'? It is obvious that the healthy AMAZON does not 'need' to be taken care of. But she might very well wish to be able to enjoy and participate in adult healthy relational life wherein she can give and receive human love.

In Shakespeare's play, the Duke and the Queen of the Amazons are finally wed. The invitation is given to consider 'peaceful equality between the sexes,' that far-off land which Herodotus wrote about nearly three thousand years ago. Fairness and equality are on the table, once

---

194 Harold Bloom's quote: (Unfortunately, we have been unable to locate this quotation, even after diligent search. If anyone reading this can inform us further, we will be most grateful. We offer sincere apologies.)

again, and the careful delineation of the 'truth' or 'falsehood' of relational life as well.

There was a lapel button worn by women for a while that made an interesting statement, 'Friendly, but not tame.' It remains astounding to discover how much can be accomplished when men and women learn to work together for mutual goals. In their professional lives, it is even more so. And it does happen. (See *Creative Collaboration*, Section I.)

If we are to study the Amazon myth thoughtfully, it might be to challenge the AMAZON types among us to assist in the search for the mythical haven of equality, peace, pleasure and freedom to which Herodotus alluded so many centuries ago.

If the AMAZON idea of domesticity is still in the forming stages, we do know that the quality of peers forming alliances is important, as is fair play. And in relationship to Wolff's paradigm, the AMAZON is well able to understand something of the mode of the HETAIRA. Do we hear a note of longing in the ancient words of Herodotus? Perhaps so. There are those among us who would like to think so.

AMAZON woman needs to find what it is she wants to give her man, and what she wants from her man, as her peer particularly; if some notes of humor, and a little magic, (so easy for Shakespeare), are included in the mix, it is bound to help.

# Chapter 20

## Of Children and AMAZON

Toni Wolff's article has very little in it about AMAZON family life. Fortunately, other writers show how her children often are enlisted in helping with her pursuits. One illustration of this is mentioned in the film study in Chapter 2. Included here are three portraits on the theme of mothers and daughters within the AMAZON constellation.[195]

The first one, part two of the story of Velta Hungerford, is written in the first person, as her daughter Lynn Hungerford Nelson gave it in her interview. She reflects on life with her AMAZON mother, some years after Velta's death:

### Narrative: Velta Lane Hungerford, Part 2 - Lynn's Story[196]

In retrospect, my life with Mother was arranged so that my sister Karen and I could be available to her in an adjacent, assisting manner. I started helping to pack peaches on the farm when I was five, in the packing shed by the railroad tracks, where the men and women sorted the fruit into baskets and loaded them onto railroad cars. I brushed a spot of glue on top of the paper that covered the baskets, and then someone else would put the label from our farm on top of my spot. I thought this was fine. I think I liked the activity, and everyone there kept a close eye on me so that I felt comfortable. To me, it seemed we all lived a fairly normal life until Daddy died. Mother liked the ocean, and Daddy did too, so they started taking us down to Panama City for brief periods in the summer before the harvest. Then Mother decided she could start a motel business down there, where we could all go and enjoy the ocean. Later she and Daddy would go down after the harvest in October, when Daddy enjoyed the fishing, and Mother would supervise her motel business. They would be gone until Thanksgiving. Karen and I would stay with Annabelle and Joe, the older couple who lived nearby on the farm, and had always worked for Daddy. This seemed very natural to us, since Annabelle and Joe had always been around the farm, and helped raise us.

---

195 Wolff, "Structural Forms," 8.
196 Velta Lane Hungerford, Interview, Author Molton.

Daddy's death was very sudden, just a couple days after Christmas, in 1951. We had been playing canasta together at the cabin one night, and we all went to bed as usual. He was fine when we retired, as I recall. Mother was awakened by his labored breathing, and roused me. She asked me if I wanted to go and call the doctor, (the telephone was at Annabelle and Joe's house a few yards up the hill), or if she should. I was only eleven at the time, and knew she should go. By the time she returned with the doctor, he was gone.

It wasn't long after that when Mother took full charge of the farm. She remained politically active until 1958, but she also decided to change peach growing to other ways of farming, because peach trees had to be replanted every seven years, and that was a very big rotation enterprise. She decided to try cattle, and then gradually replaced peach trees with pecan trees, which were easier to raise. All of that had to be done in phases, and as far as I know, she did a great job.

When I was twelve and Karen was ten, Mother decided we should be given a good education, and we were sent to boarding school in Macon. I believed this was for our own good, and that was that. This was not the sort of school where the students went home weekends. We had our vacation, winter and spring, but otherwise, we were in school. In retrospect, I also knew that she needed additional freedom to tend to her enterprises that were not only on the farm, but also in Florida.

After Daddy's death we lived in several places, an apartment here, a couple of trailers there, the big cabin by the lake, wherever Mother needed to be. We always lived like that, sort of a gypsy life, with several camps on the outskirts of her projects around Jones County. My sister Karen and I never knew for sure where we might be sleeping, but we always felt safe when we were with her. Mother never lived in any one place, after my father died. There were several fine houses on the property, but she always seemed to find income-generating uses for them, other than having a special home just for us. When Karen and I would come home from boarding school, or later college, we would just find out where Mother was, and if she was at one of the nursing homes, there would usually be an empty bed where we would sleep. When I think about Mother's life after Daddy died, the changes for her evolved slowly, and only now begin to clarify in retrospect.

Keeping a home for herself, and a social life, gradually disappeared for Mother. There was never enough time for her to do that. I recall watching her fix her hair one morning when she was fresh from the shower. She would just push it in place and it would look great. 'It's a good thing God gave me good hair,' she often said, 'I don't have time to fuss with it.' She'd look at me, and say, 'you're pretty. But not as pretty as I am...' and walk off.

As far as I know, there was never another romantic interest in her life after my father's death; she was only forty-nine years old and still a fine looking woman.

The nursing home business actually began because of my grand-mother's lingering illness. There was no available facility where she could receive the care Mother thought she needed. So finally Mother bought a large home suitable for the care of aged people, and started the first nursing home of its kind in the county, just down the road from our farm. This proved to be a very success-ful venture, and as time went on, Mother developed, owned and operated several nursing homes. By that time, I had married Brick, who was fresh out of the navy. Mother didn't like him at first, and would not even come to my wedding. Later, after our first son was born, she decided Brick was 'OK' and he became her partner in the nursing home business. Still later, when Brick and I were managing the business, we acquired the additional properties until there were twenty-six homes, throughout the state.

Sister Karen went off to study art in Mexico City. Once I was visiting her, when I was just twenty or so, still in school. As I was leaving she asked me if I had any extra money. I had a return ticket home, so I just gave her what cash I had, and got on the plane. There was a huge storm in Dallas. My connecting flight had me stranded without a penny. I called Mother collect, and asked her to wire me some money. She was quiet, on the other end of the phone. Then she said, 'didn't I always tell you to not ever give away your last dollar? Let me know when you get home.' And she hung up. I slept that night on a bench in the airport. Fortunately on the second day I ran into an old college friend, who took me home to her apartment. But I never again gave away my last dollar.

During the '80s, when I was really busy with my young fam-ily, and also working full time as a nursing home manager, she acquired a group of needy people around her, whom she would try to help 'fix.' I think she meant well, but they didn't seem ever to get fixed. They didn't straighten up like she thought they should. Then she'd discharge them, and take on others. I think maybe she needed an audience. This was as close to any social life she had that wasn't connected to the family, or her work. She was a tough lady, and not always tactful with her employees. When it was time for Mother to enter Lynn Haven as a patient herself, we all wondered what in the world would happen. We were amazed. She became as gentle and sweet as a lamb. She was a model patient, right up to the very end. It seemed like some sort of miracle.

But now that I think about it, I realize she always had taken very good care of her own needs, herself. Her 'miracle behavior' was just another way to take care of her self.

When unpleasant things happened she decided they just didn't happen. Sometimes, what carried us through difficult times together was that she managed to maintain a sense of humor. I remember after her first stroke, she was recuperating in the trailer, which was parked out behind Lynn Haven. She was seventy-nine then. She couldn't drive any more, but she got around using a cane. The kitchen staff would bring her lunch over, and my children would look in on her after school. I was managing Green Acres then, over in Milledgeville, so I drove about thirty minutes to get there after work to check on her. She had her three dogs with her in the trailer. She loved dogs, and also all kinds of bushes and flowers, which she loved to plant and tend. This particular afternoon was in the springtime, and Mother had decided she would take her cane and go out to visit her pearl bush, which was near the door. Well, she slipped and fell. When I got there, I found her under the pearl bush, with the dogs all over her. She was peacefully looking up through the blossoming branches against the blue sky.

She looked at me, and said, "Lynn, here I am, rolled under the pearl bush, stuck on my back like a turtle, and I can't get up. But I certainly do have the most gorgeous view!"

Before she died, she told me that there were two things she regretted in her life that she felt she had missed; one was being a doctor. She felt that she should have been a doctor. She probably *should* have been a doctor. I know she would have been a good one. The second was going to war. She hated not to be able to serve in World War II. She was pregnant with me in 1940, and Mac had said, 'I don't think you can go, Pat. You have a baby now.' That must have been hard for my dad, because he always wanted her to be free to do what she wanted to do. He supported her, in every way.

When Mother died in 1993, she was 87 years old. Karen spent a week with me at that time, and we talked and talked, recalling stories.

Once we had been sent to clean up the cabin where all four of us lived until Daddy died. We were often assigned the clean up tasks when Mother wanted to move from one of the other places she had set up. We found a divorce paper, thereby discovering that Mother had been married previously, before she came back to Jones County from Washington. I don't recall the names, or a date on that paper. Karen and I just sat down, stunned. We knew that Mac had been married before, but we didn't know about Mother's earlier marriage. For some reason, we never mentioned this to Mother. But we always wondered about it.

Mother and Karen...well, that is another story, and not mine to tell.

Another cameo is a series of episodes on the famous publisher Katharine Graham and her relationship with her own difficult AMAZON mother. As Agnes' daughter, Katharine's AMAZON qualities were slow to emerge. Also in time, influences from her father Eugene were crucial in her development.

## Book Study: *Personal History*

Katharine Graham (1917 - 2001)

One of the most powerful AMAZON women of recent times was Katharine Graham, intrepid publisher and businesswoman under whose leadership *The Washington Post* achieved worldwide prominence. The Post, during the second half of the twentieth century, became a veritable beacon to the world of the fundamental role of the press in the maintenance of a free society. In her remarkable autobiography *Personal History*,[197] Graham's story serves our AMAZON study by presenting her own insight into the powerful dynamics of her relational life with her parents, Agnes and Eugene Meyer, and with her husband Phil Graham, who preceded her as publisher of The Post.

Katharine's mother Agnes Meyer was herself a natural AMAZON, even as a very young woman. Her early struggle to achieve an education without family financial help is certainly indicative of early AMAZON energy. In fact, family legend has it that while she was a young woman in Paris (1908-09) studying art prior to her marriage, she was invited by the famous sculptor Rodin to pose for him as the ancient British warrior-queen, Boudicca. However, since Rodin wanted her to pose 'nude, on horseback, with javelin in hand,' she regretfully declined his invitation.

She married wealthy Eugene Meyer in a thoroughly accommodating arrangement, which allowed her freedom to pursue her own interests

---

197 Katharine Graham, *Personal History* (New York: Vintage Books, 1998), 165-168.

in art, politics, society and the world of famous people and intellectual ideas. In her own autobiography, Agnes said that marriage for her would have been impossible unless the man was financially secure, because she would have to come to a marriage with no dowry, and only her own debts and those of her father to bring with her. It had been a source of great relief for her to be able to tell Mr. Graham about the 'crushing debt' of anxiety she had carried concerning these issues, and she added, 'Let no one undervalue the importance of economic independence.'

Agnes produced five children in eight years, and called herself 'a conscientious but scarcely loving mother.' The family money provided her with the means to leave the major role of maternal nurture in the hands of a loving nurse, several tutors, and other loyal household staff people. She was, as Katharine recalls, 'completely self-absorbed.' But Agnes' daughter also lists some of her mother's considerable accomplishments. Agnes worked as a volunteer, establishing a solid reputation and visibility on the social welfare and political fronts by testifying before congress on matters related to health and human welfare, and influencing cabinet level advocacy in these areas. She also challenged the radio and film worlds regarding 'vulgarization of the public mind and debasing public morals.' She became a member of the Presidents commission on Higher Education, and served on countless boards and commissions. And Newsweek magazine cited her for her public advocacy.

While one might think that having such an energized AMAZON mother might have provided an inspiring role model for an admiring daughter, such was not the case. For the most part, Katharine's feelings of inferiority as the fourth of five siblings, and her lack of personal recognition by her mother Agnes, were very painful. She felt that her mother was responsible for the inferior feelings that she and her siblings felt, which prevented them from thinking of her as an admirable role model. Although Katharine remembered her girlhood as being 'cared for, protected and isolated,' she always felt less competent than the flamboyant and beautiful mother, whose essential character seemed more and more self-centered. Katharine felt that her mother had cast her in a particular role model, and never thought to look to see if that model were really true.

Katharine reported that as Agnes aged, she became increasingly difficult. It was hopeless to ask her a personal question or for advice. Katharine's realization of her own natural gifts was slow to manifest. Her first
priority, in her younger days, was the desire to conform, to please, to
abide by laws, 'to be a good girl.' When she went to college at the University of Chicago and developed her own interests in literature, public
affairs, and later on, journalism, she began corresponding avidly with
her father. At first to please him, she soon developed an acute interest
in the world of publishing, where he exerted considerable expertise as
owner of *The Washington Post*. She gradually began to assume, through
the letters with her father and her experiences at school, that she would
become a journalist.

It was later in her life that she began to realize that her father believed in her abilities early on, which gave her some measure of poise
and security that she felt she had really needed. Even so, her early marriage to Phil Graham and the years of becoming a parent did little to
help her self-esteem and reduced her once again to the one-down feeling that was the prevalent psychological story during childhood and
puberty.

Phil Graham consistently belittled her, even when he became, at
her father's invitation, president and later publisher of *The Post*. He
had a witty and pleasing public persona, but a personal insecurity that
seemed to carry notes of ridicule and sarcasm toward every effort she
made.

It was not until after Phil's suicide that Katharine began to emerge
from the crippling self-doubt which she later understood was directly
influenced by the inhibiting nature of her earlier experiences with her
own AMAZON mother, and painfully repeated in her marriage.

Ultimately, Katharine Graham herself became president of the
Washington Post Company and then publisher, where her remarkable
courage to muster the skill which allowed *The Post* to take on the leadership of creative reporting, which ultimately collapsed a corrupt administration. This was the accomplishment for which she is most widely
celebrated, and is a singular story of a gradually unfolding AMAZON
strength of character, skill, and stability.

A contrasting piece was written by a 36-year-old woman when it was published in *Newsweek* magazine, just eighteen days after her AMAZON mother, Madeleine Albright, was sworn in as Secretary of State.

## Narrative: "A Daughter's Story"

by Anne Albright

I was in high school in the mid-70's when somebody asked me, 'Don't you feel deprived because your mother works?' I didn't understand the question. I always thought my mother's work was very exciting, and my sisters and I never felt that she didn't have time for us. She's always done the ordinary things that mothers do: getting us up in the mornings and ready for school, helping us with our homework. We used to do our homework together: she was finishing her Ph.D. and we were in grade school. On Fridays she would do the grocery shopping while my sisters and I were horseback riding or taking ballet class or guitar lessons. We had a wonderful family life.

When she went back to work, she told us we could call her at the office if anything ever came up. So we called one time when she was working for Sen. Edmund Muskie, and the receptionist told us our mother couldn't come to the phone because she was on the floor with the senator. When she called back, we said, 'What were you doing on the floor with Senator Muskie?' She had been on the floor of the Senate, of course, but we were too young to know what she really did.

When we were children, my younger sister, Katie, wanted to be a fireman. My twin sister, Alice, wanted to be a doctor. I wanted to be a baseball player, a pitcher for the New York Mets. My mom never told us, you should do this or do that. Nevertheless, academic achievement was highly valued in our family, and we were all history majors in college, like my father. Each of us sort of assumed we'd go to graduate school; we ended up as two lawyers and a banker. The one thing she wanted to teach us was: do your best at your job, no matter what it is. She's said many times that there's no such thing as luck. What you get, you work for.

Of course, all three of us were thrilled for our mom. We went to the Senate for her confirmation hearings, to the Capitol for the presidential swearing in. But we've been proud of her all along. I remember that she spoke at my younger sister's graduation from the National Cathedral School in Washington. The ceremony was in the cathedral itself. She came down the aisle at the head of the procession, in her long, flowing Ph.D. robes. It was so exciting to see your mom that way. When I remember that, and the other highlights of her career, I know how tremendously lucky we are. As kids, we never felt we were being sacrificed for her career.

Quite the opposite.[198]

---

198 Anne Albright, "A Daughter's Story" (New York: *Newsweek*, February 10, 1993.)

# Chapter 21

## Of Amazon and the Other Types

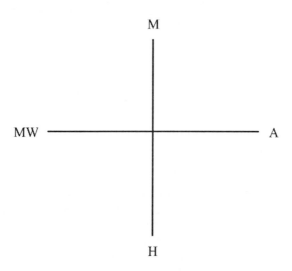

Wolff writes:

(Note: Wolff is repeating the need for the AMAZON to develop her personal relationships.)

- "A personal form must be joined by an impersonal one."

- "If the gradual integration of the next structural form does not take place, the original one will exaggerated and turn negative."[199]

(Paraphrases): Later on, a third form will have to be assimilated into consciousness, which usually lies on the same axis as the second, but has more of a shadow character and is harder to accept than the first.

---

199 Wolff, "Structural Forms," 11.

## Film Study: *The Grass Harp,* Part 2

Early in the film, the difficult dynamics and dashes of misunderstanding between the fiery AMAZON Verena and her MEDIAL sister Dolly crystallize in a pattern of threatening hostility, and become the unfolding drama of the story. (Dialog approximate.)

Verena: "Dolly, I need to talk to you."

Dolly: "What's the matter?"

Verena: "What goes into that medicine of yours?"

Dolly: "Oh, this and that. Why?"

Verena: "Well, you made enough this last year to pay income tax. That's why."

Dolly: (mystified.) "My ... my!"

> (Verena wants Dolly to patent her herbal 'dropsy cure' tonic so that it can become a commercial success. Verena has already been approached for Dolly's product by big time out-of-town 'Chemical Engineer' consultant, Morris Ritz (Jack Lemmon}. Verena has more than a business interest in Morris; she hopes that he will promote Dolly's dropsy cure. She is also impessed with his smooth attention to her. A dinner at the Talbo home is arranged to inform Dolly of the plan.) (Dialog approximate.)

Verena: "This is important, Dolly. Morris is comin' tonight especially to meet you."

Dolly: "No...please..."

Verena: "Yes. You can do this. Wear that pink dress I bought for you. Stand up straight... and try to fix your hair. You look a mess."

> (The time of the dinner arrives, and Dolly comes warily and late to the table. She is wearing a pink dress.)

Verena: "Dolly, we have a nice little surprise just for you. Morris, show Dolly those fine labels you have ordered for her medicine bottles."

> (Morris gives Dolly an envelope containing the labels. She studies them quietly, and says nothing.)

Verena: "Well, don't you like them?"

Dolly: "I don't ...know."

Verena: "Why of course you do. I told Morris about that medicine you make, and invented a lovely name for it! The Gypsy Cream Dropsy Cure. It will look very nice in advertising."

Dolly: (timidly) "I don't need... I... I label my own jars..."

Verena: "Now Dolly, Morris and I are travelin' to Washington this week to get a patent on your medicine. Your name goes on it, as the inventor, of course. Now, Dolly, you have to sit down and write all the ingredients."

(Dolly stands up quietly, and steadies herself.)

Dolly: "It won't work... No... because... you haven't the right... (to Morris) not you, either, ...Sir."

(Morris sneezes, water is spilled, he complains of the roses on the table causing his allergies. Dolly reaches to remove them, tips over the vase, glass breaks, water spills all over the food and the table.)

(Later. Dolly sits on her bed in her room while Verena paces, lecturing her, furiously.)

Verena: "Three thousand dollars I've spent for the factory already set up ... thousands for the machinery already ordered, carpenters workin' and bein' paid by the hour...and no tellin' what that specialist Morris will charge....All your fault!"

Dolly: "You're my sister and I love you dearly. I could prove it to you by giving you the one thing I ever had that is all mine... Then you would have it all. Please, Verena, let this one alone!"

Verena: (Heated) "I've worked for you all these years! I gave you this house to live in, food to eat, your clothes, everything you have!!, I've done it all, for you and Catherine and Collin!!

Dolly: (Hesitant) "We've earned...something... too... we've kept the home nice for you, haven't we?"

Verena: "Do you think I could invite anyone here? No! Because I'm ashamed of you! Look what you did tonight? You spoiled everything!"

Dolly: (Weeps, humiliated) "I'm... truly sorry! I always thought... we belonged here. (She steadies herself) "It's alright. We'll go away..."

Verena: (Screams) "And just where would you GO???!!!"[200]

---

200 *The Grass Harp*. 1999. See Film Index.

The two sisters inhabit different worlds; Dolly's is the nature world where she hears the tall grass sing, and learned the lore of healing herbs from traveling gypsies. In this sense she is MEDIAL indeed. Verena, an AMAZON, is completely focused on making a living as a shrewd businesswoman. Verena's efforts at interpersonal relationships, however, seemed doomed to failure. Morris skips town with twelve thousand of her well-earned dollars. Neither of the sisters elects to develop an adult relational life with a male partner. The HETAIRA quality is not fully grasped by either of them.

But Dolly's ability to relate in a highly personal way as part MOTHER to Collin humanized her intrinsic MEDIAL manner. After the denouement of the film, the two sisters still remain together, somehow understanding, that at some deep level, they need each other.

# MEDIAL WOMAN

## A Random Scroll

**Anna,** Biblical prophetess . . . **Annina,** in Menotti's opera *The Saint of Bleecker Street* . . . **Azucena,** in Verdi's opera *Il Travatore* . . . **St. Bernadette of Lourdes** . . . **Gret Baumann-Jung** . . . **Oda Mae Brown,** in the film *Ghost* . . . **M.J. Blavatsky** . . . **Echo Bodine** . . . **Cassandra** . . . **Clara Trueba,** in Allende's book *The House Of the Spirits* . . . **Meinrad Craighead** . . . **Daisy,** in film *On A Clear Day You Can See Forever* . . . **Deborah,** Biblical prophetess . . . **Jean Dixon** . . . **The Witch of Endor** . . . **Maria Esperanza** of Batavia . . . **Morgan Le Fay** . . . **The Fox Sisters** . . . **Liz Green** . . . **Hecate** . . . **Hildegard of Bingen** . . . **Julian of Norwich** . . . **Kuan Yin,** Goddess of Mercy . . . **Emilie Preiswerk Jung** . . . **Helene Preiswerk** . . . **Cynthia Killion** . . . **Shirley MacLaine** . . . **Maria Prophetissa** . . . **Mechthild of Magdeburg** . . . **Medea** . . . **Aunt Mozelle,** in the film *Eve's Bayou* . . . **Caroline Myss** . . . **Christine Page** . . . **Persephone** . . . **The Pythia of Delphi** . . . **Rabi'a al-'Adawiyya** of Basra . . . **The Shekinah** . . . **Sophia Eterna** . . . **Sylvie,** in the film *Moonlight and Valentino* . . . **Dolly Talbo,** in the film *The Grass Harp* . . . **St. Teresa of Avila** . . . **Evelyn Underhill** . . .

A fish cannot drown in water,
A bird cannot fall in the air.
In the fire of creation,
Gold doesn't vanish:

Each Creature God made
Must live in his own true nature
How could I resist my nature
That lives for oneness with God?

*—Mechthild of Magdeburg*[201]

---

201 Mechthild of Magdeburg, *The Enlightened Heart* (New York: HarperCollins. Edited by Stephen Mitchell. Translated by Jane Hirshfield 1998), 64.

# Chapter 22

## An Overview Of MEDIAL WOMAN

The MEDIAL WOMAN is the most mysterious of the feminine types. She is both a puzzle to herself and an enigma to those she encounters. In contrast to the other types, her primary relationship is to the other, the unknown, to God or gods. She stands at the juncture of the known and the not known; between this world as we know it and another world; between what is and what will be, or has been; between what could be and what should not be; between rationality and the domain of the irrational. She is sage, prophetess, medium, soothsayer, clairvoyant, crystal gazer, sibyl, pythia, fortuneteller, sphinx, witch, sorceress, saint and/or angel. In psychological terms, she bridges consciousness and the deepest levels of the collective unconscious. We touch her realm when we wonder about our dreams, and we come close to her when we note strange coincidences in our everyday lives. Her process is not unlike the universal rise of instinct into consciousness within the history of the human race. In all of nature, it is a like the progression of animal-like sounds emerging into the first human stuttering of language and song.

MEDIAL WOMAN'S task is to communicate her perception to the world. The origin of this perception is non-rational. She knows, but does not know how she knows. Her thought process may often seem so strange that others back away. She perceives a reality that only becomes defined when she is able to deliver it in understandable terms, a task that often overwhelms her. While her perception may be described as merely intuitive, it is somehow even beyond what is commonly described as intuition. It is a particular refinement of an advanced intuitive process.

We might ask, how is it possible to 'know' anything? How do we identify the many ways of learning, perceiving, understanding, in human experience? Science has identified certain phenomena that are perceived 'in utero' which form memories of a sort. How these primal memories are consistent in all of nature was experienced in a dream of a woman who understands herself primarily as among those described as of the MEDIAL WOMAN archetype. Her vivid and lyrical description helps us grasp something of the depth of her perceptions. When questioned about her creative process, this woman (who prefers to remain anonymous) responds in fluid metaphors: Our thanks to her for letting us share it:

> Something separates from its source, and becomes 'the separated,' which carries a sense of what has been left, be it womb or Eden, and what is calling ahead, yet to be consummated. In that juncture of 'knowing' lays the instinctual cry not yet fulfilled by an answering resonance, it's other wavering answer. First comes the instinct, then the essential thread of harmony discerned in the vastness of the void. The harmony is not exact, never exact, yet the sounds come and answer and sometimes blend. A third vehicle of knowing joins the two. We yearn for the harmony of resonance, then the ineffable dance. By the mysterious grace of the third thing, there is a blend, a meeting, and a new entity is formed, a union of both need and nurture. It happens in a flash. I draw it out in order to tell you about it.

As the history of the human race developed, an articulation of this primal joining of instinct, energy, and the mystery of life itself has been recorded and elaborated by endless varieties of religions, scientific studies, archival speculation and artistic creation. With so much diversification, it is possible that whatever the source of this particular essence of life, it can be overlooked, rationalized, lost, or 'claimed' by a confusion of shortsighted self-proclaimed visionaries and simplistic explanations. But there still remains a powerful current in the mystery of 'knowing,' which seems to be grasped, and sometimes brilliantly illuminated, by the MEDIAL WOMAN bridge that connects what is rational and what is also perceived non-rationally.

Unlike the other types, the ego structure of the MEDIAL WOMAN is more like a wicker basket than a bowl. The things that fall through the spaces in consciousness are her business, her treasures to be picked up and given a voice. She is apt to seem foolish, or say the wrong thing. She may bring an unwelcome presence to a tight-knit group. She is Cassandra, hearing her own special inner voice, and at the same time cursed by the automatic disbelief of those who hear this voice through her lips. Along with her particular gifts are her great vulnerabilities. For example, she may become psychologically inflated so that the more she believes her intuition is infallible, the less accurate her intuition becomes.

The MEDIAL WOMAN is connected to, and works with, the collective unconscious where archetypal notions keep her operating at a powerful level of abstraction. For example, the professional psychic is able, at times, to find a pipeline through ritual or questioning, and receive information that seems to have an uncanny sense of rightness to the person receiving it through her particular MEDIAL portal. Often, the MEDIAL WOMAN psychic does not even have a memory of what she has said to her client. She 'channels' the information. Her images and perceptions become completely impersonal to her, and their applicability to the client lies primarily within the client's interpretation.

The requirement for hearing the small inner voice that the MEDIAL WOMAN cultivates is, according to Jung, a sacrifice.[202] The ego sacrifices a customary sense of jurisdiction and entitlement, in order to hear this voice. There is a certain relinquishment of everyday rational control. Thus, her awareness of the daily world in which others live is apt to be diffused and sometimes fragmented. This timeless archetype, however, remains always present among us, and within each of us to some extent.

Most MEDIAL WOMEN experience energies and frequencies (auditory, visual, olfactory, or tactile) that others do not perceive. However, as with all the types, these experiences are within the range of possibility for all. At some time within most women's lives, aspects of the MEDIAL WOMAN will show up. She may attend to them, let them go, or shove them with determination out of awareness. Sometimes those special nudges are life enhancing, and should she learn to attend to them, she may also learn how to act upon them creatively, and even use them in her work. (For example, as in working internally with her own dreams, or externally by recognizing these experiences as possibly applicable for her professional interests.)

## Two Categories Of MEDIAL WOMAN

Although there are many different styles of MEDIAL WOMAN there is one distinct way in which she relates to the world of 'the other,' which

---

202 C.G. Jung, "Symbols of Transformation: 2. The Sacrifice", CW 5 ¶ 669.

produces a general categorization, that of two distinct types: The Type A MEDIAL WOMAN has a clearly defined ethereal 'other,' a personalized spirit guide, god, or goddess. This entity is familiar and established in her culture, and can be generally accepted as a 'true,' or recognizable force for the benefit of all, such as Jesus, the Virgin Mary, or whatever manifestation of the divine is prevalent in her milieu. Hildegard of Bingen and Teresa of Avila were of this genre. These women both had a strong sense of mission to their divine source. They were known to receive visions and voices in a manner that brought strength and inspiration to their particular order or discipline. Such experiences may be so compelling for the Type A MEDIAL WOMAN that others attend to her necessities of life, and protect her by the disciplines associated with communal life.

Type B MEDIAL WOMAN, on the other hand, may relate to ethereal forces which the dominant collective opinion may not recognize or grant legitimacy, or may even believe to be contrary to the general well-being or good health of the culture. The container for her visionary messages is less specific than Type A. She may focus on an object such as a candle, a crystal ball, herbal essences, tea leaves, cards, runes or astrological charts. In ancient times, animal entrails were 'read' for prognostication and augury. She generally needs such a recognizable, tangible craft, which serves as her own portal of connection with another world.

While the source of inspiration for both A and B MEDIAL WOMEN may be entirely different in context, they both bear in common a distinctly spiritual nature and a primary concern for, and preoccupation with, the phenomena associated with the collective unconscious.

Early Greek mythological tales brought to life the mysterious and feared abilities of Medea, a woman of magical gifts and of drastic temperament. Another was the female monster gorgon Medusa, part woman and part serpent, so fearful that to behold her countenance could 'turn fierce warriors to stone'. In contrast, from another culture, the centuries-old Kuan Yin of China is a benefactress to all, and generously bestows her compassion to the human race.

## Two Early MEDIAL WOMEN

1.Maria Prophetessa

This extraordinary woman from medieval Egypt was known through-out the early centuries of the Common Era as a prophetess, an alche-mist, an inventor, a philosopher, a neo-Platonist, and a healer. She has been associated with prophetic literature all the way back to Moses, and was called 'Miriam, the sister of Moses' by the noted alchemist Zosimus of Panopolis, writing in the third century A.D. Miriam is described in the book of Exodus as a prophetess who led the women in celebrations of singing and dancing for the glory of God. Of course the era of Moses is several hundred years before the Maria Prophetessa of early New Tes-tament times; she has also been called 'Maria the Copt,' a name used to identify early Christian converts in Egypt, and 'Maria Cleopha,' which associates her with the ancient time of Cleopatra. In addition, she has been claimed by some to be no less than the enigmatic Mary Magdalene of New Testament times. All of these correlations span a period of near-ly 2,000 years, and naturally do not embrace any one particular 'Maria.' The quantity of recorded fragments relating to someone called Maria Prophetessa, however, reliably validates the existence of a particular woman living in the first century, in and around Alexandria who was of Jewish origin. While none of her writings have survived, there are some elements of history bearing her name that have been confirmed in various ancient manuscripts. Among her accomplishments were her startling reputation as a healer, her work regarding the elements of na-ture, and many inventions that still carry her name. She studied the seasonal cycles of water on the planet, the relevance of moisture in the air from rain, and the daily rhythm of dew, so essential to human health and plant life. She taught that planting should be carried out in the seasons of Aries and Taurus, which is still observed today. She also taught that all creations of nature contained a life force, and were com-posed of body, spirit and soul. This teaching parallels the Quintessence theory of Aristotle, who taught that all matter is formed by air, rain, heat and fire, plus ether, (the circular movement of heavenly bodies.) It was Alexander the Great who originally brought Aristotle's insights and learning from Greece to Egypt, circa 270 B.C.

The inventions of Maria Prophetessa had principally to do with wa-ter, and how to use it different ways. She invented the double boiler, the manner in which certain foods can best be prepared without scorching, called bain-marie, or water baths. Cooks in the west still prepare their custards in this manner.

Her greatest manifestos in the ancient study of alchemy are known as 'The Axioms of Maria Prophetessa:'

1. <u>The truth is, that what is above is like what is below, and what is below is like what is above, to accomplish miracles of the one thing.</u> (Thus, the order of truth in the natural world is comparable to the order of truth in the supernatural world.)

2. <u>Out of three comes the one that is the fourth.</u>[203] (This illustrates a distinctly new entity; the alchemical combining interaction of three entities produces a fourth entity, a process of purification believed to lead ultimately to gold. This axiom was also applied in later alchemy studies to the purification of the human spirit to divine perfection.)

Her axioms were often quoted by Jung.[204]

Maria Prophetessa was an accomplished practical alchemist, who invented several devices that are still in use today. Her remarkable sense of the components of primitive chemistry indicate a sensitive, intuitive imagination, and her devout study of nature has led to her place in history as one of the earliest recorded female healers.

## 2. Rabi'a al-Adawiyya of Basra

Some seven hundred years after Maria Prophetessa spoke of the laws of nature and the miracles of healing to early Christians, another MEDIAL WOMAN was known and admired in a nearby land whose religion also sprang from the ancient Abrahamic tradition, but who followed the path of her beloved Allah. Rabi'a al-Adawiyya, (712–801 A.D.) an ascetic who lived a life devoted to prayer and contemplation, grew up in the Sufi tradition of absolute surrender to Allah. Her contemplative life led her to become one of the most powerful spiritual voices of her time, and multitudes sought her out to ask for her prayers and receive her blessing.

Like Maria Prophetessa, there is no first-hand recorded history of Rabi'a written during her lifetime. Her first biographer, the poet Farid al-Din'Attar (d. 1230) collected tales of her life some four hundred years

203 *Cambridge Dictionary of Philosophy* (New York: Audi, 1999), 18.
204 C.G. Jung, "The Father In The Destiny Of The Individual" CW 4, ¶ 743n.

after her death. In so doing, the separation of factual data from mythic tales cannot be established, but that the tales of her life and death have been retained and retold again and again is ample proof of her superior saintly status in her time. Since then, many translations from several languages have tried to capture the essence of this woman who so deeply affected the lives of those around her.

At the time Rabi'a lived, the city of Basra was a cosmopolitan enclave, with commerce from both the Persian Gulf and extensive overland trade routes that connected the city to all directions in the Middle East. It was also a lively center of culture and Islamic religious and intellectual thought.

The famous ascetic saint Hasan Basri lived there, and died in the year 728, perhaps even before Rabi'a was born. But by then, the ascetic contemplative way of life among the followers of Allah was well established as the path to spiritual enlightenment and wisdom.

The various tales associated with Rabi'a's life tell of the fourth child born into a poor family of devoted Sufis. It is believed that after Rabi'a's parents died, she was sold into slavery and trained as a musician to earn money for her owner. She sang, danced and played the flute. It is possible that she performed as an indentured HETAIRA. But she despaired of her life, and began spending her nights in intense prayer and meditation.

The tale of how she gained her freedom also carries the medial note of a miraculous intervention:

> One night, her owner happened to be awake, and overheard the earnest young woman at prayer, bemoaning her servitude, and asking Allah to help her. He was amazed to see, above her head, a lamp of brilliant light suspended in mid-air. Her owner recognized the light as that of the divine illumination known as 'Sakina.' He called her to him the next day, and asked her what she needed to do. She replied that she wished to follow a life of prayer, and he immediately gave her complete freedom to do so.[205]

> Rabi'a chose a difficult path of austere devotion, poverty and self-denial. Farid al-Din 'Attar wrote of her, as one on fire with love and longing, who was accepted as a second and spotless Mary. As an ascetic, she prayed all through the

205 Camille Adams Helminski, *Women of Sufism* (Boston: Shambhala, 2003), 25.

night, slept briefly before dawn, and wakened to rise again
'as dawn tinged the sky with gold.'[206]


She denied herself even the simplest comforts of life. At an old age
she was said to have owned only a reed mat, a broken pottery jug, a bed
of felt that doubled as her prayer rug, and a brick for a pillow. She went
straight to God without a guide for her teaching, and was one of the
first to teach that love alone was the guide on the mystic path. She felt
no reverence even for the House of God in Mecca:


It is the Lord of the house whom I need; what have I to do with the
house?

She thought of any sort of self-interest as unworthy. Her most famous prayers exemplifies this goal:

> Oh my Lord, if I worship Thee from fear of Hell, burn me
> in Hell. And if I worship Thee in hope of Paradise, exclude
> me from Paradise. But if I worship Thee for Thine own sake,
> then withhold not from me Thine Eternal Beauty.

Rabi'a's often-repeated words of wisdom are beloved by Sufis everywhere:

> You call yourself a teacher: Therefore learn.

*

> How long will you keep pounding on a open door, begging
> someone to open it?

*

> Where a part of you goes, the rest will follow. Given
> time.[207]

---

206 Mme. Widad El Sakkakini, *First Among Sufis: The Life and Thought of Rabia
   al-Adawiyya* (New York: Oxford University Press, 1978).
207 Kathleen Jenks, "Rabi'a al-'Adawiyya, an Eighth Century Saint From Iraq"
   (Santa Barbara: Pacifica Graduate Institute, January 2003).

Centuries later, MEDIAL WOMEN who were themselves cloistered or part of cloistered communities such as Hildegard of Bingen, and still later St. Teresa of Avila, have described in detail their personal meditations that tell us of their connection to the presence of God, and allowed them to glimpse and describe a divine realm in an unforgettable manner, not unlike that of Rabi'a al-Adawiyya.[208]

## Two Twentieth Century MEDIAL WOMEN

## Book and Film Study

## 1. Clara Trueba, in *The House of the Spirits,* Part 1

By Isabel Allende[209]

> Women with particularly strong medial practices seem to be common throughout the contemporary fiction of South America. The time is early in the century. In the film version of this popular book, Clara's daughter Blanca narrates the story of Clara's life as if reading sections of her mother's diary and recalling segments of their relationship, which was very tender and moving.
>
> Clara was a very unusual child. As a little girl, she was given to practicing telekinesis, and telling the fortunes of household employees to amuse herself. At one point she interpreted a dream of the Gardener, and told him to bet on a certain horse the next day. Whereupon, the Gardener found himself to be a wealthy man. Little Clara's fame as a psychic grew in the city, where her father was a wealthy landowner with political aspirations. At the age of eight years, Clara meets Esteban, who is very interested in courting her beautiful older sister Rosa. He is a young man of a formerly distinguished family, which had previously fallen into financial ruin. But Esteban is a man whose ambition is to reestablish the family holdings, and win Rosa's hand. Clara announces, innocently, that one day she herself will marry him. He secures the promise of Rosa and her family that he may make plans to marry Rosa if he works very hard. He manages to buy a forsaken old mine some distance from the city that he believes he can restore to productivity. The two promise their troth to one another, and Esteban leaves for the

---

208 Jenks, www.mythinglinks.org/NearEast~3monotheisms~Islam~Rabia.html
209 *The House of the Spirits.* 1993. See Film Index.

mine in high hope and firm resolve. Some time later, Clara has a frightening premonition that 'someone from our family will die, not by natural means.' Later, at a political celebration for father's success in running for public office, the innocent Rosa drinks the ceremonial first draft of a mysteriously be-ribboned gift bottle of poisoned brandy intended for her father. She becomes violently ill, and dies. Clara, thinking that since she predicted her sister's death, she must have caused it, decides she will not speak again. Clara becomes mute.

When Esteban hears the news of Rosa's death he is grief stricken, and races from the mines to mourn the loss of his fiancée at her funeral. Mute little Clara stands beside him, and holds his hand. He returns bitterly to the mine with only his lonely and tedious work to command his attention. Finally he sells the mine at a profit, and goes back to his distant and neglected family plantation to restore its vitality.

After Clara's brothers and sisters leave home, Clara remains with her parents, cared for mainly by the family nurse, Nana, and educated by tutors. She carries around a little slate on which she writes what she needs to communicate with others. The delicately beautiful and somehow ethereal young woman is waited on and tenderly nurtured by an indulgent cadre of family members and retainers.

Several years pass. Esteban, now a wealthy man, returns to the city. He is also miserably lonely. He remembers Clara, and goes to the family mansion once again. Upon seeing Esteban, Clara's silence is broken. She simply opens her mouth and asks Esteban if he has come to marry her. An elaborate wedding is held. After a four-month's honeymoon, Esteban transports his bride on the long trip to his restored and flourishing plantation.

Clara's interest in occult phenomena matures. She gives birth to Blanca and later twin boys. The family also establishes a gracious home back in the capital city where they both grew up. There is a gathering storm of revolution threatening the country. Amid all this, Clara's MEDIAL WOMAN interests develop as well, complete with her small table, three-legged stool, and her trance-like meditation.

Clara's life story illustrates a sensitive fictionalized version of a MEDIAL WOMAN'S relationships with her children, her husband, and her spiritualist friends.

(Further stories of Clara Trueba appear in Chapter 26)

## 2. Cynthia Killion - Psychic Reader

A young practicing professional psychic, Cynthia Killion, was just 28 years old in the year 2000. She was doing psychic readings for a call-in audience on a monthly cable television program called Psychic Live, telecast via a public access station in Kansas, and web-streamed via the internet. She agreed to relate some of her experience as a contemporary MEDIAL WOMAN who struggles to validate her own journey, and who faces difficult odds as she attempts to explain herself and her work to the world.

## Telephone Interview: Sikes, Molton and Cynthia Killion

1. Early Years and Preparation

Lucy Sikes: I would like to ask you about your childhood. Did you go to public or private school?

Cynthia Killion: Public school.

LS: Did you have 'trances?' Did the teachers find you distracted, some-times?

CK: I don't remember in class having a trance. I do remember having the experience of being out in the playground and seeing something happen, and watching it, and knowing exactly what was going to happen next. When I was in first grade I had a lot of difficulty in school. I nearly flunked kindergarten. I went to a certain school where the teacher thought I was disabled. I was really having a problem 'getting it.' Then I changed schools, and another teacher identified me as a 'gifted child,' and from that point on I did very well. Or so she said.

LS: Do you have brothers and sisters?

CK: Yes, I have. Actually, I have a lot of brothers and sisters, because my father was quite prolific. I don't know all of them. The ones I have that I would consider my brother and sister are Max and Debbie.

LS: Did they key in with you, when you were having these prophetic thoughts?

CK: Well not really. My brother is ten years older, and my sister almost sixteen years older. One of my first visions happened when I was outdoors with him. I was maybe six years old. He was setting up traps, like rope traps for deer, and I had wandered off. There was a field near the woods where a farmer had wheat. That's where I had my vision of the white buffalo, which is the first vision I can really remember in great detail. And that was with my brother. But I remember telling my family about it. Understandably, they just thought I was fantasizing.

Mary Dian: Cynthia, I want to go back to the white buffalo. You mentioned it at one time I heard you speak, that the image of the white buffalo merged with you. What does that mean? Can you explain?

CK: Well, first it wasn't just the image. I saw the white buffalo as surely as I can see the lamp in this room. It wasn't just an image in my mind. I saw this as a spirit, as a living entity. I felt that entity move into my body and into my soul, and become one with me, on a physical level. And that is the best way I can explain it.

MD: How far was it from you?

CK: Well, it wasn't far. It was in the sky at first when I saw it. But then it came, it just came forward. It was coming very fast. It was rushing. Rushing. It came down and moved through. And it was very large too. I know that as I'm sitting here. I can still experience it as if it were yesterday. But it seems odd to me that it would have merged with me because I would have been a small child. But the image, if you want to call it that, was very large. He went right through me. Like a wind, or something.

MD: Was it frightening?

CK: No, it was ecstatic.

MD: Cynthia, Have you talked to people who have given you any interpretation of that experience?

CK: Some people have offered, but I think I have to ultimately have my own. There are myths and legends about the white buffalo and I know from those legends that the white buffalo symbolizes a teacher or a prophet, so maybe that's part of it. But I just knew, something inside me knew, that I had a calling, when that happened.

LS: Did you seem to be communicating with it as it merged with you?

CK: Absolutely.

LS: How did your mother react to this when you told her?

CK: Well, I told her I had seen a white buffalo. I didn't have the language to say I'd merged with it. They just thought, I don't know, that I'd heard a story or something on TV or they just trivialized it again, which wasn't altogether bad because at least they didn't forbid it. My mother had left my father, so I didn't know him, growing up. So it would have been her, and my sister, who would have been a young adult then.

LS: Did you ever try to reconnect with the white buffalo?

CK: No, I just kept that inside me. And I knew it was for me. Not necessarily to share with other people, just for me. It was a knowing.

LS: Was your mother in any religion?

CK: I understand that she had been, before I was born. She left my father, and that was a good thing. She had been involved in a fundamentalist religion, and had actually been a very religious woman, but she became quite bitter about the church because they kept telling her to take my father back, and he was abusive. She pretty much turned away. (Later) I don't know if I have told you this, but I'm actually trained in Wicca, in white witchcraft. When I was thirteen I got involved in that and studied with a man. I was actually interviewed in the paper about that when I was sixteen. The interviewer asked my mom what she thought of it. My mom said that it was just a phase I was going through. So that was her attitude. Actually, that helped a lot, because she didn't crack down on it. She was not repressive.

LS: How did you get connected with Wicca?

CK: I had a friend who was older than I. She was sixteen, and she had a boyfriend older than she was. So I met his roommate who was involved in Wicca and nature religion. He later invited me to be his student.

LS: Did you go through the different levels of Wicca?

CK: Well, yes. I actually did all three. I'm a Capricorn, so I'm an over-achiever. But I'm not practicing Wicca now, and I think it's important, if you are writing my story, to understand that I'm not against it, but now I like to combine all of the things that I've been exposed to. I studied the runes for a long time, and many things that would enhance my ability. And then came astrology, and what happened to me when I was twenty-one.

(Killion's story is continued in subsequent chapters)


Cynthia Killion's vision brings to mind the Blackfoot Indian story, often respectfully retold by Joseph Campbell, world renowned master in the field of cultural mythology. It tells the tale of how a girl who knew the rituals of life became the Buffalo Woman Healer.

## Legend: "Chief's Daughter and Buffalo" (re-told)[210]

The Blackfoot tribe was dependent on the buffalo for their food, and so they were great buffalo hunters. They herded the animals to the edge of a cliff, and drove them over, so many were killed at a time. But after a while, the buffalo learned their lesson, and would veer off and escape their intended end. And so there was a fear among the people that the coming winter would mean starvation for the tribe. Chief's Daughter worried about this, as everyone did. One morning she was walking along, thinking about the situation.

'If only you, buffalo, would just fall off the cliff, I would marry one of you,' she cried. Sure enough, one did.

The buffalo walked right up to her and said, 'Very well. You will be my wife.' Chief's Daughter protested, but the buffalo said, 'A promise is a promise. My people have already given themselves, so now you have to follow through. You are my bride.'

That morning Chief realized his daughter was gone. So he found a magpie, which is a magic bird, and asked if he had seen his daughter.

'Oh, yes,' replied the magpie. 'She went off with a buffalo who has taken her for his bride.'

Chief said, 'Well, you could take her a message. Tell her that her father is looking for her.'

---

210 Joseph Campbell with Bill Moyers, *The Power of Myth* (New York: Doubleday, 1988), 75-76, paraphrased.

So Magpie found Chief's Daughter and when she was a little apart from the buffalo he whispered, 'Your father is coming to get you.'

'Oh no,' said Daughter. 'If he does, we will both be killed. No, tell him to wait. I will think of a plan.'

About this time, Buffalo Husband called to his wife, 'Here, come and bring me some water.' Pop! He took off one of his horns and she went to the spring to fill it with water for him to drink. Chief's Daughter acted the part of dutiful wife. Her father met her there and they talked. She told him to wait a while, and took the horn back to Buffalo Husband. But Buffalo Husband's nostrils suddenly flared, so that the blood filled his nose and he snorted and pawed. 'I smell something. I smell a man.' and he and the rest of the buffalo found the girl's father, sniffed him, stomped and gored him until he was surely dead, and trampled him so that there was nothing left even to bury. But the girl cried and cried and Buffalo Husband took pity on her and decided to give her a chance. 'If you can bring your father back to life, I will let him live.'

So Chief's Daughter called Magpie. 'Help, please help. Please find a tiny piece of my father so that I can perform the reconstruction ritual.' Pretty soon Magpie had dug enough to come up with a little bone. 'Here, this is just a bit,' he said. 'It's enough,' Chief's Daughter said, and took the bone, which was a vertebra, and put it under a blanket. Then she did the ritual dances. After a while she looked under the blanket, and saw that her father had come back most of the way, but he was still not finished. So she covered him again and danced more, and then he came back entirely and he stood before her and the buffalo. 'All right,' Buffalo Husband said, 'If you can do that, will you do the same for us?'

After that, there were always buffalo dances to honor the creatures that had given their lives, so that the people might live again.

Chief's Daughter performed the ceremony of restoration. She knew exactly what to do to restore the Chief to his tribe. To know, or invent, life-restoring rituals is a MEDIAL quality. They abound in Native American lore, and give honor to the cooperative co-existence of humans with the world of nature. To 'marry' the buffalo could mean to understand and honor what the wild buffalo spirit represents.

# Chapter 23

## Familiar Qualities of The MEDIAL WOMAN

In Toni Wolff's words:

- "'Medium' means: in between, neither this nor that, something intermediate."

- "The lucidity of consciousness rests upon dark unconscious seeds out of which will grow objective cultural values. It is this unconscious background that is perceived by MEDIAL WOMAN's structural form."

(Paraphrases): (She) is immersed in the psychic atmosphere all around, and the spirit of her era, but particularly in the collective (impersonal) unconscious. She identifies herself with archetypal contents as opposed to personal contents. If MEDIAL WOMAN works to differentiate the underlying unconscious values of the times without seeing herself as personally involved or represented, she can exert a helpful cultural contribution.[211]

## 2. Hildegard of Bingen

This outstanding woman of twelfth century Germany was an ecstatic visionary, writer, musician and Abbess who made a strong impact on the spiritual leadership of her time, as well as directly influencing the politics of the Holy See in Rome. While we know of her work in several impressive fields of leadership and creativity, it is in the detailed records of her visions and her music that her MEDIAL qualities are most conspicuous, and have provided a renewed source of inspiration for women of our time. She kept careful records of her visions by seeing to it that a capable scribe, the monk Volmar, set down her recollections for posterity. In her book *Scivias*, (her record of the visitations she experienced and interpreted from a very early age) there is an unmistakable

---

211 Wolff, "Structural Forms," 9-10.

sense that she knew the presence of the divine, and she recognized the importance of letting this be known to the world. Her powerful MEDI-AL voice comes through even in translation, as she instructs her readers how they should respond to what she says. She displays a remarkable sense of entitlement.

Like many visionaries in history, she also suffered what are now called migraine headaches. In the light of modern medicine, ecstatic visions followed by severe headaches are both characteristic symptoms of the migraine syndrome. Even as such, Hildegard's records of those experiences drew an enduring picture of what a cloistered life of medi-tation and prayer may yield to the gifted imagination. What is truly important about her visions is that she objectified and recorded them.

Fiona Maddocks in her work *Hildegard of Bingen* describes her life.[212] In the year 1114, when Hildegard was not yet twenty, she wrote a let-ter to the most important clergyman of her time, Bernard of Clairvaux, about her anxiety regarding her visionary experiences:

> Reverend Father Bernard, I beg you, Father, through the living God, to listen to me as I question you. I am greatly troubled by this vision, which has appeared to me through the inspiration of divine mystery. I have never seen it through the outer eyes of the flesh. I have seen, ever since I was a child... . Make it clear to me, if you will, through this exchange, whether I should say these things in the open or maintain my silence.[213]

Hildegard did indeed say these things 'in the open'. Maddocks tells of the woman's fame by the time she reached the age of fifty, referenc-ing Hildegard's account of her work, spoken to her scribe, in the manu-script "Vita":

> Crowds of people of both sexes come flocking to her, not only from the locality but also 'from every part of threefold Gaul and Germany.' Her celebrated powers of prophesy en-abled her to divine the inner minds and consciences of those who visited her.[214]

> Hildegard of Bingen is known for her ecstatic visions, her prophecies, her music, and her leadership. She provides an

---

212 Maddocks, *Hildegard of Bingen* (New York: Random House, 2001), 75-89.
213 Maddocks, *Hildegard of Bingen,* 75-89.
214 Maddocks, *Hildegard of Bingen,* 75-89.

excellent example of the Type A MEDIAL WOMAN, firmly
established in the institutional church of her time from
the age of eight years, and nurtured by her order. She also
became a noted musician and composer, as well as a strong
leader. While many efforts in her behalf were made after
her death to have her canonization completed, this was
never accomplished. Still, today she is venerated in Germany, and held in the highest regard world wide, with frequent festivals given in her honor. Canonization is a complex issue, and even today remains difficult to understand.
Hildegard's reliquary has survived, however, and remains
at Ebingen.[215]

Characteristic of the Type B MEDIAL WOMAN is that she works without an anchor in a religious institutional tradition. Different aspects of
the MEDIAL WOMAN, and her unusual abilities, are certainly familiar
in our contemporary culture outside the aura of church history. These
aspects are even often presented to the public in light-hearted commercial comedic style, such as television's popular past and present series *Bewitched, I Dream of Jeannie, Buffy The Vampire Slayer,* etc. Perhaps
aspects of the MEDIAL messages are easier for an audience to manage
through comedy because of the uneasiness some feel about the experiences involved.

It is our job to present as many aspects of the MEDIAL WOMAN as we
can, and continue here by sharing another segment of Cynthia Killion's
life and work as will occur throughout this section.

### Interview: Cynthia Killion 2. *A Sense of Radical Truth*

MD: On your Psychic Live TV program, you were talking to a woman and you thought there was a possibility of a change in her
health in August, either that she would get much better, or that
she might be preparing to die. You said you had to speak 'radical truth' at that time. What does that mean?

CK: To me, that's just a phrase I use when I speak of something that is
true, and not just in the literal sense. In fact, it's not even true in
the literal sense. It is more about the deep symbolic truths that

215 Maddocks, *Hildegard of Bingen,* 75-89.

simply by hearing those words, we're moved by them. That's what 'radical truth' is. When you hear it, or see it, it changes you. And that's ultimately what I look at as part of what I do. It's not just to report information but also that which will move people at their deepest levels to make the changes they need to make. When I speak 'radical truth' that's what a person needs to hear in that moment to move from a place of inaction, from a place of stifled-ness, to the point of change.[216]

MD: Cynthia, you have mentioned Mary Baker Eddy, and some connection to your family.

CK: My mother was an Eddy. They've traced her lineage back, and her family comes from around the same area as Mary Baker Eddy, in Massachusetts and the Boston area. That connection has become very important to me recently. In my spiritual path, I've been studying Divine Science, and she was the founder of Christian Science, as you probably know. Most of the new thought movements basically come out of her teachings. So it has been liberating for me, to draw upon her. I consider her to be a mystic too, and maybe even a psychic. You might not use that word necessarily, but her ideas had to come from 'that place within.' They were radical, and far ahead of her time. So it's a nice lineage to be able to draw upon.

(Killion's story continues throughout this MEDIAL WOMAN section)

## Carl Jung and MEDIAL WOMAN

Jung wrote extensively about women mediums. His mother's side of the family had strong MEDIAL histories, and his own mother Emilie exhibited some distinctly MEDIAL qualities. (See Chapter 5.) He considered the work of people devoted to Spiritualism as comparable in some respects to the discovery of the dynamics of the unconscious in psychology, because both fields deal with psychological facts. Even spirits appear to be psychic phenomena whose origins lie in the unconscious, (and are) shadowy personifications of unconscious contents.

He wrote:

---

216 'Radical Truth' in this interview may be related to the book by Brad Blanton, *Radical Honesty*, National Book Network (Irvine, CA: Entrepreneur Press, 1998.)

> Those who are convinced of the reality of spirits should
> know that this is a subjective opinion that can be attacked
> on any number of grounds. Those who are not convinced
> should beware of naively assuming that the whole of spir-
> its and ghosts has been settled and that all manifestations
> of this kind are meaningless swindles.[217]

Presenting such dramatically diverse women as examples of Medial-
ity as Hildegard of Bingen and Cynthia Killion reinforces Toni Wolff's
description of the MEDIAL WOMAN, restated at this point: *The ME-
DIAL WOMAN focuses her ego awareness primarily upon phenomena associated with the collective unconscious.* (See Chapter 1, Overview)

Jung does discriminate very carefully, however, between characteristics of the psychological factors of projection, and the characteristics of
a more mechanistic rationale of spirits presented by spiritualism. This
MEDIAL WOMAN'S characteristic awareness repeats itself over and over
in our study of this type.


## Ravenna

There is a curious story which has only been partially explored in print,
that tells the incident of a trip which Jung undertook to Ravenna in
1933 with a 'friend,' (later confirmed by the well-known analyst, Esther
Harding), to have been Toni. In this story, there is a semblance once
again of a MEDIAL quality in Toni Wolff.

During this visit to the famous shrine of Galla Placidia in Ravenna,
both Jung and Toni Wolff simultaneously experienced seeing a set of
beautiful mosaic images, which they distinctly remembered, and which
later proved to be non-existent. The historic records proved that these
mosaics had been destroyed in a fire hundreds of years before their trip.
Jung considered this experience to have been "among the most curious
events of my life. It can scarcely be explained."[218]

Something, perhaps, of the nature of their ability to inhabit the
timeless realms of myth together, suggests that the quality of their relationship at times held some moments of an inponderable reality outside of our everyday experience.

---

217 C.G. Jung, 1950-1980, "Psychology and Spiritualism," CW 18, ¶755.
218 C.G. Jung, *Memories, Dreams, Reflections*, 285.

# Chapter 24

## Less Familiar (Shadow) Possibilities Of
## The MEDIAL WOMAN

Toni Wolff says:

- "The MEDIAL WOMAN is overcome by the effect (of the collective, or impersonal, unconscious,)... and is absorbed and molded by it. She must, for instance, express what is in the air, what the environment cannot or will not admit."

- "To deal with the collective unconscious demands a solid ego consciousness and an adequate adaptation to reality. As a rule, the MEDIAL WOMAN has neither and consequently she can create confusion."[219]

(Paraphrases): It is mostly the dark aspect of a situation or idea that she catches, and she can spread what is dangerous and negative. Her ego is overcome by the power of the collective unconscious that sweeps through her, because she does not differentiate the impersonal from the personal, I from you, conscious from unconscious. She may take some things personally that do not belong to her, and experience something of a destiny that is not hers as if it were her own.

Because objective and psychic contents in herself and others are not understood, or are taken personally, she experiences a destiny not her own as though it were her own, and loses herself in ideas which do not belong to her.

Instead of being a mediatrix, she is only a means and (may) become a victim of her own nature.

Many dangerous and 'wicked' MEDIALS have found a place in literature and history. As children, most of us were told of fairy tale witches

---

219 Wolff, "Structural Forms," 9-10.

stealing children, the jealous magical maneuvers of Morgan La Fay, and Oz's Wicked Witch of the West. Shakespeare gave us the three memorable witches out on the Scottish heath boiling the bubbles of trouble. Mythology tells of Medea's spells that could rescue her lovers and wipe out all enemies. So the dark side of MEDIAL WOMAN is probably somewhat better known than that of the other three types. Since she is so popular, what is it that makes her so evil? It may be our own longing for power when we are feeling powerless. She most certainly serves as a powerful magnet for all the dark shadow projections of our culture.

There is another distinct shadow piece of the MEDIAL WOMAN, and that is her historic connection with what used to be called hysteria, studied early by Freud and others. The term describes the phenomena associated particularly with the medium, the prophetess and the channeler, characterized by her assimilation and production of voices and personalities other than her own. The object of her behavior may be to gain attention in a theatrical manner, now clinically referred to as histrionic personality disorder. However, her motives for such performances may be entirely unconscious. Clinical studies of this pathology by no means describe the broader scope of activity that identifies the MEDIAL WOMAN archetype, any more than Old Mother Hubbard characterizes every MOTHER.

## Three Films for Study:

### 1. *Moonlight and Valentino* [220]

This film presents a variety of women, among them Sylvie (Whoopi Goldberg), who has some of the unfocused MEDIAL qualities that end up working against her best interests. Caught up in her own world, she can't sort out what belongs to her and what to others. Everything flows in. Sylvie tells fortunes, reads Tarot to amuse her friends, makes pottery, and 'senses the love in her neighbor's lives,' but has difficulty sensing the genuine love that her own husband has for her. She has trouble telling him that she loves him. Out of her unconscious fears of abandonment, she has a feeling that her marriage is over and that her husband has left her. Frantically she calls her best friend and neighbor Rebecca (Elizabeth Perkins) with an urgent plea that she must come to

---

220 *Moonlight and Valentino*. 1995. See Film Index.

her house immediately. Upon Rebecca's arrival, a weeping and nearly hysterical Sylvie sobs, "Paul is gone. He took his clothes and left me!"

Not entirely distracted by Sylvie's weeping, Rebecca sees a note on the floor. After reading it, she says slowly, 'Yes, he left you.'

Sylvie moans, 'I told you so. I knew this was going to happen…'

Rebecca replies, 'Here's the note.' She reads: 'I've gone to the gym. I'll be back soon. I hope you're feeling better. I love you. – Paul.'

*

This part of the film illustrates the 'background interference' with which MEDIAL WOMAN is, or should be, familiar. So much flows through her head that she just substitutes one scenario, *which she unconsciously needs to live through,* in order to examine her own issues, for the truth of the real situation. Her own ancient anxiety produces one catastrophe after another. In time, Sylvie learns an important truth that changes things. She realizes that it is not Paul who keeps turning away, but she herself.

*

In this feature film, a well-to-do African American Bayou family presents contrasting elements of wealth, education and superstition.

### 2. *Eve's Bayou*[221]

Father, Louis Batiste (Samuel Jackson) is a handsome and successful African American physician in 1962 Louisiana. Aunt Mozelle (Debbi Morgan), Father's sister, is a seer of sorts who practices as a 'psychic consultant,' among neighbors and friends. She ministers in a helpful, personal manner when people come to her for consultations, yet her own awareness and fascination with the occult is dangerously close to the darker side of voodoo.

Roz (Lynn Whitfield), wife and mother, is beautiful and 'perfect.' She remains aloof from the impassioned needs of both her husband, and those of her two daughters. She attempts to control her girls with absurd discipline measures.

The daughters Cisely and Eve bear the family shadows surrounding them all.

---

221 *Eve's Bayou.* 1997. See Film Index.

Father is a philanderer, with many girl friends. He is also especially fond of Cisely, his fourteen-year-old daughter, and courts her rather like he does his other women, in a charming but inappropriately seductive manner. When she responds in a thoroughly innocent but similarly seductive manner mimicking adult behavior, he is horrified, and casts her furiously away from him. She does not know what it is that she has done to warrant her beloved father's rejection. She is thoroughly upset, mystified, and soon falls into near suicidal despair.

The younger sister, Eve (Jurnee Smollett), who is perhaps ten or eleven years old, is frightened by the affliction that Cisely is enduring. She senses a tragic situation and intuitively moves out of the family circle for help. She engages the assistance of 'The White-Faced Woman' (Diahann Carroll), an aged voodoo priestess of color living deep in the Bayou, who 'whitens' her own dark face in a macabre grimace. This woman responds to Eve's story by promising her a magic gris-gris charm, but only if the child brings a great deal of money. Eve scrambles and steals to acquire the sum, returns to the dark swamp, and buys the charm. The priestess's frightening energy is totally impersonal, dangerous, exploitive and self-serving. She is, in effect, the opposite of the naïve but well-meaning Aunt Mozelle.

The denouement is characteristically tragic, and a death occurs. But both young girls somehow survive. Ostensibly, The White-Faced Woman carries on her folk magic as before, exploiting the fears of the community for her own gain.

•

## 3. *The Gift*[222]

Annie, (Cate Blanchett), a young widow, seeks money to support her sons and herself by conducting readings, which she performs for friends and neighbors through the use of a set of symbolic cards. Clients give her offerings for her services.

As the film opens, she is interpreting the cards for a disheveled and frightened young woman, who is saying that her husband, Donnie, will kill her if she leaves him.

---

222 *The Gift.* 2000. See Film Index.

Annie replies that Donnie Barksdale isn't crazy enough, and that he is an insecure redneck. The woman leaves Annie's home, hurriedly.

The school counselor, Wayne, phones Annie, asking her to come in to talk about her oldest son Mack, who is in the school infirmary. He has been in another fight. Annie goes to the school and talks to Wayne, who suggests that Mack is still disturbed over his father's death. Jessica King, Wayne's fiancée, enters the office, and Wayne introduces the women. Annie feels very uneasy about this young woman, and momentarily experiences a sudden frightening vision of her.

Annie drives to a gas station for a necessary car repair, where Buddy (Giovanni Ribisi) tells her not to worry about paying, after all the readings she's done for him.

In the next scene he is test-driving her car with her in the passenger seat.

He tells her, " I felt so good yesterday, I didn't think I needed my medicine." But he suddenly becomes very disturbed. "Tell me now, am I gonna die? If someone told me to kill myself before the sun goes down...?"

Annie soothes and comforts him as best she can. But she seems not to sense how dangerously ill he really is.

She arrives at home after dark, and someone bangs on the door insistently, and yells. Hesitant, Annie unlocks the chain and lets Donnie Barksdale inside, the husband of the woman she has seen earlier in the day. He becomes furious, and starts yelling at her, calling her names. "Con artist! Satan worshiper! The devil's gonna get you burned!" He slams through the house, terrorizes her and the children, and leaves.

The next scene shows Annie at a party held in a bar. In an alcove aside from the guests, Annie sees Jessica, off in a side room. She is having sex with a man other than her fiancé, Wayne.

Later Annie is sitting at a table with Wayne. He asks her, "Did you know that something was going to happen to your husband before he died?" He speaks in a kindly and gentle manner. She replies that the night before his death, she had experienced some disturbing dreams of abandonment...

She leaves the party and picks up the children at a baby sitter's house. At home, she finds the house open, the TV on, a baseball bat in a strange place, and SATAN! Spelled out in red letters, on her bed coverlet. She suspects Donnie; She starts to call the police, but realizes the policeman is Donnie's close friend.

Just then Buddy comes to the door. He is very disturbed, and demands that she read for him. Frightened, she complies." Why am I so sad and angry?" he sobs. She replies, from her visions, "Your Daddy took things away from you when you was a little boy. You was hit with a belt..."

Buddy turns on her, "You're the damned psychic!" Furious, he leaves, overwhelmed by his painful memories.

The word is out that Jessica has been missing for four days. Jessica's father and a policeman scoff at Annie's so-called psychic abilities, and then later ask her to help them find Jessica. She agrees to try, and on the basis of her vision, she takes the police to a large pond on the property, where they find Jessica's body.

Meanwhile Buddy, in a murderous rage, has tied up his invalid father and is pouring gasoline on him. He lights the fire. A very sick man has committed a murder. Buddy is taken into custody.

Annie is now caught in disaster on all sides.

Donnie Barksdale is on trial for murder, but Annie is placed on the witness stand, and her hunch is that someone else is responsible for Jessica's death. She goes at night back to the pond, where Jessica's body was found. Suddenly Wayne appears, and discloses his murderous intent toward her, as he pushes her nearer and nearer to the edge of the dock.

Somehow, she escapes, through what seems to be the intervention of Buddy, who says," You're the soul of the town, Mrs. Wilson." And then he is gone.

Later, as she is describing what happened to the police, she is told that whoever it was that saved her, it could not have been Buddy, because he hanged himself at six o'clock that evening.


Annie, whose predilections were proven to be accurate, was nonetheless hindered by her own fears, her lack of education, and a naive sense that her own 'rightness and goodness' were sufficient to protect her. She exhibits exactly the warnings that Wolff points out: the dangerous limitations of the MEDIAL WOMAN who knows herself least of all.

## Interview: Cynthia Killion 3. Of Shadow and Darkness

MD: Toni Wolff points out some of the recognizable characteristics that MEDIAL WOMAN might have to contend with. One of them is that her ego investment is primarily focused in the phenomena that have to do with the collective unconscious, that vast other world, where there are alternative ways of connection to nature, and of experiencing existence. One of the shadow qualities for the MEDIAL WOMAN would be the tendency to neglect the real world, and its importance. She thinks in impersonal generalizations, rather than personal facts.

CK: Well, I think that's definitely a temptation, when you live so much of your life in that other world. But I feel like I've overcome that by trying to see that what others call reality, I would maybe call just one part of reality. I think that one of the ways that the MEDIAL WOMAN can help herself is by seeing 'reality' as an expression of the spiritual. And that's where I've come in my life, although I haven't always been there. It has been a process of maturation, I guess, beginning to see the physical world as first of all spiritual. But I certainly had a lot of problems, definitely with relationships, growing up, and relationships with men. That was a challenging area for me. I was promiscuous at a young age, just with boundaries. Saying no to people has always been very difficult for me. It's not just that you want to nurture. I think that with a psychic person, sometimes people misunderstand us; they think we're very nurturing, and I really don't think that's the truth. The reason is that we feel each other's feelings as if they were our own, so we begin to think those are our preferences, when in reality they might not be.

MD: To use other people's longings as your own...?

CK: Yes, Yes.

MD: That's it. We've also looked at some MEDIAL WOMEN who live pretty much in seclusion. Perhaps this is because of their introversion, but maybe because they are just easily confused by all this stuff that flows through them. You seem to be a bit more comfortable, and you carry a solid degree of extroversion.

CK. Well, that is by necessity. I have a mission. I mean I was given this mission, and I know it is to take these ideas out into the world. In order to do that, I have to extrovert some, so I've learned. But at heart I am still an introvert. There's a part of me that really loves to do psychic readings, and a part that hates doing the readings. I can't explain that. I do spend a lot of time alone. I get cranky when I don't have it. It's not just that I want it; I need it, because otherwise I go insane. But even when I am alone, I'm never alone because I'm still picking up on vibrations. But at least they're not being so forcefully driven at me.

LS. So your sense of yourself...being different...you feel you need to develop more of a sense of yourself?

CK: Yes, to develop more of an ego. And I am saying that psychic people need to develop the ego, whereas a lot of Eastern spirituality I've studied speaks about dropping the ego. And generally I think that is a good idea for many people in our society, but for the psychic woman, or person, the need is to develop the ego strength.

MD: Well, if we think of the ego as a negative thing, then people deny it. But if it is a positive thing then it helps to support the talents.

CK: Right. And it is true in my case, because otherwise I wouldn't know where I began, and where that other person ended, and vice versa.

MD: Cynthia, outside of the personal shadow work that we have been talking about, there is a huge collective shadow to MEDIAL work. Psychic gifts can be used for dark and manipulative purposes, as we all know. And perhaps you have encountered, in your work, places where you have sensed genuine danger. I made some notes during the Psychic Live television program. At one point, while you were conducting a reading, you said something about shutting off, or shutting down...and saying that 'shutting down' had to do with your going to a different place in your psyche, but that this 'other place' was still a divine place...

CK: Oh, right. And that's the place...I use the term 'inner psyche' in my own writings. But some people might call it 'the higher self,' or 'the still small voice,' or 'that place within.' Really, we have to go to that place even to be able to speak to the spirits. The spirits are here to help us but we need also to access our own divinity. Or what we call the 'inner psychic.' That's the phrase I use. Because I believe everybody has an inner psychic. It is obviously more pronounced in some than others but I believe that psychic abilities are survival instincts that are given to us basically for protection, and also for enlightenment. We've come not to rely on them as much because there are other things we rely on.

MD: I was reading your book last night. You mentioned various planes of awareness. We were amazed with your psychic reading work during the broadcast, how quickly you moved, could traverse, two or three different planes of awareness, moving deeper, going further... Is some of this speed with which you move a sort of way to protect it all, so that you don't become conflicted with other messages that might be coming your way?

CK: You know, that's a good question. I don't really know. I think that the speed part of it is that I'm just trained to do this now. I've done so many readings that it doesn't take me long. I'm never too far from the space where I could do a reading. So I guess, for me, it's an ongoing dialog. I do slip into other states fast, and part of that is, that it protects the integrity of the information. Because it comes very quickly, and I need to be able to move very quickly to get it and bring it to this side. We all live on many planes at once.

LS: When you connect with the person, going 'into their energy,' do you search for anything? Is it the first thing that hits you, like a...a taste, a smell?

CK: The way I really prefer is just to let it come to me. A reading is like surrender, and just letting go into that person's energy for a moment, and just feeling what's going to come up. But in doing the readings, I do let the people ask questions, and go searching for the answer. But I find that what is really important is what is going to come through. Not everybody can let go of control enough to go there. But for me, I really enjoy being in that space for a moment. I can't explain it, but it feels like what I was just born to do.

LS: When you surrender to the other person's energy, I suppose if you figure out that it is dark, intrinsically evil, then you immediately retreat from it?

CK: Well, what I do, and you don't see this on the show, I do the prayer before hand and that protects me. I have this belief based on my experience, that we all have light, and we all have dark in us. And the places where I usually go are some in the dark, but I mostly go into the light so I'm generally not going into dangerous places. That doesn't mean that I won't see some of the darkness, but I'm not going to go deep enough. How can I explain it? I know the prayer for protection helps and that's part of the reason I like to have the spirits with me. It's not just to get information, but that they can actually serve as protectors. For the most part, the place that I go into in the person's energy is not a place that can be dangerous to me. I've done some, not so much on the show, but I've done some pretty scary readings. I've done a reading where I realized in the middle of it that the man was a child molester, or had been. I said, "You're a child molester. You know you molested this person." And he said yes, he was. It wasn't just that I had thought this. The client confirmed me. That was pretty scary, being alone with this person. But, I wasn't harmed. When you go into that place that I talk about, not just in the client's energy, but you are going through the (your) divine self, your own inner psychic. That is a portal, through which you are going into their energy. And if you understand that this is a very safe place for you that tends to bring out the highest in others. I can't exactly explain. You are coming from a place of divinity, so it almost brings up their divinity. But there is some darkness that comes in, and I could chose to get out, that's true. So, everybody has darkness. I guess that is part of the differences you were talking about, Mary Dian, when you talked about how you don't really believe everybody could do this. You know, when I say that everyone can be psychic, I'm not saying that everyone could be a professional psychic. There is a distinction there.

MD: You are also not saying that everybody should do this, are you?

CK: Well, right. One of the things that make me a little bit different from other psychics I've met is that I've learned to be very good with boundaries. And I'm very good at knowing how to protect myself. I know how and when to pull out, and I do. Most of the time, it's not an issue as much as you might think it would be.

MD: There is something rather amazing that at your age of twenty nine years, you have this kind of ability to know how to protect yourself, and that you seem to be so well grounded.

With the MEDIAL WOMAN type, the world watches for three major shadow pieces. One is chicanery, one is the possibility of a serious delusional pathology, and one is evil intent. Any, or all three *may* play a part in the MEDIAL WOMAN shadow. Another important shadow aspect of the MEDIAL WOMAN is best understood by a look at her opposite type. For example, the characteristics of the AMAZON that best typify her are: specificity, goal orientation, and the disciplines of time, money, order, sequence and organization. The AMAZON manages these things easily. In contrast, these characteristics are those that the MEDIAL WOMAN might well find to be extremely difficult, if not impossible to even consider important. She may even decide not to bother herself with them. In that sense and to that degree, something of the world of every day reality is obscured from her field of vision, and may become irrelevant entirely. (See Adjacent and Opposite Type, Chapter 28)

# Chapter 25

## MEDIAL WOMAN and Some Career Thoughts

In Toni Wolff's words:

- "Some earlier times and cultures found her as prophetess, shaman, priestess or ... religious visionary."

- "If she has the faculty of discrimination, [this] can help her exert a positive cultural influence, consecrating herself to the spirit of her age."[223]

  (Paraphrases): In our age we have the medium of [ depth] psychology, of which the unconscious is an essential factor.

  The work of creative actresses, artists and poets reflects the images (of) the collective unconscious in artistic forms and voices.

A multitude of callings for the MEDIAL WOMAN is available in our society at this time, in addition to the ones Wolff listed above. One unmistakable characteristic necessary for all is an intuitive imagination capable of working with images, both literally and metaphorically.

To illustrate some of the professions which a skilled MEDIAL WOMAN can enhance, and for the sake of order, we have gathered them into a few broad categories: Astrology, Fine Arts, Health and Healing, Past Lives, Psychic Reading, Psychology, and Religion.

(Note: The reader will notice that of the four types, this particular section on 'Some Career Thoughts' is much longer than the others. The reason is that the MEDIAL WOMAN, as a bona fide professional, is still relatively uncharted to much of the world).

---

223 Wolff, "Structural Forms," 10-11.

## Astrology

This age-old fascination of human beings for observing the order of the stars and their circuits in the heavens dates from the very dawn of history. It is reflected in every culture throughout the Far East since ancient times, and even among prehistoric tribal lore worldwide. It is told that once an ancient Chinese astrologer was executed for becoming drunk and failing to predict an eclipse!

A recent internet study maintains that the percentage of women in today's world who consult their  daily horoscopes on a regular basis measures somewhere around 80%. Popular author Dan Brown speaks of astrology as 'the symbolic constant all over the world.' Carl Jung called astrology 'the first form of psychology.'

What is it about astrology that is so popular? And why is it considered a favorable career among MEDIAL WOMEN? There seems to be, along with the prescribed charts that can easily and even mechanically be done by computer, a manner of approaching astrology involving subjective intuition. Some people have faith in astrology's predictive qualities, while others regard astrology as descriptive and/or metaphoric at best. It may be the element of synchronicity, the acausal connecting principle, which is its ultimate draw upon our curiosity.

A further look into the role of astrology in the life of our contemporary MEDIAL WOMAN, Cynthia Killion, presents a strong illustration of the lively demand within our culture for this arcane but still highly popular tool. Of particular interest here is that Killion secured, through astrology, the subjective strata of her psyche (i.e. using intuitive rather than entirely rational tools) from which to develop her own later skills as a psychic.

## Interview: Cynthia Killion - 4. From Teenage Interests to Professional Life

CK: When I was twenty-one, I'd been studying astrology for several years already, got pretty good at it. I was living in North Carolina at the time, married to my first husband, and there was a woman there that we knew named Deborah. She ran a little new-age shop, and she said she needed somebody to write astrology reports. She also read cards and was a gifted psychic. So as she was talking about this one day, I said, 'Oh, I know about astrology…a little bit. I've been studying it for about eight years.' And she said, 'You could do the reports for me.' She would get the information and collect the money and I would write the reports. And that was when it all started. I realized that the gifts were showing through me and that there were things I was writing in the reports that I didn't think you could have gleaned from astrology. But people were coming back and saying, 'Oh, that was so right on! That's so accurate!'

LS: Was astrology a way of focusing your attention?

CK: Yes. It was also a gateway. It was much easier for me to say that I was an astrologer, rather than a psychic. So it was almost a way of hiding my gifts, too. Any divination tool can help you to your psychic gifts, and I had progressed through astrology, but it was just that I had to go beyond that…. It's about 'that place within.'

## An Astrology Story

An interesting account illustrating the importance of the astrological tradition to people living in other parts of the world was published in the *New York Times Magazine* LIVES section:

## Destiny's Child

By Bharati Mukherjee[224]

> "From birth, I waited patiently for Death. But now I may have inadvertently missed our Rendezvous."

I've always known that I would die at 63. The year of my death was foretold by my horoscope, which was cast by my family's astrologer in 1940. Like most Calcuttans of my generation, I might not have a birth certificate, but I do have a horoscope, an older authority, calculated according to the alignments of planets at what my family remembers at the moment of delivery. This scroll of yellow paper with Hindu astrological charts and Sanskrit writing describes

---

224 Bharati Mukherjee, "Destiny's Child" *New York Times Magazine*, January 5, 2003. LIVES Section.

my temperament, alerts me to cosmic incompatibility when looking for a husband and predicts when my life's important events,
both pleasant and unpleasant are likely to happen.

When I was eleven, my future was read to me. The family elders were deciding whom a distant cousin should marry. They had
just discarded their top choice of bridegroom because the couple's
horoscopes didn't match. I pestered my father to tell me what kind
of marriage I had in store. My father, who was well known for
his impassioned delivery of Sanskrit chants, read out the relevant
lines. 'There!' my mother exclaimed. 'I knew there was nothing to
worry about.' The astrologer didn't agree; after all, I would marry a
blue-eyed foreigner totally outside the Brahmanic pale of civilization. I also learned that day that I was prone to catching colds, I
would cross the oceans and settle far from home – and I would die
between July 2003 and July 2004. I accepted the prediction about
death as fully as I did the others. The shocking news was that I was
destined to live so long. I was a knowledgeable child, and I knew
that the United Nations calculated the average Indian life span to
be 37 years.

After having crossed the oceans to study in the United States
and marrying a blue-eyed American student, Clark Blaise, and set-
tling in his country, I came to believe that all of my horoscope
would come true.

In 1985, after a terrorist bombing of an Air India flight killed
329 people, I still hung on to my faith in fate even as I wondered
whether greater vigilance from counter terrorism agencies might
have saved those lost. My husband and I spoke with scores of
grieving South-Asian Canadians in the wake of the disaster; one Sri
Lankan couple that emigrated to Canada to escape ethnic violence
in their homeland, lost both of their daughters. Though the husband was a Christian and the wife a Hindu, they had found solace
in the teachings of a Hindu priest in rural India. Months after the
disaster, the swami told them to accept the inevitability of their
children's deaths on that June day. I asked the couple, 'What if
the suitcase bomb had been detected before the plane took off?'
The grieving father told me he had asked the same question. The
swami answered: 'You could have pulled them off that plane. You
could have locked them up, you could have done anything, but
you couldn't have stopped them from dying that day. Their mission was fulfilled.' Had those 329 people died that day under different circumstances, I would, of course, never known. But I was
willing to accept it might have happened.

Last month, while I was sitting in a dentist's chair for a clean-
ing, my serenity (or complacency) was thrown off. The young dentist, who was friendly but censorious of bad dental hygiene, asked,

'How long have you had this?' I guiltily assumed that I had a cavity. Even now, nobody in the Calcutta neighborhood I grew up in goes to the dentist except for emergencies. 'It's probably nothing, just a callus on the side of the tongue, but let's be sure,' he said. He made an appointment for me to see his mentor, a specialist in maxillofacial surgery, later that day. The specialist agreed that it was probably nothing. I could keep an eye in the tiny patch of white on my tongue and come back if it grew. He suggested a biopsy.

'What would you do, Clark?' I asked my husband.

'I'd want to know right away,' he said. So I agreed to the biopsy. The lab results showed that the cells were abnormal. 'It's not cancer yet,' the specialist assured me, 'but it'll have to come out.' He had a gentle voice and a tired face. I told him that the operation couldn't be scheduled before the summer because I had a lecture class at Berkeley for the university's spring 2003 semester. 'It should have been done yesterday,' the specialist said, his voice still gentle.

I just had the surgery. I'm told the cells could turn cancerous, so I must report for checkups every two to four months for the rest of my life. For the time being, I have resigned myself to the fact that modern science has probably trumped fate, and that it's very likely that I shall live beyond the age (predicted.)

This is a cause for panic. I have so accustomed myself to closure in this life, this incarnation, in 7 to 19 months, that lingering on indefinitely terrifies me. In really low moments, I tell myself, you can padlock the door, but destiny will sneak in. And that's a comfort to me.


## Education

Cynthia Killion believes that reaching the level of concentration necessary to expand one's medial capacities can be taught, and is writing a book in that regard, a task which she has found very difficult. Others such as scholar and educator Christine Page have worked on the serious job of developing strategies and curricula on this formidable task. Skilled therapists are learning to expand their clinical skills to work effectively with the flashes of metaphoric imagery that come to them in therapy sessions. There are also new frontiers in the education of children that are being developed to increase intuitive perception. This idea was illustrated by the challenging story related to the work of renowned educator George Leonard. Marianne, a workshop participant

who has spent her professional life in education, brought this story to
the group:

## Narrative: Marianne's Story

## An Image For The Future

> During the 70's, there was a great deal of thinking going on re-
> garding the possible goals for the education of young children in
> the future. I recall the philosopher and educator George Leonard
> speaking to a group of educators at a conference and describing an
> ideal school for children in the future. He might have mentioned
> that the illustration came originally from B.F. Skinner. In Leonard's
> account, he was speaking as if he were with a group of teachers
> being led by the principal of a model school. They paused by a
> swimming pool, where children of all ages were happily playing in
> both the deep and the shallow ends of a very large swimming pool.
> A visitor remarked, in alarm, 'Good heavens. There is no lifeguard
> with them!'
>
> The principal replied, 'There is nothing to worry about. If any
> child were in the slightest danger, every child in the pool would
> know it instantly, and the child would receive immediate help.'
>
> I never forgot that illustration, of a time in the future when
> teachers might know how to teach certain kinds of protective intu-
> ition to their students.

What seemed like impossibility then has certain credibility now, a small
but growing one, as the world begins to study MEDIAL WOMAN in new
and creative ways. Just because the rules that govern such phenomena
are for the most part unknown does not mean that there are no understandable rules, Jung warned us. It means that the rules are not generally accessible to us, as yet.

## Fine Arts

The arts have always carried much of the soul by lifting human consciousness to an ethereal world. Civilization has been enriched for centuries, as women of highly creative artistic skill bring their intuitive
understanding of the spiritual dimensions of life before the public.

World-renowned scholar, philosopher and theologian Evelyn Underhill
(1875-1941) wrote of the element of mysticism that she feels supports
all great art:

> This intuition of the Real lying at the root of the visible
> world and sustaining its life, is present in a modified form
> in the arts: perhaps it is better to say, must be present if
> these arts are to justify themselves as heightened forms of
> experience. It is this, which gives them that particular vital-
> ity, that strange power of communicating a poignant emo-
> tion, half torment and half joy, which baffle their more
> rational interpreters. We know that the picture which is
> 'like a photograph,' the building which is handsome and
> commodious, the novel which is a perfect transcript of life,
> fail to satisfy us. It is difficult to say why this should be so,
> unless it were because these things have neglected their
> true business; which was not to produce the illusions of or-
> dinary men, but to catch and translate for us something of
> that 'secret plan,' that reality which the artistic conscious-
> ness is able, in a measure, to perceive...
>
> An apparition from a more real world of essential life
> is the world in which the 'free soul' of the great mystic
> dwells.[225]

The task of identifying some of the great artists, whose work moves us
beyond our daily lives and into the realms of inspiration, presents an
enormous selection process, difficult to identify. So your writers each
agreed to allow themselves just three minutes to record what and who
came into mind first, and invite readers to do the same.

Our choices were completely spontaneous, and great fun to record.

## In just three minutes each:

(Molton)

The story and music of Bellini's opera NORMA, especially the aria 'Cas-
ta Diva'; Marion Zimmer Bradley's work, *The Mists of Avalon*; singers
such as Jessie Norman, whose interpretations of the great flowing river
of spiritual songs can move me deeply; Mary Zimmerman's work as
a playwright; The brilliant characterizations on film by such women

---

225  Evelyn Underhill, *Mysticism* (Meridian, N.Y.: New American Library), 7-8.

as Meryl Streep and Judith Dench; Bach's *Cello Suites*; The imaginative comprehension which Shirley MacLaine delivers; the second movement of Schubert's *Quintet in C Major*; Ray Charles singing "Georgia On My Mind"; The other-worldly photography of Jamie Tuttle, these are the artists whose work has moved me just in the past weeks. The lifetime list is endless.

(Sikes)

Annie Leibovitz's photography combined with the text of Susan Sontag in their book *"WOMEN"* catch the marvel of our gender caught in life; the wonderful vocal meditation for the Virgin Mary from *Totus Tuus* by Henryk Gorecki; a "Concerto de Aranjuez-Adagio" by Joaquin Rodrigo brings me the joy of the Spanish guitar; the breath-taking vision of Robert Wick's sculpture delivers the reality of nature to the beholder; Bette Midler's rendition of "The Rose"; Woody Guthrie's ballads; the searing reality of some of Embima Smith's poetry; Rosa Bonheur's painting, "The Horse Fair" – these have enriched my life and led me far away.

\* \* \*

Physician, scholar and innovative writer Leonard Shlain, in his book, *Art and Physics*,[226] relates an episode in his life wherein he takes his twelve-year-old daughter from California to New York, to the Museum of Modern Art. He wanted her to see what the East coast, and much of the world, rewards by preserving in great museums. His reason for doing so was to try to open this world for her, to share with her his own passion for modern art. Finding it fairly comfortable to address her curiosity through the work of the Impressionists, as the works became more and more abstract, he found himself becoming increasingly uncomfortable. Her innocent, honest and wonderful question, repeated over and over again in all of our lives to some degree was, 'What makes it great art?' He knew that the answer to her question about art was somehow related to the great-unanswered questions, which the world of contemporary physics confronts. Shlain attempts to answer the question by showing her that the intuitive mind of the artist even anticipates the discoveries in science, and proposes that the essence of truth is just 'Out there.'

226 Leonard Shlain, *Art and Physics* (New York: HarperCollins, Perennial), 7-8.

We all ponder the same questions. Is it that the artist has seen or experienced something of the ineffable, the consummate, the hidden order of the universe, perhaps, and beheld a vision that renders language insufficient to describe?

Is it that almost inexplicable element in truly great art that touches what we call and immortalize as genius? It is possible that at some point of her own experience, the gifted MEDIAL WOMAN may be tapping in to that enormous, seemingly irrational mystery, like the artist searching, only in another language?

## Health and Healing

### Book Study: "M'Dear" from *The Bluest Eye* by Toni Morrison

'Aunt Jimmy' is a frightened and sick old woman, whose only relative in her home is a bewildered teenaged grandson, Cholly. She is in need of help beyond the skill of her neighbors and friends.

'M' Dear'

Finally it was decided to fetch M'Dear, a quiet woman who lived in a shack near the woods. She was a competent midwife and decisive diagnostician. In any illness that could not be handled by ordinary means - known cures, intuition, or endurance – the word was always, 'Fetch M'Dear.'

When she arrived at Aunt Jimmy's house, Cholly was amazed at the sight of her. He had always pictured her as shriveled and hunched over, for he knew she was very, very old. But M'Dear loomed taller than the preacher who accompanied her. She must have been over six feet tall. Four big white knots of hair gave power and authority to her soft black face. Standing straight as a poker, she seemed to need her hickory stick not for support but for communication. She tapped it lightly on the floor as she looked down at Aunt Jimmy's wrinkled face. She stroked the knob with the thumb of her right hand while she ran her left one over Aunt Jimmy's body. The backs of her long fingers she placed in the patient's cheek, then placed her palm on the forehead. She ran her fingers through the sick woman's hair, lightly scratching the scalp, and then looking at what the fingernails revealed. She lifted Aunt Jimmy's hand and looked closely at it – fingernails, black skin, the flesh of the palm she pressed with three fingertips. Later she put her ear on Aunt Jimmy's chest and stomach to listen. At M'Dear's request, the women pulled the slop jar from under the bed to show the stools. M'Dear tapped her stick while looking at them.

'Bury the slop jar and everything in it,' she said to the women. To Aunt Jimmy she said, 'You done caught cold in your womb. Drink pot liquor and nothing else.'

'Will it pass?' asked Aunt Jimmy.

'I reckon.'

M'Dear turned and left the room. The preacher put her in his buggy to take her home.

That evening the women brought bowls of pot liquor from black-eyed peas, from mustard greens, from cabbage, from kale, from collards, from turnips, from beets, from green beans. Even the juice from a boiling hog jowl.

Two evenings later Aunt Jimmy had gained much strength.[227]


The MEDIAL WOMAN stands between two worlds. In this case, M'Dear stands between the world of illness, and the world of health. Or perhaps more accurately, between life and death. She knows what needs to be done through experience, through trial and error, and through a profound, accurate intuitive 'knowing.'

## Two Contrasting Profiles

The conventional medical world now recognizes the link between energy and illness. When the energy for life is at low ebb, illness follows. Energy for life is both a physical and a spiritual/psychological problem. In the past decades, enormous strides have been made in the acceptance of alternative medical models of treatment. How MEDIAL qualities assist in both physical and spiritual healing practices characterize a significant portion of the professional options open to the MEDIAL WOMAN.

While some MEDIAL women in this field work from within the rational scientific medical system and forge new bridges of mutual respect and understanding, others prefer to practice the healing of illness and injury by addressing their own psychic resources alone. Caroline Myss and Echo Bodine pursue two very different perspectives in their

227 Toni Morrison, "M'Dear," *The Bluest Eye* (New York: The Penguin Group, Plume 1994), 136-137.

approach to healing and medicine, yet both demonstrate a unique gift of finely tuned MEDIAL intuition.

## 1. A Medical Intuitive: Caroline Myss.

Caroline Myss has done a great deal to legitimatize the world of intuitive medicine, and to develop respect for the various areas of holistic and alternative healing within in the practice of traditional medicine. She combines the psychic's gifts of clairvoyance with the manner in which humans experience illness and healing within psyche.

The discovery of her own MEDIAL skills was a surprise to her, and like most MEDIAL women, she had a tendency to overlook this particular ability, perhaps out of some fear of what it might require of her. In the introduction to her early book, *Anatomy of the Spirit*, Myss describes her earliest sense of the presence of her own gifts:

> Over lunch one day, when I was seated next to him (Dr. C. Norman Shealy, neuro-surgeon), I told him that I was able to diagnose people at a distance. He didn't seem the least impressed. Rather, he peeled an apple and asked me, 'How good are you?' I told him I wasn't sure. Then he asked, 'Can you identify a brain tumor in someone? Can you see a disease forming in a person's body? I don't need anyone telling me that someone's 'energy' is low; I can see that for myself. I need someone that can scan a person like an x-ray machine.'
>
> I told Dr. Shealy that I was uncertain of my accuracy since I was relatively new at this. He said he would give me a call sometime, when he had a patient he thought might benefit from my skill. The next month – May 1984, he phoned me at Stillpoint. He had a patient in his office, he told me, then gave me the patient's name and age and waited for my response. I recall the evaluation I gave vividly because I was so nervous; I spoke of my impressions in images rather that in physiological terms. I told Dr. Shealy that I felt as if his patient had concrete running down his throat. Then I commented on the emotional issues that, from my point of view, preceded the development of his physical condition. The patient, an addict, was so terrified to admit his condition that he was physically unable to speak the truth about it. The words froze in his throat.

When I finished, Dr. Shealy said 'Thanks.' and hung up. I had no idea whether I had done an adequate job, but later he told me that the man had cancer of the esophagus.[228]

\* \* \*

In her book, Myss mentions the importance of remaining totally impersonal as she works: She said that keeping yourself emotionally detached from the subject on which you are reporting, and seeking out only the facts that describe the situation, are important for her. Cynthia Killion mentions something comparable. It is this capacity, perhaps as Killion, Myss and other MEDIAL professionals seem to imply, this impersonal approach helps to objectify and isolate where problem areas are, and assists the practitioner to work from a distance as well as in person when necessary. The MEDIAL WOMAN is *impersonally* related to her subject.

Myss has taken great care in educating herself to work creatively with the existing medical establishment, a factor that has placed this part of her work within the boundaries of conventional medical wisdom and consciousness. The combination of her distinctly MEDIAL ability and that of the professional physician has made a significant impact on the manner in which some medical practice is beginning to redefine itself throughout the world. Her perspective illustrates an essential effort that the MEDIAL WOMAN must undertake, if she seeks a professional accountability

## 2. A Spiritual Healer: Echo Bodine

Working from an entirely different perspective, Echo Bodine is widely known in the United States as a spiritual and psychic healer. She travels and lectures extensively and has written several books. It was some years before Echo Bodine learned to develop and control these gifts that led her to her acclaimed professional work. In Kansas City in 2001, she presented a Cornerstone Foundation lecture in which she gave this account of her early experiences working with a young boy's critical

---

228 Caroline Myss, *Anatomy of the Spirit* (New York: Three Rivers Press, 1996), 21-23.

condition, using her techniques that are outside the traditional treatment of trauma injury:

> I got a call from a woman whose son had fallen 18 feet and landed on his head. He was in a coma. She called and asked if I would please channel some healing to him. Well, the first time that I went there, a male nurse was there talking to the family, telling them that their son would never come out of the coma, and if he does, the best thing that they could do for him would be to put him in a nursing home.
>
> A voice of fear came to me, and I thought, O.K. This is just a waste of time. Then another voice came to me, and said, 'Go talk to God.' So I excused myself from the mother and went down the hall to talk to God. I said, 'What shall I do?'
>
> And the voice within me said, 'Are you going to listen to the fears of the world, or are you going to get to work?' I said I was going to get to work.
>
> I went back to the room and asked if the family would mind if I was alone with the boy. I placed my hands on his body. He was in a coma, as I said, and there was no response. I was channeling healing to him for about five minutes. And from behind, me I heard a voice say, 'would you please heal the speech part of my brain? I'd really like to talk again.'
>
> I slowly turned around. And standing up against the wall, just like leaning up against the wall, ...this young boy...well, he was something.... I didn't know what he was, repeated, his arms folded, 'would you please heal the speech part of my head? I'd really like to talk again.'
>
> I said, 'Who are you?'
>
> He replied, 'I am the soul that lives in that body. Uh...and I'd like to talk again.'
>
> I said, 'Sure.' And sssSSSH! He left the room.
>
> His soul communicated to me every day, about what he needed. And at the end of two months...he walked out of the hospital into his life. That's the kind of work that I have been fortunate to be a part of.[229]

---

229 Echo Bodine, paraphrased from Lecture Notes on Tape (Kansas City: Cornerstone Foundation, Edge Newspaper co-presentation, Unity Temple, May 18, 2001). Audio Cassette.

## Yoga, Massage Therapy, and Other Body Work

Another dimension of psychic/physical healing is encountered in the various practices of Yoga. Of the many forms of Yoga systems, the Tantric and Kundalini approaches are arguably the most prevalent available, and practiced by thousands of people in the west. Caroline Myss is a firm believer in the healing effects of the latter ancient form, as are many well-known people. The flow of consciousness through the body's energy centers, combined with focused meditation is known to lead to an inner world beyond physical health alone. But various physical discomforts can also be helped through Yoga.

Related bodywork fields in the realm of massage therapy and breath work constitute rapidly growing areas of mind/body health study. Reiki, Rolfing, Pilates, marshal arts and nutritional programs proliferate, and offer an open field of study and training for the MEDIAL WOMAN who feels inclined to focus her intuitive gifts in the health arena.

## Past Lives

From the world of the astrologist, it is just a small conceptual step away from what used to be considered as 'Reincarnation,' a spiritual concept favored by much of the world's inhabitants. It is now more popularly referred to, at least in the west, as 'Past Lives' or in its practical/ application, 'Past Lives Regression.'

Alice Howell, a well-known astrologer and psychotherapist relates this encounter with a client:

> A woman had brought in a dream in which a gypsy appeared. She asked me, directly, 'Was I once a gypsy?'
>
> I had no way of answering. To tell her outright she was once a gypsy would be overstepping the line by far, for me. I stick with the image, and if it speaks to the client in a meaningful way, I am content to see it as a metaphor and to use the expression, 'It is almost as if you have a kind of gypsy in you.'[230]

However, I should mention that an analyst friend of Jung's, Erlo van Waveren, has written a book called *Pilgrimage to the Rebirth*. In it he not only discusses recall of his own former lives, but also seriously suggests

---

230 Alice Howell, *Jungian Symbolism in Astrology* (Wheaton: Theosophical Publishing House Quest Books 3rd Edition, 1987), 62-63.

that these lives live on in us as sub-personalities, sometimes as complexes in conflict. It would seem sometimes as if this could be the case. Nowadays, many are taking a serious look at past-life-regressions.

Another of Howell's clients came for an astrology reading but his astrology configurations, as explained by Howell, brought the image of a monk, a hospice and a monastery rolled into one:

> When he offered this as an image for consideration, I replied with my usual response, 'It is almost as though you have a monk in you.' The client laughed and said he knew from past life regressions that in fact he had been a monk in several lifetimes.[231]

Of the well-known women who speak out on the subject of reincarnation, possibly one of the most renowned is the actress Shirley MacLaine, whose book *Out On A Limb*,[232] describes her own experiences in a realm of past lives, and how she interpreted the meaning of them. What may be a literal belief for her may be a more plausible metaphoric truth for others. In any case, her straightforward story remains a stirring documentary of her own experiences in this realm.

## Psychic Reading

### Miss Cleo

In our everyday world, we can feel ourselves shake our heads at those who might be gullible enough to call, 'Miss Cleo's Mind And Spirit Network' for a free three-minute consultation. However, 'Miss Cleo' is spokesperson for a million-dollar phone syndicate controlled by two South Florida businessmen. At this early decade of the new millennium, many shadow projects were unveiled. And who is to say whether the people offering consultation are tricksters conducting a hoax, or genuinely gifted MEDIAL WOMEN doing their work? That their services are in demand is the point. An audience is there, awaiting what the MEDIAL voice has to offer. And that there is such a thing as authenticity within the whole spectrum of MEDIAL WOMAN's abilities is no longer a matter of automatic dismissal.

---

231 Howell, *Jungian Symbolism in Astrology*, 64.
232 Shirley MacLaine, *Out on a Limb* (New York: Bantam Books, 1983).

Neither is the fine line between genuine ability and trickster manipulation quite so easy to determine, even by the MEDIAL WOMAN herself.

## Psychology

In Toni Wolff's words, repeated:

- "Today, at least, we have the language of [depth] psychology in which the unconscious is an important and often vital factor whose inclusion into one's life can not only have a healing effect, but may even lead to greater consciousness and to being rooted meaningfully in the laws of psyche."[233]

Throughout the development of modern psychiatry and psychology, attention has been paid to qualities of the human psyche that are described as MEDIAL, i.e. the distinctly prophetic quality of some dreams, the nature of phenomena associated with telepathic experience, or the phenomena associated with synchronicity. In the study of the human psyche, there are qualities of cause and effect that lie beyond rational explanation, given what is empirically known and rationally described. Freud was one of the earliest to introduce the 20th century world to the practical ways of working with the unconscious, and made a great leap into the inner world of our human mental apparatus. His theories explained the irrational part of human behavior primarily by what he determined to be the instinctual design of the central nervous system. Scientists such as Adler and Jung studied the nature of the unconscious further, and successive research established what is documented as 'known', and what is yet still to be known.

The MEDIAL WOMAN knows, but does not know how she knows. Characteristically, she does not know the limits of her own vision, nor how the images appear to her and are made conscious to her.

Gifted MEDIAL clinicians in the field of medicine and psychology stand between the worlds of consciousness and the unconscious, the latter being considered for centuries nonexistent, evil, or forbidden except for priests and saints. MEDIAL WOMAN 'knows' through images that appear to her psyche and tell her something. The access to her im-

233 Wolff, "Structural Forms," 10.

ages, which are inexplicable to most of us, are beginning to be understood or at least considered as true manifestations of a world the order of which is still relatively unknown.

Some people have had the experience of working with highly intuitive and skilled therapists who work with dream images, the metaphoric manifestations of what is going on in the unconscious. The work is both archaic, and is also significantly avant-garde. While all MEDIAL WOMEN are, in a sense intuitive, not all intuitives are MEDIAL. But a skilled intuitive clinician, trained in the disciplines of practice, can learn how to do this work effectively. That is probably what Toni Wolff was referring to, when she talked of 'using the language of psychology and working within the laws of psyche.'

Other possibilities for the MEDIAL WOMAN are within the field of research, in which the 'inductive leap' of hypothesis leads to, and may be validated by, the deductive processes of accountability.

Gifted therapists abound, many who have developed helpful paradigms for working with individuals, couples and families. Since Toni Wolff's time, the work of many professional women such as Carol Gilligan, Virginia Satir, June Singer and Harriet Lerner have presented their methodologies to the world through their books as well as their practices, and have opened the field to women of talent and imagination. May their tribe increase!

## Religion

The religious life has always provided a haven for MEDIAL WOMAN. As mentioned earlier concerning Type A, those associated with a known and established religious system such as Catholicism in the West, and Type B, those who are not. Within the Type A, there are also various categories that designate the particular gifts of the participants.

Religious mystic Evelyn Underhill has written extensively regarding these aspects of religious life, and makes a distinction between the genius of the gifted (MEDIAL) mystics, and those members of the community of faith whose work is determined by their individual gifts, which may not include ecstatic revelation.[234] Hildegard had visions, as did many other famed saints of the faith, cloistered or otherwise, such

---

234 Underhill, *Mysticism*, 10.

as Joan of Arc, Bernadette of Lourdes, and Teresa of Avila, each of whom carried the aura of ecstatic genius.

Underhill describes this genius in terms of transcendence, but also implies that in its transformative power, there is a new manifestation of the human spirit:

> The ego acquires a fresh center. The *élan vital* is oriented in
> a new direction and begins the hard work of cutting a fresh
> path. New levels of reality are disclosed.[235]

Underhill maintains that the initial revelation also requires an understanding of the beholder's own passage, having glimpsed the eternal qualities of The Divine. She now has a personal mandate, a requirement into the process of delivering the best of her own selfhood to the needs of the world.


In today's world, the ecstatic visions of MEDIAL women still challenge, revive and inspire the church, such as the singular life of Mother Teresa of Calcutta and the recent reported sightings of the Virgin in Medjugorje and Batavia in Venezuela, or the established shrines such as those of Guadalupe. Other religions also report miraculous events at their sacred shrines. Sometimes, visitors to those shrines come away with new understandings of themselves and their own missions in life. The spiritual impulse, or spiritual capacity within the human psyche, has been challenged, stimulated, and insistently pressed for a means of expression.

Well-known Gnostic scholar Elaine Pagels writes of the visions of the Gnostic scholars recorded in the ancient Nag Hammadi texts: "Yet the Gnostic writers do not dismiss visions as fantasies or hallucinations. 'They respect—even revere—such experiences, through which spiritual intuition discloses insight into the nature of reality.'"[236]

For the MEDIAL WOMAN, this idea seems as natural as breathing. For her, it is only a matter of describing the image, which the vision produces for her.

Jung points out attributes of the 'religious tendency' among people who possess exceptional MEDIAL qualities:

---

235 Underhill, *Mysticism*, 44-69, paraphrased.
236 Elaine Pagels, *The Gnostic Gospels* (New York: Random House Vintage, 1979), 12.

I have observed and also partially analyzed people who seemed to possess a supranormal facility and were able to make use of it at will. . . . This faculty was clearly coupled with a religious attitude, which enabled them to give suitable expression to their sense of the ego's subordination to the archetype. . . .

The religious tendency is obvious enough in nearly all serious-minded mediums. As a rule, they cannot exploit their 'art' for egoistic purposes, and this proves that their faculty is not subject to the will of the ego but owes its existence rather to the overriding dominance of the unconscious.[237]

The following poem from the ancient *Nag Hammadi* texts forges another link to the ecstatic visionary from the anonymous voice of the Divine Feminine. It is as MEDIAL in character as one could imagine, both immediate and transcendent. It is exciting to hear the roll of the voice from thousands of years ago speak in such contemporary terms. A brief exerpt:

The Thunder, Perfect Mind

I was sent forth from the power,

And I have come to those who reflect upon me,

And I have been found among those who seek after me.

Look upon me, those who reflect upon me,

And you hearers hear me.

You, who are waiting for me, take me to yourselves.

And do not banish me from your sight.

Do not be ignorant of me anywhere

For I am the first and the last...

I am the honored one and the scorned one.

I am the whore and the holy one.

I am the wife and the virgin.

I am, the mother and the daughter.[238]

—Translated by George W. MacRae

---

237 C.G. Jung, *Letters*, 542.
238 "Thunder Perfect Mind" from *The Nag Hammadi Library in English*, 3rd Completely Revised Edition by James M Robinson, General Editor.

Underhill wrote:

> In religion, mysticism has been described as 'the science of
> ultimates,' the union with the Absolute, and nothing else.
> It is the person who attains to this union, and not the per-
> son who talks about it. Not to know about, but to *be*.[239]

By virtue of this description, the woman who *claims* to be a mystic,
quite possibly is not.

It has been said that humankind is incurably religious. The ideal of, and
longing for, perfection hovers in the psyche, and can be a trickster. It
is always difficult to know what is, and what is not, anchored in genuine spiritual authenticity. The Old Testament relates that thousands of
years ago, King Saul condemned the 'Witch of Endor,' then later, when
in severe distress, disguised himself and consulted her regarding his
own destiny. She recognized him, and called his bluff. It is clear, that
in our time, the inherent challenge of spiritual capability lies within
the purview of some MEDIAL women. The enrollment in theological
seminaries and training for leadership credentials as clergy, spiritual
directors, advisors and liturgists has multiplied at an unprecedented
rate. Also, the nonsectarian 'priestess societies' are flourishing, wherein
women find community and support for their personal spiritual development. Religion, spirituality, spiritualism, healing, hospice workers,
past lives, the arts, all contain elements of the expression of a spiritual
essence. It would seem that a talented woman with MEDIAL abilities
has never before lived in a world of so many options.

---

239 Underhill, *Mysticism*, 72.

# Chapter 26

## Of Men and MEDIAL WOMAN

Toni Wolff wrote:

- "She will often personify the impersonal side of [a man's] anima and thus unknowingly draw him into chaotic turmoil by which she will be carried away herself."

- "She may devote heself to the life and work of a single man."[240]

  (Paraphrases): With men, she may sense and animate psychic contents which should be made conscious, but which do not belong to his ego and cannot be easily assimilated without preparation. In such cases, her influence is destructive and bewitching.

While Toni Wolff said very little about the MEDIAL WOMAN from the man's point of view, she did imply that MEDIAL WOMAN holds a curious fascination for the man. It also seems clear that because MEDIAL WOMAN'S own awareness is apt to be defused, her own identity remains a mystery to her. Because her ego is weakened, she may well be very vulnerable to receiving the man's unconscious script, and following his wishes entirely without distinguishing herself from him.

### Study: Carl Jung and the Preiswerk Women

Carl Jung, as a young medical student at the turn of the century, pondered the occult first of all within his own family. His mother, Emilie Preiswerk Jung, had what he called her 'Number 2 personality,' which carried a dark and somehow menacing authority for him as a child. When she was a little girl, she had been given the task of regularly attending her famous father, Hebrew scholar and pastor Samuel Pre-

---

240 Wolff, "Structural Forms," 9-10.

iswerk, on Saturday evenings, as he prepared his Sunday sermons. She was stationed behind him with a towel in her hands, in the dining room as he worked. She was instructed to swish this towel in the air to fend off the evil spirits that would distract him from the intricate and sacred tasks of sermon preparation.

By day she was a loving mother, but by night she was uncanny. Then she was like one of these seers who are at the same time a strange animal, like a priestess in a bear's cave, ancient and as ruthless as truth and nature.[241]

Emilie's grandson, Carl's son Franz Jung, liked to tell old stories about her. In 1988 he related this little story to writer Mary Dian Molton, who was studying in Küsnacht at that time. It is reminiscent of his grandmother's childhood duties with her father's sermon preparation. Franz told me that his grandmother lived just a few blocks from the family home on See Strasse in Küsnacht. He recalls that when he was a boy, he and his sister used to pass her house on the way to school, and often stop to visit with her in the mornings, usually in hope of collecting some cookie treat to eat as they strolled along the rest of the way. But also, they wanted to see if Grandmother had evidence of unwanted nighttime visitors. Franz said that at night when Grandmother went to bed, she would place small seals of pasted paper on all the doors, from the inside. Then in the mornings, she would carefully inspect these stickers. If any were broken, which she deemed to be evidence of an invasion of spirits, she would then gather up her dish towel and shoo the certainly annoying, or perhaps even evil, intruders out of her house. Thus reassured that all was in order and the pesky ones were vanquished, the day could begin. Franz and his sister Helene considered this to be a most endearing but strange habit of Grandmother's.

There was a young cousin on Jung's mother's side, one Helene Preiswerk, six years Carl's junior. He had heard, while away at school, that spiritiual séances were being conducted under her leadership. Some years before, Jung's paternal grandfather had soundly condemned such things as 'nonsense,' but it was from his mother's family that these ideas continued to challenge and interest Carl, as a young medical student. He became so interested, in fact, that he devoted his doctoral thesis to the parapsychology and pathology of 'So-called Occult Phenomena,'

241 C.G. Jung, *Memories, Dreams, Reflections*, 50.

based on the experiments he and Helene carried out together, from as early as 1895 to 1900. In his work, after a time, he produced the thesis, which described what occurred, and how he understood and observed such phenomena. He maintained that a young woman could develop a secondary personality, whereby she was able to absorb information, ideas and even other personalities through an unconscious mode, and reproduce them under her self-hypnosis as 'the voices of spirits,' This included, in his particular family, Helene's reproduction of the voice of their deceased patriarch, Grandfather Preiswerk.

Jung also wrote that it was important to understand that this feat was accomplished through entirely unconscious means.

Gerhard Wehr, one of Jung's biographers, describes this situation:

> Before long Helly's possibilities as a medium were exhausted. The experimenter recorded a gradual decrease in the vitality of her ecstasies, and her utterances became more colorless and trivial. Finally he [Carl] caught her simply trying to produce any kind of phenomenon at all, obviously for her cousin's sake. Jung terminated the experiment. He later wrote, 'Very much to my regret, for I had learned how a No.2 personality is formed, how it enters into a child's consciousness and finally integrates into itself. All in all, this was one great experience, which wiped out all my earlier philosophy and made it possible for me to achieve a psychological point of view. I had discovered some objective facts about the human psyche.[242]

These two women, Emilie and Helene, both MEDIAL, had a powerful effect on Jung as a physician and scientist. So much so that he devoted considerable energy and thought, during his adult professional life, to their unique psychologies. Were they unduly influenced by the power of his personality, or he theirs? A case may be made from either point of view. It is clear that their inner worlds held a great fascination for him. Only as he matured was he able to see this part of their nature from an objective perspective.

As Wolff suggested, the MEDIAL WOMAN can take on the unconscious script of the man in her life as his anima woman, and be completely

---

242 Gerhard Wehr, *Jung: A Biography*, 73-74.

absorbed by him. That she does so unconsciously is also true, an indication the fragility of her own ego resources.

Isabel Allende gives an interesting portrait of 'Clara' as an adult whose ego seems to be very strong; her relationship to her husband Esteban, is presented by the author through his eyes:

## Book and Film Study: *The House of the Spirits,* Part 2[243]

Clara and Esteban


They were married in a small service. As a wedding gift Esteban gave her a set of diamond jewelry, which she thought 'lovely.' She packed it away in a shoebox and quickly forgot where she had put it. He adored her, but was somehow mystified regarding what it was she wanted. Esteban swore that sooner or later she would come to love him as he needed to be loved, even if he had to resort to extreme measures. He finally realized that Clara did not belong to him, and that 'if she continues to live in a world of apparitions, she probably never would.'

Clara's 'impudent sensuality' was also not enough for him. He wanted far more than her body; he wanted control over that undefined and luminous material that lay within her and escaped him even in those moments when she appeared to be 'dying of pleasure.'

After the three-month honeymoon in Europe, Clara and Esteban arrived at their new home. Esteban discovered that Clara lived in another world. She grew increasingly distant as time went on. He felt that her spirit was not with him, she hardly spoke to him, and her fresh laughter disappeared. When he came to her room and she was busy at her little three-legged table, he tried to share these aspects of her life with her, but she witheld her notebook testimonies from him, and would not let him or anyone read her thoughts. When he tried to join her in her contact with spirits, she told him he interfered with her concentration. So he stopped trying.

She finally had a bolt installed on her bedroom door, and only allowed him to enter if refusing his entry meant 'the end of the mar-

---

243 Isabel Allende, *The House of the Spirits* (New York: Alfred Knopf Bantam, 1993), 178-179.

riage.' But he still felt she was the only woman for him, and always would be.

For Clara and Esteban, there was a final encounter years later, when Esteban in his fury and frustration lost all control and hit her, badly bruising her and knocking out several teeth. She never spoke to him again. Over the years, she took refuge in her own silence as she had done as a child, a power move of self-protection. They continued to live in the same household, and accommodated to the difficult times of their lives, like caring for the children and grandchildren during the war. Clara spoke to him with civility but only through others, the children, or servants. It was very painful for Esteban, but for Clara it seemed to matter 'little if at all.'[244]

* * *

A MEDIAL WOMAN with a strong ego such as Clara's does what she wishes, and places her own interests above all else, and everyone else. In our day and time, such a woman, who perhaps never has to gain entrée into the world's business and earn a living, and who has always been regarded as precious, angelic, special and perfect, is somewhat handicapped regarding her adult maturity. But Clara's ego is absolutely intact. She remained herself, and did not yield to the external pressures of others.

As with the AMAZON, MEDIAL WOMAN must struggle to keep her personal relationships alive and cared for. Only by so doing is she able to keep involved in the reality of daily human life.

This next film differs from Wolff's statement above because the effect on the man seems to be chaotic at first, but ultimately deemed accurate. It illustrates the *required impersonal nature* of the MEDIAL intervention.

### Film Study: *White Palace*[245]

Max (James Spader), a serious, young, upwardly mobile middle-class man in a lucrative advertising business, has suffered the tragic acciden-

---

244 Allende, *The House of the Spirits*, 178-179.
245 *White Palace*. 1990. See Film Index.

tal death of his adored wife, and has since been in a bleak depression for over a year. All efforts of his many friends to introduce him to other 'nice girls' of his class fail to interest him. After a party and more than a bit drunk, he meets and flirts with a waitress, Nora, (Susan Sarandon) in an all-night hamburger joint. He meets her again by accident at a bar. They soon become lovers.

After a fight and reconciliation, we see him alone in her messy apartment, sprawled on the bed, still in his underwear. Another woman enters the room, an older version of Nora, with frizzy blond hair, flowing skirt and jacket, many beads and an embroidered vest. It is Norah's sister Judy (Eileen Brennan). Awakened by her entrance through the beaded curtain, Max hastily tries to dress. (Dialog approximate):

Judy: (Without any shock or seeming surprise) "...Tell me...you are... Ray?"

Max: "No."

Judy: "Ted?"

Max: (Struggling to get into his trousers.) "No."

Judy: (She continues...eyes closed, appearing as though she is trying to remember or intuit something.) "... I see three letters..."

Max : "Max."

Judy: "Aaah, ahha.... And who am I?"

Max: (Somewhat irritated) "I have no idea."

Judy: "Well, Judy's my name. I'm Nora's big sister."

Max: " Sister?"

Judy: "Where is she?"

Max: "She's working."

(Later. Judy and Max are sitting at the table.)

Judy: "I'm not surprised if she didn't say anything about havin' a sister... I left her alone with Mr. and Mrs. Robles. I know how she looked, when I walked up the road that day... I probably should have taken her with me. But I just...didn't know... how. I didn't know where I was going, either. God, I was just seventeen. I heard a voice that told me to pack up and go. So I did. And there was her little face watching me leave her behind. She didn't even have a warning.... (then sweetly) But here we are.

(and, triumphantly) "I could feel it back in Albuquerque! I had some precognition. You ever have precognition?"

Max: "No, not me. Never did."

Judy: "Aahh, you've got such beautiful eyes...but I see pain in them, though."

Max: (changing the subject) "Think I'll have a drink. Would you like one?" (He goes to the refrigerator.)

Judy: "Max! You're putting me off...Don't do that..."

Max: "Well, it's just hard for me to believe this way..."

Judy: "That don't even matter... . Ah, I'm seeing something strong bothers you, works on you, now, in your life."

Max: "I'd agree with that.."

Judy: "I can see that you are a smart man. Intelligent... but you're not satisfied in your work...you're a teacher..."

Max: "I once was..."

Judy: "You will teach again. What you need is a little faith. Your life is sadly about women. There's an older woman...it's your mother. She' hard, a hard woman."

Max: "Oh, Yeaas!"

Judy: "Now I'm seein' Nora. You'd like to have room for Nora. Is there another woman in the way ?...someone gone, on the other side? I see something wrong with her neck... it's broken."

Max: (alarmed) "How can you know about that?"

Judy: (Partly awakened from her trance).... "About what, Max?"

Max: "How could you know that?"

Judy: "Know what, Honey? Don't be afraid. Just talk to me. This is not no evil here. You just need a little faith in the unknown. You'll come to know that, one day. Honey."

(Later, Max talks to Judy, as she is ready to take off in her car.)

Max: "I thought you were a fake."

Judy: "Well proof's in the parting, they say. Nothin' to be afraid of, you know? But I don't tell people what they're better off not knowing. You know, I try to stay on the good side. When I see something bad, I just keep quiet. I gave Nora a reading...when her boy Charlie was a little baby. I saw then just how he'd end up. I never told Nora, of course. Just had to carry that secret all those years because...I just saw him, you know, lying down there in the Du Par River. They, found him right there, some fourteen years later. They all said it was an accident, but he was full of whiskey, and full of drugs. I believe Nora really believed that boy would make her proud. But with that sonbitch husband, and her not believing much in herself, she lost again. I think maybe she just gave up trying after ... maybe till you came along... Well, I gotta go now; My friends in New York told me to come and bake a turkey by Thursday. So I'm bakin' a turkey... Ha Ha!"[246]

Judy understood Max and helped him to find his way. However, had the two of them been romantically involved, the impact of the MEDIAL WOMAN, who sees *impersonal* categories, may well have been negative. She might have led Max into a path for which he was ill-equipped, either in talent or ego strength, to pursue. The MEDIAL relationship is certainly more complex when there is a personal connection because MEDIAL WOMAN loses her 'impersonal' touch and can become manipulative, and/or easily manipulated.

There are dynamics of relational life that the MEDIAL WOMAN is apt to overlook, just as with the AMAZON. She can easily loose herself in someone else's life; or, she can get so involved in herself that she neglects the personal side of relational life entirely. It is also highly possible that she can be easily overwhelmed.

---

246 *White Palace*. 1990. See Film Index.

# Chapter 27

## Of Children and MEDIAL WOMAN

Wolff is curiously silent about the subject of the MEDIAL WOMAN and children, in her essay "Structural Forms Of The Feminine Psyche." One reason for the omission on Wolff's part might be that she herself never had a child, and as far as we know, never particularly wanted one. Her major love, which was Jung himself, had his own children, or at least three of them before he and Toni became involved. Her major interest was in the HETAIRA type, about which she had a great deal to say.

### Mythology: Cassandra and Medea

Cassandra, the youngest child of King Priam, received the gift of prophesy from Apollo, as mentioned. But she refused to serve as the Pythia for the Oracle at Delphi. Her father, aware of her prophetic gifts, kept her confined during the Trojan War so that she remained available for him to consult. Agamemnon carried her home to Mycenae as his concubine, a spoil of war. Her young life was marked principally by war, terror and uncertainty. When she arrived at Mycenae with Agamemnon after ten long war years, his furious wife Clytemnestra promptly murdered both of them. Scarcely more than a child herself, Cassandra bore no children. She remains one of the first of the mythological queens to bear the names describing MEDIAL WOMAN, that of both 'sorceress' and 'prophetess.'

Medea, however, knew every trick of sorcery necessary to serve the needs of her beloved, Jason. She helped him win the Golden Fleece and to escape with her from her father's kingdom by secretive and magic means. She married her love, accompanied him on his long journey home, and bore him three children. When he abandoned her for another king's daughter, she callously murdered their children for her own purposes of revenge.[247]

---

247  Hamilton, *Mythology*, 123-130; 242-243.

We might draw tentative assumptions from these ancient metaphors that perhaps the children of such women endure a highly unique and particular set of dynamics in order to reach their own adult lives.

In fairy tales wherever there is a 'good' queen and/or a 'bad' queen, there is ususlly a witch nearby, and an enchantment of sorts. Children are frozen into statues, awaiting the special touch of liberation, freedom, exorcism, true love, or a 'God Mother.' Trees bloom on graves of the 'good mother' enabling the daughter to bloom into adult life, etc. The role of MOTHER, in any case, is a bewitching experience for the children concerned. But there are also the positively charged experiences of MEDIAL mothers and their children.

Killion speaks of her life with her young son:

## Interview: Cynthia Killion - 5 Alex and I.

LS: What does your son Alex think about your abilities?

CK: He's only eight. He's been raised around this and very openly. He knows his mom's psychic. He doesn't really question it. He does think too that I'm kind of like a witch. He'll say that sometimes. Because I use drums for medicine and when he's sick, it's not like I don't go to doctors too, I believe in doctors — but if he gets a little 'Ow-ee' I'll lay hands on him and send healing energy through. Of course, I do my work through the home. If he's around he has to go play outside, and I'll tell him, 'I'm talking to the spirits now,' so I don't sense any fear there. It's just part of his childhood. As you know as therapists, whatever you experience in your childhood, that's what normal is for you. This is his 'normal'.

MD: Have you seen anything in Alex that suggests he might have some of these abilities?

CK: Well, absolutely. I think he really does. He has interesting dreams sometimes. I know one time, you might say it's just a child's nightmare, but I had a feeling it's more than that. We had a tree at the side of our house and it was starting to scrape on our roof, and we had to get rid of it, which I was very much against, but we had to because it was going to cave our roof in. So we had the tree people come and take it out, and that night my son had a dream that the tree was beating on the window and it was mad. I'm pretty sure that he was picking up the vibrations of the tree. He exhibits other things like that; he has a heightened sensitivity. But it's different for him because it is just part of his environment. Whereas for me, growing up, it wasn't part of the environment; it was part of me.

## Narrative: Echo Bodine and Her MEDIAL Mother

I was raised Presbyterian. My psychic journey began when I was seventeen. There were four children. Nothing unusual in the family. We never talked about psychics. My mother, however, was very intuitive, and always seemed to know everything that was going on with all four children. We used to tease her about being a gypsy. She had dark hair, and liked to wear large hoop earrings.

One evening at the dinner table, my younger brother age 14 excused himself and went downstairs to practice his drums; He was clanking away, and sounded really rough. The rest of us were still sitting at the dinner table. Suddenly, really nice drumming music started coming from the den. We all looked at my Dad. He said, "I don't know. It must be the record I bought him." It was the nicest music. But it didn't have the record quality.

We were all frozen, just listening to the music. About two minutes later, my brother flew up the stairs, 'Did you hear it? Did you hear it?' We said we did, and asked him what happened. He told us that a white figure floated in, put his hands on top of his, and played through his hands. Then it stopped. The guy backed away, and went out the door. My brother was so freaked, he could barely tell the story.

My mother was attending a prayer group (during that period). There was a woman in the group who had heard a famous medium from England speak. Mom called the lady and asked if she could call the speaker, a Mrs. Olsen. She called her, and gave her name. Mrs. Olsen replied, something like 'Oh, yes, Mrs. Bodine. Your son just met his guardian angel, Mr. Fitzgerald. When he was alive, he was an accomplished drummer. He will teach your son. I need to see you. You and your children have some unusual gifts.' Mom was very uncomfortable, and said, '...Uh...we will get back to you.'

All of us were uncomfortable. What did it mean? That was when I started sleeping with the light on. I feared that something was going to come floating through the door at me. I just couldn't sleep. I had Catholic friends who would talk about guardian angels, but it wasn't part of my reality. However, our curiosity did get the best of us, and we called and set up an appointment for the next week.

At our session, I was told that I had been born with the three means: *clairvoyance*, (the ability to get information through seeing images), *clairaudience* (the ability to hear), and *clairsentience* which used to be understood as intuitive smelling, but is also understood as the ability to sense a mood when you enter a room. She also said I had the gift of healing. She told me never to forget that it was God working through me, I am just a channel... I was seventeen, in high school. I thought, 'this woman is crazy.'

She also told my Mom that she had psychic abilities, and all the children as well.[248]

In addition to her work as a healer, psychic reader and intuitive, Bodine travels and lectures widely, and has written several books. One wonders how her life might have developed had her mother not been present during this unusual set of circumstances.

248 "An Evening with Echo Bodine," Lecture Notes, Audio Cassette.

# Chapter 28

## Of MEDIAL WOMAN and The Other Types

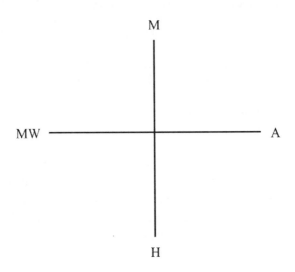

Wolff's ideas here:

> (Paraphrases): In much the same way as the AMAZON absorbs the impersonal cultural values of her time through collective consciousness, so does the MEDIAL WOMAN perceive the unconscious elements of her culture, or that of a single person, or a situation. And as the AMAZON mistakes mannish behavior for genuine masculine activity, so does the MEDIAL WOMAN mistakenly concretize 'spirits' into the unconscious spirit. It is her cultural task to find out and express this meaning, and in this manner accomplish a life-giving contribution to the world.[249]

For the MEDIAL WOMAN, te two adjacent types are the MOTHER and the HETAIRA. Her fourth, or opposite type, is the least known and the most alien. For the MEDIAL WOMAN, the opposite type is the AMA-

---

249 Wolff, "Structural Forms," 11.

ZON, who relates primarily to collective consciousness, the world of 'reality' in the practical, everyday sense of the word.

A woman in one of the workshops brought this story to the group. She was pleased to share her story, but asked that her name not be included:

## Narrative: A MOTHER Speaks about an adjacent MEDIAL Experience:

When my third child was born, I had what I later learned is called an 'out of body' experience. While I was in labor with my youngest son, I know I left my body and went to a strange place. It did not seem so strange while I was there. But it was not just a dream. It was far more vivid than a dream.

My first sensation was that I found myself high above the delivery room, and could clearly see that there was a little baby boy beside my body, I could see my own body below me, lying, beside this little child. He seemed to be sleeping, and he wore a placid half-smile on his face. I knew he was all right. Then I felt myself moving, and soon I was in another place. This place was like a way station, a connecting place, in a grayish netherworld. There were wooden benches lined up, almost like pews, but also like in a bus or train station. I was alone there at first, and then I was aware of a being of some sort, who seemed to be male. He was trying to assist me, in a kindly manner, to navigate myself without a body. He was very reassuring, and told me not to worry, I would soon become accustomed to it. I felt awkward in this new manner of movement. But it was my job to learn how to do this, in this place, under the instruction of this gentle being.

My next awareness was that I needed to go back to my baby. When I woke up, I was alone in the hospital recovery room, and in a very messy state of a hemorrhage, lying in a puddle of blood. I managed to find a bell to summon a nurse, who came in and saw that I was in distress. She brought in a doctor, and they took care of the situation. Soon I was in my own hospital room, holding this lovely baby, still wearing his little half-smile.

As he grew, people often remarked that he had a special light in his eyes, and a special capacity for genuine joy. He still does, even though he is a grown man now. And his laugh is just glorious and infectious, a gift of utter delight to the world. And certainly to me. I know that he called me back, somehow.

I do not know exactly where this place was that I visited. But I have never since had any real fear of death, nor any doubt about there being yet another existence after death.

I have read that such experiences are not uncommon to women during childbirth. But if the consummate MOTHER type has some understanding of the MEDIAL WOMAN, then this was my experience of her.

## Historic Study: Marie Laveau, Voodoo Queen (1794-1897)

The interception of MEDIAL WOMAN'S abilities with a darker world is perhaps inevitable despite her good intentions. Yet there are also those stories of witchcraft, Voodoo and other occult arts and practices that often carry a distinctly malevolent cast.

A case in point is the interesting story of the New Orleans doyenne of magic arts, Marie Laveau. She is still recalled when great Voodoo stories are told. That she had some MEDIAL qualities lies beyond doubt. She also used her MEDIAL intuitive gifts with her talents of extroverted showmanship, and an almost uncanny manipulative ability to exploit both the fears and the longings within the darker recesses of the human psyche. It was probably in that realm that she was most skillfully successful. So in order to determine a type that best describes Marie, we must examine both her MEDIAL and her AMAZON skills as being her secondary, or auxiliary talents. Her primary typology must lie in either the MOTHER or the HETAIRA archetype. A closer look at her history may yield a possible explanation, or maybe more than one.

Marie was born at the close of the eighteenth century in the racial, cultural, commercial and gastronomic carnival known as New Orleans. She was mulatto, meaning that her bloodline was of black, white and Indian descent. She grew to be tall and strikingly handsome, with curly black hair, reddish skin, and fine features. She also was blessed with a very quick mind.

At the time of her first marriage in 1818 to Jacques Paris, a free man of color from Haiti, she is listed in city records as the illegitimate daughter of Charles Lava and Marguerite Decanter. But she was also later described as a descendant of French aristocracy, and/or/ the illegitimate daughter of a wealthy white planter from the East Indies. In New Orleans, she earned her living first as a hairdresser, catering to wealthy white and Creole women of society who confessed to her their secrets, fears, jealousies, lovers, husbands and their mistresses, financial conditions, and fondest hopes.

Jacques Paris died five years after the marriage, which was childless. Later she took as her lover and lifetime partner Christophe Duminy Glapion of Santa Domingo, with whom she bore fifteen or sixteen children.

As Marie Laveau's career developed, she became known for her skill in the making and uses of gris-gris charms, and the secret meetings and practices of Voodoo as it had been brought to New Orleans by both the slave trade from Africa and the Indies. Out of this mix, there emerged the hybrid New Orleans practice of Voodoo. The phenomena associated with Voodoo were particularly vital and threatening to the civil authorities of predominantly Catholic New Orleans. There were secret rituals involving the bloodletting of small animals, snake worship and intense orgiastic chthonic dancing, most often leading to random sexual expression. There were also rumors of people who just disappeared.

After 1817, Marie managed a trade in procurement of women, and quietly established her place of pleasure and entertainment called *Maison Blanche*. But her greatest success began with the secret ritual ceremonies conducted out at Lake Pontchartrain, late at night. The steady intense drums, whirling half-clad dancers and animal blood letting ritual unleashed powerful primal emotions. She led the action, and her fame grew. She became secure enough in her own power to invite the press, general public and police to these occasions, and even charged admission. She was allowed to proceed with her businesses without prosecution, since legal officials and police of the city were either patrons of her arts, or else intimidated by threats of Voodoo and gris-gris. She knew the multiple uses of the manipulation of fear and guilt through 'magic.' She is said to manipulate ways to throw elections, find new lovers and get rid of old ones, and even destroy enemies, for substantial fees. Yet, she always incorporated the aura of 'religious' work in what she did. She was a conspicuous Catholic, combining holy water and familiar prayers with the rituals of Voodoo, and presented herself to the public in almost saintly terms, with all the dignity of a royal priestess on a divine mission. With the knowledge of the private affairs of so many socially and politically prominent people in the city, and formidable theatrical skills, she eventually became one of the most powerful women in New Orleans. It was understood that whites sought her help, and people of color saw her as a leader.

In her later years, Marie did a great deal of prison work, visiting inmates regularly, and tending to their families. This she continued nearly until her death, at the age of 97.

Perhaps her greatest MEDIAL quality was her ability to balance the two worlds of consciously ordered daily city life, and the wild world of passion and intrigue that lies just beneath the surface of the human psyche. This was Marie's enormous intuitive gift. Yet her skills were more clearly defined by AMAZON energy, with her success in business and her preoccupation with collective consciousness. The mystery to her being equipped with MEDIAL as well as AMAZON characteristics lies in the story of her personal history about which little is known. Her life with her partner Christophe Duminy Glapion was certainly stable, and fruitful as well. This implies that she may possibly be best described as either an HETAIRA, or MOTHER, which would explain her having access to both MEDIAL and AMAZON skills. There is one story about a daughter who became Marie Laveau II, passing herself off in public events as her mother for a time as the ageing queen began to fade. Daughter Marie II didn't have the talents of her mother, however, and soon passed out of the public spotlight.[250]

## Narrative: Lucy Sikes, 'S', Mother To The Tribe

Lucy Sikes brought this story about a distinctive adjacent type to the MEDIAL WOMAN. 'S' is MOTHER to her tribe, among the Bushman (The San) of Botswana. 'S' combined her MOTHER skills with both MEDIAL and AMAZON qualities, in a powerful manner:

> In April 2002, I traveled to Botswana, Southern Africa, in search of the women of the Bushmen tribe, written about as a people 'left behind in time.' At that time, we were deeply involved in Toni Wolff's work on the four major archetypes of women. I was curious to find examples in other countries and cultures to illustrate these four types.
>
> I hoped that by visiting an indigenous people under foreign skies, in a very different world far away, I might find the equivalent of Toni Wolff's types represented. We traveled by a small airline from Johannesburg to a little town called Maun, then by private

250  Francine Prose, *Marie Laveau* (New York: G.P. Putnam's Sons, 1977).

plane further into the bush, then by Range Rovers along dirt tracks deep into the country, far from passable roads, radios, electricity, plumbing, newspapers and/or railroads.

We spent a few days becoming acquainted with the San tribe through our guide, who spoke the characteristic ('click') Bushman language. We followed the yellow-beige women as they dug into the desert, finding plump tubers unerringly, with little hindrance from the infants and small children strapped on their sides. Gradually the people became accustomed to our presence.

We were invited to watch the San tribe perform a traditional ritual. In so doing I was fortunate enough to see 'S', the leading matriarch of her tribe, at work in her essential role as guardian of the health of the tribe.

She was the official caller who brings the scattered members of the group together for the ancient ceremony, now called the "Trance Dance." 'S' focuses an intention of healing through facilitating the movement of energy in the group, thus providing a container in which change can occur.

I hoped to film this ceremony at the gathering, using night-sensitive film. We waited at our camp for the stars to come out, well past sunset, and then the Land Rover carried us over the rutted road far away from camp with only the small headlights in the darkness, until we came to a wide circle of trees. The night had grown chilly. We waited.

In a while, two middle-aged Bushmen men came and created a fire, then disappeared into the dark. Later, another man came and put more wood on the fire, and he too disappeared.

'S' finally emerges from the dark bush night, alone. She is wrapped in a shawl, and carried a long white peeled staff. In the firelight I can see her dark wrinkled skin. No one in her group is present. She began clapping and calling in a singsong voice, calling, calling, and thumping her staff as she walks back and forth, under an enormous tree. After some time, a scrawny dog appears. She begins clapping and continues calling, calling and about twenty minutes later some teenage boys appear. They strap on their rattles of caterpillar shells with dried larva inside, tied with string made out of twirled grasses. Experimentally, they begin to stomp.

Others begin to come, honoring the persistent call of 'S'. Older men appear, tie on their rattles, and begin to stomp. Women with infants slung over their shoulders or bound to their breasts begin to settle around the campfire in a circle, and the male dancers gradually surround them and the fire in a larger circle. After about an hour there are enough settled around the fire to create the clapping which carries the dancers along with their atonal a capella chant.

I am busy filming the flickering fire as it played over the faces of the dancers. In a while, one of the men whom I had met before comes to give me a gift of some rattles and urges me to join the Trance Dance. He shows me how to wrap them around my legs. Later I learn from our guide that this was unusual.

The dance goes on and on. A few dancers begin to faint. When we depart hours later, I see 'S' join the circle of dancers. Though she doesn't faint like some do, she seems entranced. There is a sense of something moving through all of us present. This is the purpose of the ritual for health and purification.

I must have been touched with Bushman magic. On the way home on the first flight, my little duffle bag was lost. People looked and looked in every airport. My trance dance beads were in that bag, so I came home, distressed.

On the first night home back in Kansas, I had a dream:

I was in Africa, in an old pale blue and yellow painted bus. The driver opened the folding doors near his seat, and pointed out across the verdant green plane. "MAUN! " he said.

I woke up and phoned Botswana, and the Maun airport. A woman took my call. I explained about the missing bag, and she looked for it. She came back and said, "It's not here."

"But," I said, "I had a dream that it is there!"

"Just a minute," she said. In a few minutes she returned.

"It's here," she said.

"I began to describe how she could return the bag but she said, "Just tell me the airport near where you are."

Picturing all the airlines and airports, I didn't think I would see the bag again, but indeed, the next day it was in Kansas City!

'S' was the MEDIAL WOMAN as Priestess and Healer, the MOTHER, and the AMAZON, a well-evolved woman who had incorporated at least three of the archetypes into her own personality. Wolff described the MEDIAL WOMAN as immersed in the psychic atmosphere of her environment and in the impersonal unconscious. It seems there could not have been, anywhere on the face of the planet, a better example of Wolff's MEDIAL WOMAN than 'S'.

# SUMMARY

Toni Wolff maintains that the psyche of women contains four major archetypes: the MOTHER, the AMAZON, the HETAIRA and the MEDIAL WOMAN. By the time a woman reaches maturity, each of the types has set, consciously or unconsciously, its own particular ego orientation that has established its primary objectives. Two of the types MOTHER and HETAIRA, have a primary personal orientation, while AMAZON and MEDIAL WOMAN are oriented primarily to impersonal collective life.

Once a woman figures out which of the types is closest to how she manages her world, she realizes that there are two adjacent secondary types with which she also may have some familiarity, and a fourth opposite one with which she is less familiar and somewhat uncomfortable. Each type has its distinctive familiar characteristics, its less familiar (shadow) side, its career possibilities, its particular manner of relating to men and children, and its particular relationship to the other types.

A woman's self-nurture includes an invitation for her to explore and integrate all four of the types into her awareness and understanding, one by one, over time. If she remains caught in her primary type, her development and growth become stifled, her particular shadow side more powerful and destructive, and her world seriously limited.

# Appendix

## List of Films and Credits

*Accidental Tourist, The.* 1988. Based on book by Anne Tyler. Screenplay by Lawrence Kasdan and Frank Galati. Directed by Lawrence Kasdan. Actors: William Hurt, Kathleen Turner, Geena Davis, Amy Wright, Ed Begley, Jr.

*African Queen, The.* 1951. Horizon, Based on the novel by C.S. Forester, 1935. Screenplay by James Agee, John Huston and Peter Viertel. Directed by John Huston. Actors: Humphrey Bogart, Katharine Hepburn, Robert Morley, Peter Bull, Theodore Bikel.

*Angels and Insects.* 1995 – U.S, British. Based on a novella by A.S. Byatt, *Morpho Eugenia* by Philip Haas. Screenplay by Philip Haas and Belinda Haas. Directed by Philip Haas. Actors: Mark Rylance, Kristin Scott Thomas, and Patsy Kensit.

*Bagdad Café.* 1987. MGM. Also known as *Out of Rosenheim*, 1988; Screenplay by Eleonore and Percy Adlon. Directed by Percy Adlon. Actors: Marianne Sagebrecht, CCH Pounder, and Jack Palance.

*Charms for the Easy Life.* 2002, TV. Based on the book by Kaye Gibbons. Teleplay by Angela Shelton. Directed by Joan Micklin Silver. Actors: Gena Rowlands, Mimi Rogers, Susan May Pratt.

*Disclosure.* 1994. Based on a book by Michael Crighton. Screenplay by Paul Attanasio. Directed by Barry Levinson. Actors: Michael Douglas, Demi Moore, Donald Sutherland.

*Elizabeth I.* 1980. (Also, known *as Elizabeth the Virgin Queen*). Channel Four Films. Written by Michael Hirst. Directed by Shekhar Kapur. Actors: Cate Blanchett, John Gielgud.

*English Patient, The.* 1996. Based on the book by Michael Ondaatje. Screenplay by Anthony Minghella. Directed by Anthony Minghella. Actors: Ralph Fiennes, Juliette Binoche.

*Eve's Bayou.* 1997. Screenplay by Jack Lemmons. Directed by Kasi Lemmons. Actors: Jurnee Smollett, Meagan Good, Samuel L. Jackson, Diahann Carroll, Vondie Curtis-Hall.

*The Gift.* 2000. Screenplay by Tom Epperson and Billy Bob Thornton. Directed by Sam Raimi. Actors: Cate Blanchett, Giovanni Ribisi, Keanu Reeves.

*Gone with the Wind.* 1939. Based on the book by Margaret Mitchell. Screenplay by Sidney Howard. Directed by Victor Fleming. Actors: Clark Gable, Vivien Leigh, Leslie Howard, Olivia de Havilland, Hattie McDaniel, Butterfly McQueen.

*Grass Harp, The.* 1998. The. Based on the book by Truman Capote. Screenplay by Stirling Silliphant and Kirk Ellis. Directed by Charles Matthau. Actors: Piper Laurie, Sissy Spacek, Walter Matthau, Mary Steenburgen, Nell Carter.

*Hannah and Her Sisters.* 1986. Screenplay by Woody Allen. Directed by Woody Allen. Actors: Woody Allen, Mia Farrow, Michael Caine, Carrie Fisher, Barbara Hershey, Lloyd Nolan.

*House of the Spirits, The.* 1993. (German - Danish- Portuguese - U.S.) Based on the book by Isabel Allende. Screenplay by Billie August. Directed by Billie August. Actors: Meryl Streep, Jeremy Irons, Glenn Close, Winona Ryder, Vanessa Redgrave.

*Moonlight and Valentino.* 1995. Screenplay by Ellen Simon. Directed by David Anspaugh. Elizabeth Perkins, Whoopi Golberg, Kathleen Turner, Gwyneth Paltrow.

*Postcards From the Edge.* 1990. Book and Screenplay by Carrie Fisher. Actors: Meryl Streep, Shirley MacLaine, Richard Dreyfuss.

*Runaway Bride.* 1999. Screenplay by Josann McGibbon and Sarah Parriott. Directed by Gary Marshall. Actors: Julia Roberts, Richard Dreyfuss.

*Tampopo.* 1985 and 1986. Japanese. Screenplay by Juzo Itami. Directed by Juzo Itami. Actors: Ken Watanabe, Tsutomu Yamakazi, Nobuko Miyamoto, Koji Yakusho.

*To The Lighthouse.* 2004. BBC TV in three parts. Based on the book by Virginia Woolf. Screenplay by Hough Stoddart. Directed by Colin Gregg. Actors: Rosemary Harris, Michael Gough, Suzanne Bertish Wright.

*White Palace.* 1990. Based on the book by Glen Savan. Screenplay by Ted Tally and Alvin Sargent. Directed by Louis Mandoki. Actors: Susan Sarandon, James Spader, Eileen Brennan.

# Bibliography

Adler, Gerhard. *The Living Symbol*. Princeton, NJ: Bollingen Series LXIII Pantheon, 1961.

Allende, Isabel. *The House of the Spirits*. New York, NY: Bantam Edition, 1993.

Armstrong, Karen. *A Short History of Myth*. Edinburgh: Canongate, 2005.

Anthony, Maggy. *The Valkyries - The Women Around Jung*. Longmead, Shaftsbury, Dorset: Element Books, Ltd, 1990.

Bair, Deirdre. *Jung A Biography*. New York, NY: Back Bay Books, Little Brown and Co., 2003.

Beauvoir, Simone de. *The Second Sex*. New York, NY: Random House, Vintage, 1989.

Berger, Arthur Asa. *The Art of the Seductress*. Lincoln, NE: Writer's Club Press, 2002.

Blackman, Ann. *Seasons of Her Life, A Biography of Madeleine Korbel Albright*. New York, NY: Scribner, 1998.

Bornoff, Nicholas. *Pink Samurai*. New York, NY: Simon and Schuster Pocket Books, 1991.

Burge, James. *Heloise and Abelard, A New Biography*. San Francisco: Harper San Francisco, 2003.

Butler, E.M. *Rainer Maria Rilke*. New York, NY: Octagon Books, Farrar, Straus and Giroux, 1973.

Byatt, A.S. *Angels and Insects: Two Novellas*. New York, NY: Vintage International, Random House, 1994.

Champernowne, Irene. *A Memoir of Toni Wolff*. San Francisco: C.G. Jung Institute of San Francisco,1980.

Campbell, Joseph. *The Power of Myth*. New York, NY: Doubleday, 1988.

Carson, Anne. *Eros the Bittersweet*. Normal, Il: Dalkey Archive Press, Illinois State University, 2003.

Castillejo, Irene Claremont de. *Knowing Woman*. New York, NY: Harper Colophon, 1973.

Curie, Eve. *Madame Curie*. Translated by Vincent Sheehan. New York, NY: Doubleday, 1937.

Davies, Margaret. *Colette*. Edited by A. Norman Jeffreys. Edenburgh: Oliver and Boyd, Evergreen Pilot Books, Ltd., 1961.

Delbée, Anne. *Camille Claudel*. San Francisco: Mercury House, 1992.

Dietrich, Bill. "Amazons and Art." *Seattle Times*, WA: July 7, 2002, K9.

Drury, Michael. *Advice To A Young Wife From An Old Mistress*. New York, NY: Random House. Third Edition, 1993.

Ellenberger, Henri F. *The Discovery of The Unconscious.* New York, NY: Basic Books. Second printing, 1970.

*Encyclopedia Mythica.* "Inanna", http//pantheon.org/articles/i/inanna/html; "Dumuzi" (Tammuz) www.templezagduku.org/dummuzi.html.

Faber, Michael. *The Crimson Petal and the White.* U.S. edition. New York, NY: Harcourt, 2002.

Fitzgerald, Rachel. "Toni Wolff's Vision of Archetypal Femininity," 2001, www.caplocator.com/interest-areas/Wolff'sVision.html. (Website now dismantled).

Fitzgerald, Rachel. *She Moves in Circles,* Xlibris 2010.

Freud, Sigmund and C.G. Jung. *The Freud/Jung Letters.* Translated by Ralph Manheim and R.F.C. Hull. Princeton, NJ: Princeton University Press, 1974.

Friedan, Betty. *The Feminine Mystique.* New York, NY: W.W.Norton and Co., Paperback edition, 2001.

Fuerst, Norbert. *Phases of Rilke.* New York, NY: Haskell House, 1974.

Gay, Peter. *Freud: A Life for Our Time.* New York, NY: WW Norton, 1988.

George, Margaret. *Helen of Troy.* New York, NY: Penguin Viking, 2006.

Gibbons, Kaye. *Charms for the Easy Life.* New York, NY: Avon Paperbacks Hearst Corp,1995.

Gold, Alan. *Warrior Queen: The Story of Boudica, Celtic Queen.* London: New American Library (Penguin), 2005.

Golden, Arthur. *Memoirs of a Geisha.* New York, NY: Vintage Contemporaries, Random House, Inc., 1997.

Graham, Katharine. *Personal History.* New York, NY: Random House Vintage, 1998.

Grimal, Pierre. *The Dictionary of Classical Mythology.* Basil Blackward, Editor. Cambrige, MA, 1960.

Hall, Nor. *The Moon & the Virgin.* New York, NY: Harper and Row, 1980.

Hamilton, Edith. *The Greek Way – The Roman Way.* New York, NY: Bonanza, 1986.

Hamilton, Edith. *Mythology.* New York, NY: New American Library, 1969.

Hannah, Barbara. *Jung: His Life and Work.* New York, NY: Perigee, G.P. Putnam and Sons, 1976.

Haskins, Susan. *Mary Magdalene, Myth and Metaphor.* New York, NY: Riverhead Books, 1993.

Haule, John R. *Divine Madness: Archetypes of Romantic Love.* Carmel: Fisher King Press, 2010.

Hayman, Ronald. *A Life of Jung.* New York, NY: WW Norton, 2001.

Helminski, Camille Adams. *Women of Sufism.* Boston and London: Shambhala, 2003.

Henry, Madeline. *Prisoner of History: Aspasia of Miletus and Her Biographical Tradition*. New York, NY: Oxford University Press, Inc., 1995.

Hepburn, Katharine. *Me*. New York, NY: Ballantine Books, 1992.

Herm, Gerhard. *The Celts*. New York, NY: St. Martin's Press, 1975.

Hickman, Katie. *Courtesans*. New York, NY: HarperCollins, 2004.

Howell, Alice. *Jungian Symbolism in Astrology*. Wheaton, IL: Quest Books, Theosophical Publishing House, 1985.

Iwasaki, Mineko with Rande Brown. *Geisha, A Life*. New York, NY: Washington Square Press, 2002.

Jacobs, Donna. Academic Thesis. "Virgil's Camilla: Amazon, Hero or Woman?" Austin: University of Texas at Austin, 1990.

Jenks, Kathleen. "Rabi'a al-'Adawiyya, An 8th Century Islamic Saint From Iraq: The Near East, Islam. Geographical Regions". Pacifica: CA. Pacifica Graduate Institute, MYTH LINKS, January 2003.

Jensen, Ferne. Editor. *C.G.Jung, Emma Jung, Toni Wolff, A Collection of Remembrances*. San Francisco, CA: Analytical Psychology Club of San Francisco, Inc., 1982.

John-Steiner, Vera. *Creative Collaboration*. New York, NY: Oxford University Press, 2000.

Johnson, Robert. *Balancing Heaven and Earth*. San Francisco: Harper San Francisco, 1998.

Jong, Erica. *Sappho's Leap*. New York, NY: W.W. Norton and Co, 2003.

Jung, C.G. *Memories, Dreams, Reflections*. New York, NY: Random House Vintage Books, 1965.

Jung, C.G. *Collected Works*. Vol. 4, 5, 7, 9i, 14, 18. Princeton, NJ: Princeton University Press, 1972.

Jung, C.G. *Letters*, 1951-1961. Edited by Gerhard Adler and R.F.C. Hull, collaborator Aniela Jaffe. Princeton, NJ: Princeton University Press, Second edition, 1991.

Kidd, Sue Monk. *The Secret Life of Bees*. New York, NY: Penguin Books, 2002.

King, Karen L. *The Gospel of Mary of Magdala, Jesus and the First Woman Apostle*. Santa Rosa, CA: Polebridge Press, 2003.

LeLoup, Jean-Yves. *The Gospel of Mary Magdalene*. Translated and commentary by Joseph Rowe. Rochester, VT: Inner Traditions International, 2002.

Leppmann, Wolfgang. *Rilke: A Life*. Translation by Richard Exner. New York, NY: International Publishing Corp., 1984.

Lord, M.G. *Forever Barbie*. New York, NY: Walker and Co., 2004.

MacLaine, Shirley. *Out on a Limb*. New York, NY: Bantam Books, 1983.

Maddocks, Fiona. *Hildegard of Bingen*. New York, NY: Doubleday, 2001.

Madsen, Axel. *Hearts And Minds: The Common Journey of Simone de Beauvoir and Jean-Paul Sartre*. New York, NY: William Morrow and Co., 1977.

Masuda, Sayo. *Autobiography of a Geisha*. Translated by G.G. Rowley. New York, NY: Columbia University Press, 2003.

Michener, James. *The Source*. New York, NY: Random House, 1965.

Moore, Robert and Douglas Gillette. *King, Warrior, Magician, Lover*. New York, NY: HarperCollins, 1991.

Morrison, Toni. *The Bluest Eye*. New York, NY: The Penguin Group, 1994.

Morrison, Toni. *Jazz*. New York, NY: Random House, Inc., Vintage International, 2004.

Myss, Caroline. *Anatomy of the Spirit*. New York, NY: Three Rivers Press, 1996.

Myss, Caroline. *Sacred Contracts*. New York, NY: Harmony Books, 2001.

Otto, Walter. *Dionysus: Myth and Cult*. Dallas, TX: Spring Publications, 1986.

Pagels, Elaine. *The Gnostic Gospels*. New York, NY: Random House, Vintage Edition, 1989.

Panati, Charles. *Sacred Origins of Profound Things*. New York, NY: Penguin Arkana, 1996.

Peter, H.F. *Rainer Maria Rilke*. New York, NY: Gordian Press, 1977.

Peters, Sarah Whitaker. *Becoming O'Keeffe, The Early Years*. New York, NY: Abbeville Press Publishers, 1991.

Picknett, Lynn. *Mary Magdalene*. New York, NY: Carroll and Graf Publishers, 2003.

Prioleau, Betsy. *Seductress*. London: Penguin Books Ltd., 2003.

Pizan, Christine de. *The Book of the City of Ladies*. New York, NY: Penguin Group, 1994.

Pressfield, Steven. *The Last of the Amazons*. New York, NY: Doubleday, 2002.

Prose, Francine. *The Lives of the Muses*. New York, NY: HarperCollins Perennial, 2002.

Prose, Francine. *Marie Laveau*. New York, NY: Berkley Publishing Corporation, G.P. Putnam's Sons, 1977.

Qualls-Corbett, Nancy. *The Sacred Prostitute*. Toronto: Inner City Books, 1980.

Renn, Jurgen and Robert Schulmann. *Albert Einstein - Mileva Maric, The Love Letters*. Translated by Shawn Smith. Princteton, NJ: Princeton University Press, 1992.

Rilke, Rainer Maria. *Selected Poems*. Translation and Commentary by Robert Bly. New York, NY: Harper and Row, Perennial Library, 1981.

Robinson, Roxana. *Georgia O'Keeffe, A Life*. Lebanon, NH: University Press of New England, 1999.

Salomé, Lou Andreas. *Looking Back Memoirs*. New York, NY: Paragon House, American Edition, 1991.

Salomé, Lou Andreas. *You Alone are Real to Me*. Translated by Angela von der Lippe. Rochester, NY: Boa Editions, ltd., 2003.

Shlain, Leonard. *Art and Physics*. New York, NY: HarperCollins, Perennial, 2001.

Sharp, Daryl. *C.G. Jung Lexicon*. Toronto: Inner City Books, 1991.

Shamdasani, Sonu. *Jung Stripped Bare by His Biographers, Even*. London: Karnac, 2005.

Shamdasani, Sonu. *Jung and the Making of Modern Psychology: The Dream of a Science*. New York, NY: Cambridge University Press, 2003.

Smith, Margaret. *The Way of the Mystics and the Rise of the Sufis*. New York, NY: Oxford University Press, 1978.

Talbot, Margaret. "Little Hotties", The New Yorker, December 4, 2006, 74-83.

Trask, Willard. *Joan of Arc: In Her Own Words*. Compiled and translated by Willard Trask. New York, NY: Books & Co., 1996.

Ulanov, Ann and Barry Ulanov. *The Healing Imagination*. New York, NY: Paulist Press, 1991.

Underhill, Evelyn. *Mysticism*. Meridian, NY: New American Library, 1955.

van der Post, Laurens. *Jung and the Story of our Time*. New York, NY: Random House, Vantage Books, 1977.

von Franz, M.L. *The Feminine in Fairy Tales*. New York, NY: Spring Publications, 1972.

Vygotsky, L.S. *Thought and Language*. Cambridge, MA: MIT Press, 1962.

Weill, Sabrina. *The Real Truth About Teens and Sex*. New York, NY: Perigee Penguin Group, 2005.

Whitmont, Edward C. *The Symbolic Quest*. Princeton, NJ: Princeton University Press, 1969.

Woolf, Virginia. *To the Lighthouse*. New York, NY: Harcourt Brace, 1927, 1951,1981.

Wolff, Toni. "Structural Forms of the Feminine Psyche." Der Psychologie, Bern: Heft, 7/8 Band III, Herausgecher: Dr. phi. G H Graber, 1951.

Wehr, Gerhard. *Jung: A Biography*. Boston: Shambhala, 1987.

Wheelwright, Joseph B. Editor. *The Reality Of The Psyche*. New York, NY: G.P. Putnam's Sons, 1968.

Wheelwright, Joseph B. *Saint George and the Dandelion*. San Francisco: C.G. Jung Institute Of San Francisco, 1982.

Willard, Thomas (trans). "Toni Wolff Eulogies." Funeral comments presented at St. Peter Church, Zürich, March 25, 1953. Privately printed, 2000.

Woodman, Marion. *Addiction to Perfection*. Toronto: Inner City Books, 1982.

Wormald, Jenny. *Mary, Queen of Scots*. London: Tauris and Co. Ltd., Tauris Parke Paperbacks, 2001.

Yalom, Marilyn. *A History of the Wife*. New York, NY: HarperCollins, 2001.

Zweig, Connie and Jeremiah Abrams. *Meeting the Shadow*. New York, NY: G.P. Putnam's Sons, 1991.

# Copyrights notices continued from page vi:

# Index

## A

Adler, Gerhard
*The Living Symbol* 298
Adlon, Eleanor & Percy
*Bagdad Café* 11, 39, 63, 296
Aeschylus 19, 176, 197-199
*The Eumenides* 197-199
*The Oresteia Cycle* 19, 197
Agamemnon 19, 198, 284
Albright, Madeleine 217
Allende, Isabel
*House of the Spirits, The* 22,
233, 279-280, 297-298
Allen, Woody
*Hannah and Her Sisters* 11, 54,
297
Angry Wife 55
anima woman 79, 120, 135,
278
'animus hound' 133
Anthony, Maggy
*The Valkyries* 298
Antiope (Hippolyta) 177
Aphrodite 81-82, 84
Apollo 19, 198, 284
Armstrong, Karen
*A Short History of Myth* 298
Aspasia of Miletus 12-14, 77,
139, 300
Astarte 80-81
Attanasio, Paul
*Disclosure* 16, 192, 296
Auden, W.H.
*Lectures on Shakespeare* 207

## B

*Bagdad Café* 11, 39, 63, 296
Bair, Deirdre
*Jung: A Biography* 111-112,
115, 298
Barbie Phenomena 96
Bastet 80
Beauvoir, Simone de 14, 85- 86,
115-117, 119-121, 126,
133, 140, 145-146, 160,
166, 301
*A Farewell to Sartre* 120
*Force of Circumstance* 119
*Memoirs of a Dutiful Daughter*
116
*The Second Sex* 85-86, 121, 298
Berger, Arthur Asa
*The Art of The Seductress* 298
Bernadette of Lourdes 273
Berry, Patricia 38
Blackman, Ann
*Seasons Of Her Life* 298
Blanchett, Cate 15, 248, 296-
297
Bogart, Humphrey 14, 296
Bolen, Jean Shinoda
*Goddesses in Everywoman* 33
Bornoff, Nicholas
*Pink Samurai* 298
Boudicca (Queen) 180-181, 186,
214
Bradshaw, John 68
*Meeting The Shadow,* 68
Burge, James
*Heloise and Abelard* 87, 90, 298

*You might also enjoy reading these Jungian publications*

*The Creative Soul* by Lawrence Staples
ISBN 978-0-9810344-4-7

*Guilt with a Twist* by Lawrence Staples
ISBN 978-0-9776076-4-8

*Enemy, Cripple, Beggar* by Erel Shalit
ISBN 978-0-9776076-7-9

*Divine Madness* by John R. Haule
ISBN 978-1-926715-04-9

*Farming Soul* by Patricia Damery
ISBN 978-1-926715-01-8

*The Motherline* by Naomi Ruth Lowinsky
ISBN 978-0-9810344-6-1

*The Sister From Below* by Naomi Ruth Lowinsky
ISBN 978-0-9810344-2-3

*Animus Aeternus* by Deldon Anne McNeely
ISBN 978-1-926715-37-7

*Becoming: An Introduction to Jung's Concept of Individuation*
by Deldon Anne McNeely
ISBN 978-1-926715-12-4

*Like Gold Through Fire* by Bud & Massimilla Harris
ISBN 978-0-9810344-5-4

*The Art of Love: The Craft of Relationship*
by Bud & Massimilla Harris
ISBN 978-1-926715-02-5

*Resurrecting the Unicorn* by Bud Harris
ISBN 978-0-9810344-0-9

*The Father Quest* by Bud Harris
ISBN 978-0-9810344-9-2

*Phone Orders Welcomed*
*Credit Cards Accepted*
*In Canada & the U.S. call 1-800-228-9316*
*International call +1-831-238-7799*
*www.fisherkingpress.com*

Lightning Source UK Ltd.
Milton Keynes UK
UKOW04f1641201013

219390UK00011B/186/P